Historians of Medieval India

Historians of Medieval India

Edited by

Mohibbul Hasan

AAKAR

Historians of Medieval India
Edited by Mohibbul Hasan

First Published 1982
First Aakar Edition 2018
Reprinted 2019
Reprinted 2024

ISBN 978-93-5002-536-9

Published by
AAKAR BOOKS
28 E Pocket IV, Mayur Vihar Phase I
Delhi 110 091, India
www.aakarbooks.com

Printed at
D.K. Fine Art Press, Delhi

INTRODUCTION

Muslims have always had a great sense of history which could be traced to Prophet Muhammad himself. That is why from the earliest days of Islam works began to be composed on the lives of the Prophet, the Caliphs, Sultans and nobles. These were at first exclusively written in Arabic, the language of the Quran and of the intellectual classes. But from the second half of the tenth century, with the revival of Persian nationalism and the adoption of Persian language and culture by the Turkish dynasties, historical works began to be written in Persian too. When the Muslims came to India, they brought with them the Persian tradition of history writing, and it was kept up by the emigrants from Persia and Central Asia. From the eleventh to the eighteenth centuries, therefore, a huge mass of historical literature consisting of general, dynastic, and regional histories, biographies and memories, was produced.

It is these historical writings in Persian which have served as the main source of the history of medieval India. But, unfortunately they have not been properly assessed and studied with reference to their author's social, cultural and religious backgrounds, methods, forms of expression and concept of history. This has resulted in an incomplete and distorted picture of the past.

The period of the Sultanate of Delhi and the local dynasties is extremely rich in historical writings. But to use these properly it is necessary to have a clear understanding of the mentality of the men who wrote them. The first question that arises is, why did they write at all ? The answer is that they wrote for different reasons, for fame, for reward, for pleasing their patrons, for the edification of their contemporaries and the future generations, for preserving the memory of the achievements of Muslim rulers and for justifying the ways of God to man.

The medieval historians took their craft seriously and held a very high view of history. Barani, for instance, considered history and the *Ilm-ul-Hadis* as twins, and believed that a historian should be devoted to truth and should eschew exaggerations and verbose language. But unfortunately, because most of the medieval historians were connected with the court, they were not only not able to write what they felt to be true, they indulged in panegyrics of their patrons. Besides, many of them, like Minhaj-us-Siraj, Hasan Nizami, Amir Khusrau and Barani were of aristocratic origin which led them to weave their story round kings and nobles and ignore the life and conditions of the common people. Furthermore, since they were orthodox Muslims and lived in an age when men's minds were dominated by religion, they adopted an idiom and technique which would make their narrative intelligible and appealing to their readers. This explains why they tried to depict the medieval rulers as champions of Islam and to prove this they indulged in gross exaggerations and rhetoric. Their statements should not, therefore, be taken too literally. It is necessary to go beneath the surface of their verbose and hyperbolic language to get at the truth. They furnish, as Peter Hardy observes, the raw material of history, but it has to be processed and refined before being turned into the finished product.

The medievel historians constantly refer to God as the final cause of all happenings. But this was inevitable in a society dominated by the Asharite theology. However, this does not mean that material factors were entirely ignored. Many instances can be cited to show that medieval writers do try to explain events in terms of human factors—court intrigues, administrative measures, foreign policies or ambitions of kings and nobles. After all, despite their religious pretensions, they were wordly men writing about worldly things for worldly men to promote worldly aims.

What the medieval historians lack most is an understanding of the social and economic forces that bring about vital changes in societies and fall of kingdoms. However, it would not be correct to say that they 'treat history as a sequence of events, often isolated and without obvious relationships.' The historical writings of the period reveal that the medieval historians—and this includes the Mughal historians also—were conscious of change and of relationships between ideas, events and institutions of one reign with those of another. The very fact that many of them were not content to write merely the history of a single reign, but wrote accounts of dynasties, shows that they were aware of the social, political and religious developments and relationships between events.

When we come to the Mughal period, we find a qualitative change in historical writings. The person who was responsible for this was Abul Fazl, the friend and adviser of Akbar. Abul Fazl no doubt has many limitations. His language is ornate and verbose; he exalts Akbar's virtues but glosses over his faults; he is so much engrossed in describing the achievements of his master that he ignores the life and conditions of the common man; he is, like Barani and Badauni, intensely subjective, but unlike them he does not reflect the spirit of his age. However, despite all this, it was Abul Fazl who for the first time rebelled against the accepted technique and trend of history writing and struck a new path. He was the first Indian historian to adopt a rational and secular approach to history. He does not regard history as allied to theological studies, but tries to establish a close relationship between history and philosophy. To him Indian history does not consist in a conflict between Hindus and Muslims, but between the forces of stability and disintegration—the former represented by the Mughal government and the latter by the *zamindars*. He does not accept the traditional view of his predecessors that Indian history should concern itself only with the achievements of Muslim rulers, but believes that it should also describe the history, philosophy and religion of the Hindus. He extended the evidential basis of his works by consulting the archival records and other accounts, whether written or oral, and accepting them only after carefully weighing and sifting. His technique was followed by Abdul Hamid Lahori and Khafi Khan and other historians of the seventeenth and eighteenth centuries: but they made no significant contribution to historiography.

The study of medieval Indian history along modern lines was started by British scholars in the late eighteenth century, and the first phase of this study lasted till about the middle of the ninteenth century. The British historians of medieval India were influenced by the methods, trends and ideas of contemporary historical writings in Britain. Although they assumed the superiority of the social, political and cultural institutions of the West, their approach—this is particularly true of Dow, Duff, Erskine and Elphinstone—was, on the whole, sympathetic. Some of them, like John Briggs, were against dogmatic judgements, and held the view that there was not enough evidence available for pronouncing moral judgements on

India's past. They were not only interested in wars and conquests, but also in administration, social customs, religious beliefs and the influence of Islam on Hinduism. And they laid strees not only on Persian historical works and European traveller's accounts, but also on *firmans*, literary sources, and archaeological evidence for writing a history of medieval India.

With Elphinstone closes the liberal phase of the history of British historical writing on medieval India. Elliot, who initiated the second phase, had a very poor opinion of medieval historians ; he had also not only no sympathy for an understanding of India's medieval past, but adopted a prejudiced and even a contemptuous attitude towards it. His example was followed by the subsequent British historians, who ignored the healthier trends and methods of contemporary European historiography. Since most of them were administrators, they narrowed down the scope of history to politics and administration, ignoring other aspects of life and failing to understand the working of human society. They mainly relied upon Persian historical works and European travellers' accounts, which they accepted without making any effort to analyse, interpret and understand.

As regards the Soviet historians, they have only recently started taking interest in medieval India, particularly the Mughal period. But their interest in it is only subsidiary : it is the outcome of their desire to understand better some of the aspects of modern Indian history which have roots in the past. Although they are doing valuable work, their investigations suffer from three drawbacks. Firstly, their application of Marxist ideas to Indian conditions is somewhat rigid. Secondly, they select only such examples from the Mughal history as support their theories. Thirdly, they rely mainly upon the European travellers' accounts and the published Persian texts and their English translations, ignoring the large body of unpublished manuscripts and records which throw considerable light on the economic history of the Mughal period.

Historical writing on medieval India in Urdu started in the early part of the nineteenth century. But the first original work to be written was Sir Sayyid Ahmad Khan's *Asar-i-Sanadid* in 1849. Sir Sayyid's models were the works of medieval historians ; and it was only later that he acquainted himself with western techniques of history writing. These he seems to have applied in editing various

Persian historical texts. Unfortunately, however, his career as a historian was cut short owing to his preoccupation with the Aligarh movement.

Two other writers who deserve to be mentioned are Zakaullah and Shibli. Zakaullah wrote extensively, but he lacked critical judgement and merely paraphrased the writings of medieval historians. Shibli wrote much more about the past of Islam outside India than about Islam in India. However, the little that he wrote, he wrote as an apologist. Although he claimed to believe that a historian should be devoted to truth and objectivity and laid down certain principles for the guidance of historians, he himself did not follow the principles of scientific historiography.

The Indian scholars who began the study of medieval India along western lines in English in the early part of the nineteenth century, followed in the footsteps of the British historians of medieval India. It was only from the late ninteenth-twenties that some of them, influenced by nationalist ideas and imbibing the latest trends in European historiography, began to adopt new methods of research and open up new fields of investigation. In recent years Indian historical writing on medieval India has made further progress under the influence of historians like Sir Lewis Namier, Marc Bloch and Lefebvre.

It was in 1956 that the first attempt to study Indian historians was made at a conference organised by the School of Oriental and African Studies, University of London. But the section on medieval India formed only a small part of it. The first major systematic work to appear on the subject was Peter Hardy's *Historians of Medieval India* in 1960. Although it has opened the way to the study of medieval historians, its scope is very limited—it deals only with five historians of the period—and it has all the shortcomings of a pioneer work.

Although the present volume, covers a sufficiently wide field and long period, still important gaps have remained. However, by bringing out the trends and methods of some leading medieval and modern historians of medieval India, and by pointing out the significance of the sources in Indian languages, this work will, it is hoped, enable the student to have a better insight into an understanding of medieval India and to avoid the pitfalls into which his predecessors had fallen while writing about it.

It has yet to be fully realised that the history of medieval India cannot be properly reconstructed unless and until the medieval historical works are studied with reference to the spirit of the medieval age and the social and religious background, the psychology, the habits of thought and techniques of medieval historians. If the present volume can stimulate thinking along these lines, the purpose of its publication will have been served.

M. HASAN

CONTENTS

1

Fazlullah Rashid-ud-Din Abul Khair

Rashid-ud-Din was born in Hamadan in 1247. He studied medicine and acquired so much proficiency in it that the Il-khan Abaqa appointed him the court physician. During the reign of Ghazan his fame rose high and, in 1298, he was made the prime minister. In 1303, he accompanied Ghazan on an expedition and conducted his Arabic correspondence. At the time of Uljaitu Khuda-banda his prestige rose even higher. A suburb of the new capital Sultaniyya was named after him as Rashidiyya, and many magnificent buildings, mosques, schools and hospitals were built there. In 1309, he founded another town called Rab-i-Rashidi, near the tomb of Ghazan to the east of Tabriz, and got a canal, cut through the rocks at tremendous cost, to bring water of the Saravrud river. It was divided into many sectors, having 30,000 houses, with a separate sector called *kucha-i-ulama* where six or seven thousand scholars and students lived. Its bazars consisted of 1500 shops, it had 24 caravansarais and numerous gardens, mosques, baths, godowns, factories, paper mills and a mint. In its hospital (*dar-us shifa*) worked many physicians and surgeons from India, China, Egypt and Mesopotamia, and each one of them had to teach five students. The grand building of the library of that city was a wonder of that age. According to the *Tarikh-i-Wassaf* a sum of 60,000 dinars was spent on the calligraphy, illustration, binding etc. of his (Rashid-ud-Din's) books. But his career was not smooth. A quarrel started between him and Ali Shah which touched off an intrigue against him in the court. In October, 1317, Abu Said Khan deposed him and on July 18, 1318, sentenced him to death. All his public works were set at naught, and it was given out that by birth he was a Jew. Hence Timur's son, Miranshah, got his body taken out of his grave and interred in the graveyard of the Jews. In this way this great man was disparaged.

Rashid-ud-Din was a great scholar and prolific writer of his age. Among his works the most important are : the *Jami-ut-Tawarikh* with a world-geography appended to it, which relates the history of the world; the *Kitab-ul-Ahya-wal-Athar* (treatise on buildings and animals), which deals with agriculture, botany, mining and metallurgy, animal husbandry, invertebrate zoology, metereology, architechture, fortification, ship building etc. in 24 chapters; the *Tauzihat* (Explanations), which contains discussions on theology and mysticism in 19 letters and an introduction; the *Miftah-ul-Tafasir* (Key to Commentaries), which offers a penetrating study of good and evil, heaven and hell, fate and destiny and many other questions about the Quran, and refuts such views as transmigration and metempsychosis; the *Risalai-i-Sultaniyya* (Royal Book), which is an anthology of the discourses on theology delivered to Uljaitu in the Ramazan of 1307; *Lataif-ul-Haqaiq* (Deeper Truth), which is a collection of 14 letters on various theological problems; *Bayan-ul-Haqaiq* (Description of Truth), which has 17 letters treating theology, small-pox and varieties of heat. Besides these books, he wrote four treatises on medicine and Mongol administration and got them published in Arabic, Persian and Chinese editions, which are now lost. Some manuscripts of his 53 letters, entitled *Munshat*, are however available. These letters were addressed to his sons and other officials and relate to political and financial affairs. They throw much light on contemporary events and administrative conditions. Letter no. 34 was written to his son, Khwaja Majd-ud-Din, to communicate an order to make military preparations for an invasion of India. It shows that attempts were being made for an expedition against India. Letter no. 29 was sent by him to Maulana Qutb-ud-Din Masud of Shiraz from Multan in Sindh, and contains a description of his journey in India, which he undertook at the instance of the Il-Khan to establish diplomatic contacts with Indian rulers, and as a result of which he acquired the knowledge of many drugs and medicines not known in Iran. This journey must have kindled his interest in Indian life and culture and given him an opportunity to study it. These letters show the unique calibre and broad outlook of this scholar and the vast range of his interests and pursuits.

Rashid-ud-Din took pains to publish and preserve his books. He got his Arabic books translated into Persian, and Persian works rendered into Arabic, and his medical writings issued in Chinese, and deposited many of their copies in the library of Rab-i-Rashidi. Besides this he got all his writings collected under the heading *Jami-ut-Tasanif-ar-Rashidi*, had it furnished with maps and pictures and appendices and placed it in the said library. Every year two copies of each of these works were prepared on the quality paper of Baghdad at state expense, and sent free of cost to the famous libraries of the Islamic world. Everybody was allowed to copy these books in the library. But, inspite of these efforts, many of his books were lost due to the carelessness of his countrymen.

An estimate of Rashid-ud-Din's love of learning can be formed from the fact that his library had 60,000 volumes on poetry, history and science, including 100 choice scripts of the Quran done by eminent calligraphists. This explains his anxiety to take steps for the preservation of his encyclopaedic writings.

Though Rashid-ud-Din wrote on a variety of subjects, the pillar of his fame is his *Jami-ut-Tawarikh*. The first part of it is a history of the Turks and the Mongols and a detailed account of happenings from Chingiz Khan to Ghazan Khan, and its second part contains the succession from Adam to the Prophet, the story of Iran before the advent of Islam, the annals of the Caliphate till the invasion of Hulagu, the chronicle of Persian dynasties following that period and the history of the Jews, Franks, China and India, with a long account of Shakyamuni Buddha and his religion. In writing the history of the Mongols he drew on the data furnished by Ghazan Khan and Pulad Ching Chang. In the account of China he received information from two Chinese scholars, Li-ta-chi and Mak-sun. About the Franks he learnt a lot from a merchant of Pisa, named Iolus, and in his work on India he was assisted by the Buddhist scholar from Kashmir, Kamalashri. Thus, this book is the first expression of an international consciousness of human history. Speaking of it, Rashid-ud-Din observes :

'When Chingiz Khan, his noble family and great descendants acquired universal sovereignty, all the countries of the world, Chin and Machin (South China), Khitai (North China), Hind and Sindh, Mughalistan, Turkistan, Sham (Mesopotamia), Rum, As (Alain), Rus (Russia), Sirkas, Kipchak, Kalar, Bashkir, in one word, all countries of the four quarters became subject to him. Chingiz Khan gave a uniform shape to the world and instilled in the hearts of all men the feeling of equality. Now that the world from one enp to the other is under one or the other branch of the Chingiz-khanids, the philosophers, astronomers, scholars and historians (*hukama wa munajjiman wa arbab-i-danish wa ashab-i-tawarikh*) of all sects and religions (*adyam-wa-milal*) connected with Khitai, ancient India, Kashmir, Tibet, Uighur and other people like the Turks, Arabs, Franks are before our eyes in large numbers and everyone of them has books containing the history, chronology and religious thought of those countries and they are also conversant with these subjects.'

The *Jami-ut-Tawarikh* is an embodiment and expression of this international atmosphere and cosmopolitan outlook of the Mongol period. In this paper we propose to deal briefly with the section on India given in this work. This section consists of two parts (*qism*) divided into ten and twenty chapters (*fasl*) respectively. Appended to the second part (*qism*) is a *risala* devoted to the refutation of the doctrine of transmigration and metempsychosis (*tanasukh, naskh*). The first four chapters of the first part are based on the *Kitab-ul-Hind* of al-Biruni and give general information on India. Part of the fifth chapter, dealing with the chronicle of the kings of Delhi (*dar tarikh-i-salatin-i-Dilli*), is derived from al-Biruni and Juzjani, and here Rashid-ud-Din has also something to say of his own. The sixth chapter on Kashmir contains entirely new information regarding the history of Kashmir, especially in the Mongol period. Chapters 7 to 10 dealing with the four ages or *yugas* and the kings, who reigned in them, are quite original. The second part deals in 20 chapters with the life and teachings of Gautama Buddha. It is a unique work on Buddhism in the Persian language.

Coming now to the new information on Indian history that we get from Rashid-ud-Din, we may begin by saying that he has seen India through Buddhist glasses, just as al-Biruni has done from the orthodox brahman stand-point. In the account of King Harishchandra of the Krta age, it is stated that he, with his wife and son, is 'at the same stage of metempsychosis as Shakyamuni.' This was the period of the rule of the kings of the Iksvaku family. The Treta age is marked by the reigns of Dilipa and his son Raghu. The latter had a daughter Sundaravati who married Brahma's son *Vdlak* or *dlk* (?) and bore him a son without her father's knowledge. That son claimed the kingdom, whereupon Raghu cursed him to go to hell. There he served the inmates and ultimately rose up to Bodhisattva Avolokiteshvara (Amita Burkhan). This story is unknown in the Indian legendary accounts and may have been borrowed from some Buddhist source. Then follows the story of the *Ramayana* in a brief form. The account of Dvapar-yug opens with the story of the fight between Kartavirya and Parashurama and goes on to describe the events of the time of the Kauravas and the Pandavas leading to the war of the *Mahabharata*. The history of the Kali-yug starts with the ascent of Yudhishthira to heaven and the division of his empire among his descendants, among whom the Shakyas founded the town of Kapilvastu and produced Shuddhodana and his son Gautama Buddha. Here again, the attempt to connect the family of the Kauravas and Pandavas to that of the Buddha shows the Buddhist outlook of Rashid-ud-Din. Then comes the history of the Nandas and Mauryas of Magadha. In it the author describes Chandragupta as a scion of the earlier Nanda dynasty. About him he gives an information not known from any other source, namely, that his ministers assassinated his queen, since he neglected the affairs of the state on account of his excessive love for her. About Chandragupta's successor, Bindusara, he says that he had two sons by a brahman queen, Ashoka and Vigatashoka. The king wanted to appoint the elder son, but the ministers appointed the younger one till the return of the others from the battle front. But in the mean-time, he conducted himself so well as to outshine his brothers. Hence the government remained in his hands, and his younger brother Vigatashoka became a *brahman*. Then Rashid-ud-Din skips over the period of six hundred years after Ashoka and comes to the time of Shri Harshadeva of Kashmir. It is said that a poet of his court coveted one of his wives ; he gave that woman to him and charged both of them to go to Turkistan. Their descendants are the Mongols. This is a quaint device to connect the Mongols with India. Probably this was an ingenious invention of the minds of those Kashmiri Buddhists, who, in order to win the favour of their Mongol masters, concocted an Indian ancestry for them. The Mongols or Tatars invaded Kashmir when Vikramaditya was ruling over India.. He inflicted a defeat on them. Here, obviously, we have a reference to Chandragupta Vikramaditya of the Gupta dynasty and his fight with the Shaka invaders described in the Devichandragupta of Vishakhadatta. Then Rashid-ud-Din refers to Lalitaditya Muktapida of Kashmir and calls him Iskandar. Here also we note the tendency to establish a parallelism between Indian and Western conquerors. The most remarkable part of Rashid-ud-Din's work is that dealing with the Mongol invasion and conquest of Kashmir. He lets us know, on the authority of Kamalashri, that during the reign of King Ramadeva in Kashmir a great Mongol army, led by Ukutu Noyon, invaded Kashmir by order of Uguday Khan, besieged the capital and conquered it. Ramadeva fled before the Mongols on his black mare, and escaped from his pursuers by a daring jump on his horse across the broad Black River, which probably refers to the Kshiptika, a tributary of the Jhelum. After this, the Mongols plundered the town continuously for six months. Then they retreated after having appointed a governor there. Seven years later Ramadeva succeeded in expelling that governor and recovering his kingdom. At the time of Mangu Khan, another Mongol army invaded Kashmir under Sali Noyon and Takudar, plundered its cities and killed and captured its people. Ramadeva died and his son Lakshmanadeva (1273–1286) accepted the Mongol tutelage. Under his son Simhadeva (1286–1301) and then under Suhadeva (1301–1320) Kashmir seems to have been under the suzerainty of the Mongols. Commenting on this account Karl Jahn shows that Ramadeva of Rashid-ud-Din's narrative stands for two kings, called Rajadeva, who ruled from 1212 to 1235 and 1252 to 1273 respectively. It was during the reign of the first Rajadeva that the first Mongol invasion of Kashmir took place. According to him, the credit of expelling the Mongols may really go to Rajadeva's successor Samgramadeva (1235–1252). He has also shown that Lakshmandeva (1273–1286) received the appointment from Qubilai Khan (1259–1294) and Abaqa Khan (1265–1282), rather than Mangu Khan and Hulagu Khan. It may well be that it was Lakshmanadeva's predecessor who got the investiture from the Mongols, and his successors who got it renewed from them. However, Rashid-ud Din makes it plain that in the thirteenth century Kashmir passed under the suzerainty of the Mongol Il-Khans of Iran.

The second part (*qism*) of Rashid-ud-Din's *History of India* deals with the life and teachings of Buddha in 20 chapters. It is well-known that Buddhism was popular among the Mongols in the thirteenth century. Before launching his campaign against Yunnan and South China. Mangu Khan built a monumental stupa at Qaraqorum to ensure the success of his undertaking in the name of

'Sagamoni Burcan' the Mongol name of Shakyamuni Buddha. Hulagu, the conqueror of Bodhisattva Maitreya, Arghun (1284–1291) and Ghazan (1295–1304)—the later before his conversion to Islam—were ardent champions and followers of this faith. In this period Iran was full of Buddhist shrines and had a large number of Buddhist priests called *bakshis*. The Persian historian Ala-ud-Din Ata Malik Juwaini has referred to the Buddhists as *toyin*, a word derived from the Chinese term *tao-jen*, and in his *Tarikh-i-Jahan-gushai* (1, 44) has praised their religion as inculcating a virtuous life. He states that among them are good teachings and injunctions resembling the views and doctrines of all prophets ; among them some teach man to avoid sin and misdeeds, and doing violence to others, and enjoin on him to repay evil with good and not to indulge in cruel behaviour towards living beings. The importance of the Buddhists in Iran can be assessed from the fact that, even after the persecution following the conversion of Ghazan to Islam in 1295, they made a bid to re-convert Uljaitu to their creed in 1309–10. However, in the first half of the fourteenth century Buddhism succumbed to the impact of Islam.

In the spread of Buddhism in the Mongol world the monks of Kashmir played an important part. Two Kashmiri monks, whose names are given in Chinese versions as Watochi and Namo, introduced Lamaism among the Mongols. Marco Polo observed that the Buddhists, led by the monks of Kashmir, were noted for their piety and wisdom. Among these monks was Kamalashri, who collaborated with Rashid-ud-Din in the compilation of his history of India and treatise on Buddhism. As a result of the work of Kamalashri and his compeers, the Buddhism of Iran was nearer to that of Kashmir than to that of Tibet. In this respect it differed from the Buddhism of the eastern Mongols, who drived their inspiration mostly from Tibetan Lamaism.

A question arises as to how and why Rashid-ud-Din gives, at the instance of Kamalashri, such a detailed treatment to Buddhism. The answer is to be found in the religious crisis in Iran in the last decade of the thirteenth and the first decade of the fourteenth century. After the conversion of Ghazan to Islam in 1295, obviously for political reasons, the Buddhists were faced with persecution, and many of their shrines were destroyed. Hence, in order to defend their position, the Buddhists were making an attempt at explaining their religion to the Muslims and emphasizing the common points between it and Islam. This is why in Rashid-ud-Din's treatise Buddhist terms are rendered in Islamic concepts. For example, the Buddhas are described as prophets, the gods are referred to as angels, and the demons as devils and Mara is mentioned under the name of *Iblis*. In it, the Buddha Shakyamuni is presented as a prophet of charity and kindness in contrast to other prophets, who are marked by arrogance, egotism and self-interest. It says that before the spread-of Islam the people of Mecca and Medina were Buddhists, and wor shipped in the Kaba idols resembling the Buddha. It goes on to state that the people of Turkistan were originally Buddhists, and that, even after their conversion to Islam, there were many Buddhist temples in that country. According to it, Buddhism had spread to the interior of Abyssinia and some Negro countries. It makes it clear that the people of Manzi followed the Hinayana, whereas those of Tibet and Tangut were the adherents of Mahayana. The life of Buddha, commencing from chapter IV, is more or less the same as known to Buddhist legends current in Mahayana circles, except that here and there we come across Islamic ideas, as in the reference to *murids* and *pirs*, *madrasa* and *khanqah*, *bihisht* and the *huris*, and the theistic character of *mabud* etc. In the list of books, appended to the work, we have references to Buddha working at the command of the Exalted Creator, Allah. For example, a text says : 'Shakyamuni said that, at the command of Allah, the Exalted, and by virtue of the testimony of the Angels, he is omniscient and miraculous and rules over all the demons'. Another treatise states : 'Shakyamuni says that the Exalted Creator had commanded temples to be built and images of Shakyamuni to be placed in them.' Such utterances remind one of the prophets working at the behest of the Supreme Creator, the Exalted Allah. Thus, to sum up, we observe that Rashid-ud-Din's treatise on Buddhism reflects the tendency of the Buddhist monks, led by men like Kamalashri, to present the main tenets of Mahayana Buddhism with a tinge of Islamic concepts and without the least trace of Tantric ideas, which could be naturally adhorrent to the Muslim audience. We may presume that Kamalashri's project of bringing out a treatise on Buddhism through Rashid-ud-Din's work in such a way as to command itself to a people and court, recently converted to Islam, was a link in the same chain of events which culminated in the effort to win back Uljaitu to the

Buddhist fold in 1309–10.

The above summary of the contents of the section on India in Rashib-ud-Din's *Jami-ut-Tawarikh* shows how important it is for some details of Indian history and the Muslim understanding of Indian culture and religion. All the data, furnished by it, deserve to be thoroughly studied with reference to all the evidences at our disposal. Here, for the sake of illustration, I propose to take up the study of a passage relating to Indian history after the establishment of Muslim rule. The importance of this information is very great since it must be based on almost contemporary sources. I base myself on a manuscript, preserved in the Raza Library of Rampur, from which the relevant extracts have been copied for me by the Librarian, Mr. Imtiaz Ali Arshi, for which I am deeply indebted to him.

These extracts (*Fan-i-Tarikh-i-Farasi* No. 186 folio 121) relate to Shihab-ud-Din Ghuri. They begin with his war with an Indian king in which the latter lost his life. In this war, the Indian king was reported to be accompanied by seven hundred elephants and 'thousand thousand men'. Obviously here the reference is to the battle of Taraori between Shihab-ud-Din and Prthviraja Chauhan. About the end of this battle it is said that Prthviraja was captured by Shihab-ud-Din, who thought of reinstating him on the throne of Ajmer. The *Prthvirajaraso* states that he was taken to Ghazna and some Muslim writers, like Hasan Nizami, suggest that he was carried to Ajmer. On the basis of a coin, bearing the names of both Shihab-ud-Din and Prthviraja, Dasharatha Sharma holds that the Ghuri conqueror had really an intention to reinstate Prthviraja as a vassal chief. (D. Sharma, *Early Chauhan Dynasties*, p. 87; D. C. Ganguly, *The Struggle for Empire*, p. 112). But Minhaj-us-Siraj expressly states that 'pithaura alighted from his elephant, mounted a horse, and galloped off, but he was captured near Sarsuti (Sarsi) and sent to hell' (*Tabqat-i-Nasiri*, Elliot and Dowson, *History of India*, II, p. 297). The author supports this version of the events.

Folios 165–167 of Vol. I of the said manuscript deal with the last days of Shihab-ud-Din and the events following his death. When Shihab-ud-Din was defeated and routed by the army of Kharakhtai (Qara Khitai), which had come for the assistance of Sultan Muhammad Khwarazmshah, it was rumoured that he had died. Hence the Indian tribes and chiefs, subjugated by Shihab-ud-Din, considered it a good opportunity to overthrow his yoke. The son of Debal ruling over Koh-i-Jud, who had become a Muslim, re-embraced his ancestral faith. In particular the Khokars, who paid tribute to him, rose up in revolt and took to robbery and plundering. One Amakmal got hold of Multan. Shihab-ud-Din gave top priority to the situation at Multan and captured and killed the usurper and appointed Muhammad b. Abu Ali as the governor of Multan and Lahore (Lahawar) and commissioned him to send the tribute for two years which was in arrears. But the new governor was powerless to cope with the menace of the Khokars and reported that on account of their menace on the way it was not possible to send the tribute. Thereupon, Shihab-ud-Din ordered his commander-in-chief in India Qutab-ud-Din Aibak to deal with the Khokars, but his threats and promises proved of little avail. On all sides there was upsurge and uprising in India. Hence Shihab-ud-Din was forced to suspend his projected campaign against the Khitai, and on the fifth of Rabi-ul-Awwal of 602 A. H. marched into India. Moving swiftly, he overpowered the Khokars on the twenty-fifth of Rabi-ul-Akhar in a grim encounter. By the time of the second prayer, Qutab-ud-Din also arrived with his army and fell on the Khokars. Caught between the two assaults, the Khokars gave way. A large scale slaughter followed. The remnants of the Khokars fled towards a high hillock and set fire to the neighbourhood. But when the Musalmans approached near them they preferred suicide to surrender or slaughter at the hands of the enemy and jumped wholesale in the fire to be burnt alive. This unique information is against that which says that the Musalmans set fire to the refuge of the Khokars and burnt them (*The Struggle for Empire*, p. 124. A. B. M. Habibullah, *The Foundation of Muslim Rule in India*, p. 77). This is an instance of a supreme heroic sacrifice, a sort of collective *jauhar*, performed by men, to save their honour on a desperate occasion, the like of which is not easy to find elsewhere. But the days of Shihab-ud-Din were also numbered. As he started homeward, after a brief halt at Lahore, and camped at the village of Damel on the bank of the Indus, two or three Hindus, chagrined by the defeat and slaughter of the Khokars, one day emerged from some hiding in the river and slashed him with twenty wounds of the dagger. The amirs and nobles led by the *wazir* Muyyad-ul-Mulk, stitched his wounds and took him to Ghazna under cover of illness. But no sooner had the account of his death become known than dissensions flared up on all sides.

As soon as the death of Shihab-ud-Din became known, some of the jurists of Ghazna began the rumour that Maulana Ustad-ul-Bashar Fakhr-ud-Din Razi was hand in glove with the Khwarazmshah and at his instance got Shihab-ud-Din killed. In order to escape the storm, the Maulana took refuge with the *wazir*, who knew things as they were and, accordingly, saved him from the mischief by sending him away to a far off place. At that time, two factions were prominent in the Ghurid empire—one favouring Baha-ud-Din, the ruler of Bamyan, and the other inclining towards Ghiyas-ud-Din Mahmud, son of Sultan Ghiyas-ud-Din. Baha-ud-Din of Bamyan was the son of Shams-ud-Din Muhammad bin Masud by the sister of the Ghuri chiefs, Sultan Ghiyas-ud-Din and Shihab-ud-Din. He was in the good books of the Ghurids, and with their help ousted his consanguine brother Abbas which his father had by a Turkish wife. Hence the Ghurids invited him to Ghazna after the death of Shihab-ud-Din, but, on reaching Ghazna, he had a terrible attack of headache, which made him feel that his end was near. He called his sons, Ala-ud-Din and Jalal-ud-Din and advised them to come to terms with Ghiyas-un-Din Mahmud on the understanding that Ghazna and India would belong to them and Ghur and Khurasan would be under the latter. He appointed Ala-ud-Din as his successor. However, in India the Amirs placed Aibak on the throne, who came to be known as Shams-i-Hindustan. He consolidated his hold on Sindh, Lahore and Multan. Taj-ud-Din Yalduz captured Zabulistan and Ghazna. Amir Mahmud, son of Sultan Ghiyas-ud-Din, controlled Herat and Firuzkoh and Aziz-ud-Din Husain Khermal, the ruler of Herat, allied himself to Sultan Muhammad Khwarazmshah. In this way, these dissensions resulted in the fall of the Ghurid empire and brought in instead the rule of the Khwarazmians. Since the Mongol menace started the Khwarazmshahs in the face, they could not take any interest in India and the successors of Aibak could enjoy a secure rule there.

These few data pertaining to the Ghurids show how important this account is for the history of Asia as well as that of India.

2

Amir Khusrau

Unlike the philosophic Hindus who viewed this world, including human life, as an illusion and had, consequently, a certain disregard for history, the Muslims, like the ancient Chinese and the Greeks, seem to have had from the very beginning a keen desire to know the past and to collect and keep a record of men and events, happenings and occurrences. Their innate sense of enquiry and historical consciousness made them interested in the course of human affairs and anxious for rescuing the past from oblivion. They began to compile books containing biographical sketches, historical anecdotes and chronicles of events, public or private. Historiography, accordingly, flourished under the early Turks in India. Different types of historical literature were produced in India during the early medieval period. Historical writings of the period were of different variety in respect of style, literary form, outlook, method, content and value. The works of Minhaj Siraj, Hasan Nizami, Fakhr-i-Mudabbir are so different from one another, and also from those of Barani, Afif and others. But they were all professional historians and have been accepted as such by even modern European writers of history. The case of Amir Khusrau who, besides his five *diwans*, has four 'historical *masnavis*', and two prose works, also containing historical matter, is a little different, according to some writers,[1] as we shall see hereafter. The fact is that the view of history in that age was, as a whole, quite different from what we find today. The old medieval tradition of historiography that historical works could be written in a special style and might combine oratory and poetry, cannot commend itself to a modernist who abhors or finds very inconvenient the old patterns of rhetorical history. It is quite

[1] Chapter V of P. Hardy's *Historians of Medieval India* deals with the treatment of History by Amir Khusrau.

natural that the views on history and other subjects held by modern thinkers should have changed with the change of time, and the perspective of historians should not be the same as it was before.

History is now taken in a more comprehensive sense. Some centre their narratives on wars or conquests, others concentrate on law and government, state and politics ; and yet others view the economic, social, religious and cultural factors to be important determinatives. Nowadays we think that it is not the factual details, the mere narration in a dry as dust manner, of the series of events that actually happened—which count and constitute history. The more important thing is to say 'how this has come out of that.' A historian is expected to probe into the causes and effects and to find out the forces that helped to shape the events as they occured. The essence of history lies in an enquiry into the past, dedication to truth, objectivity, cause-effect nexus of events and movements, sound and critical judgement, and a sense of reasonableness in historical interpretation. The task of the historian is not like that of an advocate to prove or disprove a major fact or event, but to sift and evaluate the varied and multitudinous source-material and to act in the capacity of a judge and jury. He is mainly concerned with a diagnosis of the total situation on the basis of all available and verifiable evidence. He must tap and state all his source-material.

Judging by the standard laid down above, is one in a position to say that Amir Khusrau made some significant contributions with regard to history ? Can one concede about him what Elliot and Dowson have said about Benakiti[2] that he was a poet as well as a historian ? But a modern Western scholar opines that 'Amir Khusrau did not write history : he wrote poetry.'[3] The task of the historian is to reconstruct the past. He seeks to prove into things said and done so as to understand the present and predict the future. But the past did not have any spell for Amir Khusrau except when he was impelled by hopes of reward and desire for undying literary fame to carry out the behests of the ruling sovereigns. All his six historical works are characterized by disjointed themes, lacking in chronological sequences by florid, fanciful, verbose style and hyperbolic tone, by artificial literary devices, poetic imageries and literary art forms, sacrificing

[2] See H. Elliot and Dowson, *History of India as told by its own Historians*, Vol. III, Chapter XII.

[3] Hardy, *Historians of Medieval India*, 43.

perspicacity, continuity, and accuracy of historical and topographical details. Looking at Amir Khusrau's life and career, the formative influences on him and the operating principles which might have guided him, a modernist may justly feel disappointed. He had a fairly long life, was possessed of potential capacity to understand and act upon his environment, and to utilise the accumulated experiences of past generations, interpreting them in such a way so as give them a realistic historical pattern and make them meaningful and useful for future generations. He allowed his opportunities to lapse. History does not involve, as Amir Khusrau might have thought, the assumption of unintelligible and inscrutable ways and course of Fate and intervention of the Divine in human affairs, nor stereotyped descriptions of events connected with the deeds of kings, courtiers and nobles, unwholesome eulogium on those who were in power, and condemnation of those undeservedly praised during their life time, in total disregard of their good and bad, just and unjust, religious and impious actions. The historian is concerned more with groups than with individuals, more with human decisions than with Divine causation, more with the study of the past than with the delineation and appraisal of the facts and changes occuring in one's life-time.

One cannot deny the aptness of much of such remarks, specially if one ignores the 13th Century tone, and the situation and the atmosphere of the age in which Amir Khusrau lived. He has been appraised mainly on the basis of his poetical and prose works, and, undoubtedly, he occupies a very high position as a talented litterateur and artist which he so eminently deserved. But his competence as a writer of history is questioned. Would it be fair, however, to say that his works do not contain all that a modernist likes to be the concept and appreciation of history. To what extent are we justified in blaming him for his failure to realise the need of a wide historical panorama, of a continuous, objective, critical, chronological, factual narrative, true to facts and morally instructive, and for his not rising above the pride and prejudices, fashions and traditions of the time ? Did he really miss the bus ? It is true that, as the son of an Amir of Iltutmish who was of Lachin Turkist extraction and the grandson, on his mother side, of a high official of Balban's court and of Indian origin,[4] he had excellent connections in political circles, and had

[4] He and his maternal grandfather were very enthusiastic about the characteristic Indian 'chew'. See the writer's fairly long paper entitled '*Betal*

opportunities of observing many of the important events and gathering extremely important historical information from the notable and learned personalities he had contact with.

But history was not his prime concern. Religion, love of art and literature, search for beauty and the fulfilment of his economic needs by legitimate means were his dominant life motives. There was a possibility of his being deeply involved in contemporary politics by virtue of his upbringing and position, but as a Sufi and as one of the famous disciples of Nizam-ud-Din Aulia, he was of the world and also out of it in the sense that although he had to earn for his bread by his literary trade, he kept himself out of the controversial questions and situations arising from the ups and downs in the field of politics and religion. He was a man of learning and intelligence and was capable of handling historical subjects critically and chronologically, giving a connected and systematic account of the past and making valid historical analysis. But history with Amir Khusrau was contemporary history, and, he could not shake off his obsession with literary accomplishments.

Amir Khusrau has nowhere claimed to be a historian, and has frankly told us that he wrote his desultory studies on important historical topics either on the suggestion of, or for presentation to, the reigning sovereigns. There was no inner urge to do so. History cannot be written without some basis of selection from the multitude of happenings which constitute the quarry. Amir Khusrau's selection appears to be arbitrary and not in accord with what was inherent in the events and themes dealt with. But the principle of selection in most cases was not of his choice, but was dictated. He pours fourth his eulogium with hyperbolic exaggerations not only on Ala-ud-Din, who was great in many ways, but also on his worthless and despicable successor in the *Nuh Sipihr*, and even in the prefactory[5] remarks of the *Ijaz-i-Khusrawi*. Even the best and the greatest of

---

Chewing and the early Muslims'. Amir Khusrau writes about Imad-ul-Mulk, the Rawat-i-Arz or Ariz-i-Mamalik : 'I am the first of significant knowledge to owe my decent from that black-cheeked one (black *ariz*), and I have pointed out each and every particular of my family origin or lineage. That black one was the most elegant preamble to the state. I am a creation of the tip of the pen of destiny and a citation of that black one. I drown the dry grass (mean, base and ignoble thing) and bring out the pearl. Behold what a wonderful (ever-flowing) river has come out of that black cloud.'

[5] Khusrau, *Ijaz-i-Khusrawi*, Lucknow, 1865, Vol. I, 28–31.

sovereigns had their virtues and vices, but Amir Khusrau is said to have been concerned with all that was good and he skips over all that was bad. Even a cursory glance over some of the pages of the ponderous volume of[6] the *Ijaz-i-Khusrawi* and over his observation in his romantic Masnavis, the *Hasht Bihisht*[7] and the *Matla-ul-Anwar*,[8] in respect of woman, would suffice to enable one to revise such an opinion about him.

Many of the connected facts may have been known to him, but he has omitted some material which, circumstanced as he was, might have been embarrassing for him to recall. Perhaps he dared not mention in the *Khazain-ul-Futuh* or the *Tarikh-i-Alai* the brutal murder by Ala-ud-Din of his uncle and father-in-law, the mild good-natured founder-Sultan of the Khalji dynasty, on 16th Ramazan, 695. He mentions this date as the date of the accession of Ala-ud-Din to the throne. Even in his unofficial work, the *Ijaz-i-Khusrawi*, he ignores the heinous actions of his patron Sultan. We know from Barani about the critical situation created by the Mongols led by[9] Qatlagh Khawaja and Targhi, but Amir Khusrau has nothing to say about the discomfitures of the terrible and unscrupulous Sultan at the hands of his enemies, external or internal. He has made no reference to the uneasy relations between his spiritual[10] guide and Kaiqubad, Mubarak Khalji and Ghiyas-ud-Din Tughlaq in the *Qiran-us-Saadain*, *Nuh Sipihr* and *Tughlaq Nama*.

But before challenging the character and questioning the intellectual honesty of our poet-historian, we have to take into account the prevailing atmosphere of the days of the despotic, meddlesome rulers and the need of advisable appropriate conceal-

[6] Strong and weak kings, Wazirs and other officials *Ibid.*, Vol. IV, 40–44, good and bad artisans, Vol. IV, 48–49 ; also bad *Qazis*, corrupt officials, lawyers indulging in hair-splitting trivialities ; theologian ; Mashaikhs, good or bad, men of perverted tastes, *mukhannas*, dancers slaves, males and females etc.

[7] See Khusrau, *Hasht Bihisht*, Lucknow, 1873, 21–25, for the letter addressed to his daughter, Mastura.

[8] Khusrau, *Matla-ul-Anwar*, (Lahore, 1280 A. H.), the 10th Maqala, 192–98.

[9] They had advanced up to and invested the Imperial capital between 697–705 A. H. See Barani for a detailed account.

[10] The question of court attendance, change of residence, rivalry with Khizr Khan, devotion to the saint, acceptance of Khusrau Khan's money, and *sama* were the chief factors.

ments. Partial omission of some provocative particulars, colourful verbose, literary presentation of facts and characterisation of high dignitaries were permitted by the stultifying conventions of the time, and they do not necessarily mean a tendency towards wilful suppression of truth. In fact, some of Amir Khusrau's seeming over-dramatizations, or over-simplifications or even omissions and gaps do not matter much, for what emerges from his ornate and embellished picture is generally an accurate presentation of historical matters, including some new[11] facts not noticed by others. Amir Khusrau was a man of religion with a sense of dignity and responsibility. We may not forgive the historian in him for not bringing forward all the facts known to him, but considering his difficulties and limitations we cannot charge him with deliberate distortion of facts. On the other hand, we have evidence that he had an open, impartial and even a magnanimous mind. While writing about the apostates, oppressors and exterminators of the Alai family, regarded as their worst enemies by the contemporary Muslims, he gives an unmistakable proof of a refreshing candour and objective attitude.

Those who have gone through the pages of Barani relating to the atrocious deeds committed by Khusrau Khan and his accomplices, may compare his fulminations and invectives against the people described by him as accursed and foul Parwari outcasts and scavengers, with the following verses of Amir Khusrau on page 19 of *Tughlaq-Nama* : 'Many Hindus who are known as Bradus had joined him and had become his accomplices in his perfidious deeds. Bradu is the descriptive epithet of those interpid Hindus who risk their lives (heads). These martial people are reckless of their lives and also know how to knock down the heads of others. This class of people are always in the front rank of their rulers, and are ever prepared to sacrifice their lives at the behest of their rulers. The unbelieving infidels, not looking into their futurity, are, in a war fought all at once, like ten-headed demons. Hasan (Khusrau Khan) assembled and stationed them all at a place (treasury) and put on their feet fetters of gold.' Again, on p. 124 we are told about the fierce offensive taken by those dauntless warriors and the initial success that they achieved. When the two armies came to face each other with firm determina-

[11] Some of his versions are indirectly confirmed by other sources, *e.g.*, Ibn-i-Battuta describes Khusrau Khan's followers as being the bravest and the greatest who defeated Tughlaq's troops and pillaged his camp.

tion to create cracks in the opposite ranks, conquer and overthrow them from the side of the luckless Khusrau, one flank of his army sallied out and rushed like a river full of raging waves. In this furious (sweeping) charge they showed such firmness and constancy that one wing of the army of Malik Ghazi was dislodged and overthrown. Having penetrated through the opposite array of forces they fell on the rear. So much tumult and uproar arose among the people that one set of them fell upon the other. Many of the strong and sturdy troops took to flight and every one turned his bridle towards different directions. (But) Malik Ghazi did not leave his place with a small company of his troops, for he felt a pleasure in fighting for his life. Besides a single company of 300 cavalry behind him, none remained either in front or at the back. When Malik Ghazi saw the situation he was furious with rage and burst out angrily before those who were present. 'So long as my head remains in its place I shall not be alone. I would not look for help towards others for God is my helper.'

These extracts speak for themselves about the sane and sober attitude and methods of Amir Khusrau. But they may not be taken into account by those who think that 'Amir Khusrau's figures are either Virtuous or Vicious. They are gods or devils, not men.' The reference in the last sentence to the prospective Tughlaq Sultan's reliance on God may be provoking for one who contends that not only for 'Amir Khusrau but for all medievel Muslim historian and biographers, human characteristics are created outside the world of time and events, that is by God.' The orientalist and occidentalist ways and systems of religious and social thought do not always tally. It is the orientalist view that outstanding individuals are important in history, but an Invisible Power also plays at times, a large part in making or marring their fortunes. The effort and endeavours of men are really responsible for the outcome of events and occurances, but human actions are always subject to the Divine ordination. Ali, the fourth Caliph, said : 'I have realised the existence of the Divine Power by the failure of my firm resolutions.' The Quran says : 'It often happens that the armies which are very small in number come out victorious over those which are numerically very large and superior.' The Western scholars, wedded to the materialistic view of life and actions, cannot appreciate these statements. But historical literature is not wanting in illustrative instances of unexpected occurances. It is worthwhile quoting some more verses from the same work.

Continuing his narrative of the second fight, on the initiative taken by Khusrau Khan, on Saturday the first of the month of Shaaban, 720, near Hauz-i-Khas of Delhi, our author says that a contingent of the usurper's army of prabably ten thousand warlike Bradu (also spelt as Braus) cavalry broke through and paralysed the forces of Ghazi Malik, who was left only with 300[12] soldiers to rely upon. Nothing daunted, he stuck to his place. His bold stand and brave words inspired some of his followers led by Bahram Aiba, Baha-ud-Din Shaista and Malik Shadi. But they were hardly 500 in number. Let us read what Amir Khusrau has written in the *Tughlaq-Nama*: 'When all these gathered together they came to 500 and even less than that. When Malik Ghazi looked in front and behind he found only this small force and nothing more. But he did not care about the huge horde which he fancied was surrounding the umbrella (*chhatra*). He cried out 'God is great' at the top of his voice, and rushed forward foaming (as waves) towards the (opposite) umbrella and its bearer. He delivered his assault, boiling with rage, with such a fury that the entire battle-field began to resound with it. The impetuous attack of that excellent one of faith caused the confused assembly to become doubly confounded.... In whotever direction Malik Ghazi turned his reins, no sooner the enemies saw him than they seemed to be giving up their ghost. A man suddenly appeared before him and at once received a fatal wound from an arrow. Then boldly, and with a fierce charge, he struck down the umbrella (*chhatra*) with such a hard blow that it fell upside down on the head of the luckless fellow (Khusrau). With the fall of the umbrella on the ground the order and arrangement of the enemy and the ceremonial dignity and insignia (carried as ensigns upon the elephant) fell in disorder. Hasan (Khusrau) was in headlong flight with his fleeing forces and the trumpet was blowing heralding proclamation (of Victory).'

Fortunately for the valiant Tughlaq his chief opponent was spiritless and over-awed. But by unloosening the purse-strings of the accumulated treasures, and playing, perhaps, on the explosive senti-

[12] See Khusrau, *Tughlaq-Nama*, ed. Syed Hashim Faridabadi (Aurangabad 1933), The published text which contains many errors wrongly gives '*si sad*' (3,000).

ments of his erstwhile fellow-religionists he had gathered an immense horde around him. There were the intrepid, desperate, 'Braus, arrayed in front of the war elephants.' 'Ten thousand cavalry of Ranas and Rawats', and self-seeking Muslims 'who had become the attendants and servants of the Hindus and their constant companions and shadows.' In fact his army was so heavily manned by Hindus and Muslims as to astonish both the infidel and the faithful.[13] 'The Braus, each one of whom was swift and agile on the back (of the horse), had not lost their heart after their earlier discomfitures.' 'Malik Ghazi was standing in the battle-field, while his cavalry was engaged in plunder and pillage. All of a sudden a tumultuous Hindu horde, lying in ambush, appeared to deliver a severe assault. More than a thousand of Braus of black visage made a furious onslaught, and the Hindi daggers moved swiftly in shedding blood. That contingent of the Braus force fell on the standard and the rods of the banner were broken into pieces. The banner and ensign of Malik Ghazi were laid low on the ground. All glory to God. 'What a bold heart was possessed by Malik Ghazi that in spite of this severe and surprise attack he did not stir out of the place he was occupying !'[14] This is followed by the lines indicating the measures adopted and the efforts put up to retrieve the situation. Here our poet-historian philosophises : 'When fortune places the crown on the head of a person, his enemy is annihilated in consequence of the damage done by him. Whatever lock is handled by him, every one of his fingers does the work of the key. If you see with discernment, you will find the quality of capability and fitness in everything through the ordination of Providence.'[15]

Was Tughlaq's victory and his eventual enthronement a mere accident, or was it destined by the Causer of Causes that he should act in a way so as to prevail ? Amir Khusrau's critic has a fling at the 'moral Islamic way' in which vicissitudes of fortune overtaking the Alais' family was lamented, but he does not fling his searching eyes on some significant lines which could provide answer to one of his charges about the non-mention of the sources of information. 'Such misfortunes and calamities about which I used to hear before

[13] *Ibid.*, 112.
[14] *Ibid.*, 128–29.
[15] *Ibid.*, 132.

have now been seen by my own eyes.'[16] This observation occurs in connection with the detailed and pathetic account of the gruesome murder of the two princess, Farid and Abu Bakr, aged 15 and 14, who had received good education and also learnt the Quran. One was practising archery, another was an intelligent boy interested in calligraphy, and both were in the act of prayer after performing the ceremonial ablution with dust in the absence of water when they were cut down by the sword of the ruffians. The sad and piteous tale of the blinding of the three surviving princes, Ali, Baha, and Usman, aged between 8 and 5 has been described on the testimony of a reliable eye witness. 'It is from the afflicted heart of one who was an eye witness of the calamity that such things have dripped out.'[17] Elsewhere, after dilating on the virtues of truth and fidelity, our author refers to a well-informed witness. 'Thus said one who was very well-acquainted with affairs that when Ghazi Malik came to know that the Delhi forces of Khusrau had already advanced upto Sarsuti, instead of being frightened by the numerousness of the enemy army he felt happy. He showed mirth and hilarity at his prospects like the ferocious wolf at the abundance of sheep and ram.'[18]

Amir Khusrau has been charged with not 'conceiving of human individuals as acting in or being acted upon by historical situations as modern historians would conceive them.' Some of his lines are well worth one's consideration in this connection. 'Such is the sure and certain narration of the story that whatever happened to Qutb-ud-Din (Mubarak Khalji) it was pre-ordained by the True Power.'[19] One single significant line tells us a lot about the whole background of Khusrau Khan's episode : 'If unfitting things had not been practised upon me such things would not have come out from me. I would not have committed this treachery.'[20] This laconic but meaningful reply, given in explanation of his misdeeds, refers to the root cause and to, perhaps, not an unjust grievance. What has been displayed in all its nakedness by Barani has been left unspecified by our refined and cultured poet-historian. He has not, however, spared his estwhile deceased patron, has laid bare his character and

[16] *Ibid.*, 23.
[17] *Ibid.*, 232.
[18] *Ibid.*, 83–84.
[19] *Ibid.*, 23.
[20] *Ibid.*, 149.

conduct which caused his ruin, and has waxed eloquent on the consequences of licentiousness and negligence of rulers. 'Wine and love, lust and youth, pleasure and enjoyment, dominion and success. How can one whose mind is filled up with such air currents give thoughts to, and feel concerned with, the future ? It does not behove the ruler to become immersed in love and lust. A king is the constant protector of God's creatures. It would be wrong for such a guardian to remain intoxicated. If the shephered spoils himself by the use of pure wine, the herd goes in a state of sleep in the stomach of the wolf. In law, which means the rules and regulations of the Government, the stability of (political) affairs lies in vigilence and watchfulness. How can it befit a man who holds in his fists the cash of regions to lie carelessly on his back in his bed. It is not becoming on the part of a person to sleep over his affairs, for eventually he may be weighed down by the burden of his own remorse. This is specially the case with a king, for the enemies near his skin are much greater in number than his friends.'[21] If history has a moral purpose, such views and observations against the background of political events, as we find here and elsewhere, cannot be dismissed merely as trivial, unrealistic and conventional.

Amir Khusrau's critic does not find the particulars of geographical areas and topographical details given by him to be illuminating and useful. There is not much to feel enthused over the ornate description of Delhi, of the Congregations at the Mosque, the lofty minaret Mazina, and the Hauzi-Shamsi or Sultani. The outer and inner Hisar (fortified enclosures) of the capital city, situated on the hills, the Shahr-i-Nau, wrongly said to have been built by Kaiqubad, the Rauza-i-Bagh and the river near by. The descriptions of the routes adopted from Delhi to Awadh (*Qiran-us-Saadain*), Dipalpur to Delhi (*Tughlaq Nama*), Delhi to the extreme southern regions across the Narbada and the Vindhya range (*Khazain-ul-Futuh*), are not enlightening to some. The detailed account of the march of his army threading its way, stage by stage, from one place to another such as Alampur, Hansi, Madina, Rohtak, Mandoli, Palam, Kashanpur, Lahravati (*Tughlaq-Nama*) is, perhaps, not of sufficient importance to catch the critic's eye, nor does the receipt of the letters by the provincial rulers of very distantly placed regions within the shortest possible time throw any light on the means of transport and commu-

[21] *Ibid.*, 16.

nication available in the 14th century. As regards Ala-ud-Din's campaigns in the north and the south, though the dates, even months, have been given, the names of places, rivers and passes have been mentioned, and some indication is there, such as the reference to the availability of diamonds in abundance, the scheme of topography and chronology falls short of a historian's handiwork. It is not realised that many of the places mentioned are not easily identified because of their changed names on modern maps.

If the function of the historian is to enlighten and illuminate by throwing fresh, almost new, light on, and adding to the existing stock of knowledge of the past, then the wealth of solid, factual information, not available elsewhere, and furnished by Amir Khusrau's works, specially the *Miftah*, *Khazain* and *Tughlaq-Nama*, entitle the author to be called a historian. Though the *Ashiqa*, *Nuh Sipihr*, *Qiran-us-Saadain* and even the *Risail-i-Ijaz* are not wanting in valuable information of political value, they are works of solid worth for those working in the field of social and cultural history. Of these the highly verbose, artificial, wearisome style of the *Risail*, which contains, in four big volumes, the accumulated mass of specimen letters and documents emanating from the inventive mind and prolific pen of Amir Khusrau between 682/1283 and 725/1325 have scared away scholars, and has been dismissed as a book of imaginary epistolary correspondence, full of frivolous futile matters, having no bearing on the political, social, intellectual and cultural life of the age. Actually, very few have cared to scrutinize its contents, carefully and critically, and an ardent student of history is bound to be rewarded with useful information lying scattered here and there in it.

That the works of Amir Khusrau form a handy mine of factual information, which should not be taken to be historical irrelevancies, can be easily established. The historian Barani, at times, quotes him to confirm some of his views. In many particulars Barani's assertions are supplemented by the facts furnished by Amir Khusrau. There are many things which are found in his works alone. An example here will do. Barani tells us very little about the early life of the founder-Sultan of the Tughlaq dynasty. Amir Khusrau has put the following into the mouth of those who exhorted him to assume the crown : 'When the men of sober counsels heard this, they said what you have said befits you and is true ; but in throwing away your office you are taking away the pearl from yourself and putting it on others. All of us know what came about on account of your sword as that cannot be described by the tip of the pen. When the Khan (Ala-ud-Din) attacked the fort of Ranthambhor and laid siege to it, then the Rai Karad[22] made a stormy attack so that he should cut the iron siege by the sword of steel. He sent a strong force from within the fort which was like a mountain torrent sweeping off goods and chattels. There was such a loud and confused outcry in the camp of the Khan that one was falling on the other. You were ordered by the Khan to advance, and you went ahead of other chieftains. You displayed such valiant exertions in that battle as to make a whole world distressed. Two-thirds of the Rai's army was cut down and the remaining one-third managed with hundreds of pretexts to stay on. When you returned victorious from there you became a (Much sought after) hawk in the hands of the Khan. This was the beginning of your good luck and the dawn of your rising fortune. When the Sultan was gone, the faith and the fidelities of the Tughlaqs remained with you.... When another infidel (Mongols) marched against Baran (Bulandshahr) and made many Muslims his slaves like the Hindus, the king (Ala-ud-Din) sent you in that direction. You alone were responsible for the flow of the streams of their blood. There were four Tumans (each being the head of 10,000) and four Mirs (Chiefs) who were all princes of the Tartar dominion. When you encountered that agile, swiftwinged force, you did what you did for a small return. When you decided to face the ill-starred Iqbal you came out victorious over him also through good fortune. Again, in the battle of Turtaq and Ali Beg you knocked down many heads like so many cauldrons. Your next target was the army of Kapak[23] and Taibu. You were responsible for the killing of the infidels, one by one. Again, near Bunbal, by the side of the river (sea), the army of the infidels had assembled like a river. It consisted of one Tuman (10,000) of fighting infidels. Similar was

[22] There is a significant line in M. F. 'Kare Nami Bahadur Shah Sawaran Barun Zad Naubate Ba Chand Yaran' (Kare, the renowned brave Warrior and master of the horse came out and beat the forum with some of his followers), But Kare could not be Karad.

[23] Amir Khusrau who was so fond of playing upon words with double meanings has given *Kabak* (partridge) and *Taihu* (Quail). In K. F. he mentions the Mongol chiefs, Iqbal, Tai, Bu and Kapak.

the number of the Rai of Bunbal.[24] The earth was bending under the weight of the infidels like a river. Your glorious name was Tughlaq-i-Ghazi and the Mughal also bore the name of Tughlaq. You Tughlaq had taken the sword in hand for the sake of the holy war. That Tughlaq had kept the arrow in the handle of his bow for the sake of the infidels......You pierced the heart of the infidels with your glance and made them all captives or slaves. You also exacted money from the Rai of Bunbal, and realised the river tolls for the year. You then marched against Haider and Zirak and broke the rank and file of those valiant ones. In this way you fought eighteen battles here and there, and in all these you came out victorious.'

The *Tughlaq-Nama*, like other works, is not devoid of things of social and cultural import. That it was a well established custom of the time to give a feast and entertain the guests at the first sign of the incipient beard,[25] is evident from the pathetic words of prince Abu Bakr, addressed to his miserable mother, just when he was about to be killed by the assassins. 'The down on the cheek of the youth is the signal for festive hospitality; you may mourn for me without any mourner.'[26] We get here a glimpse into another prevalent practice. You see many jacket (or gown) wearing brides wandering about in the street of this city full of lusts.[27] Referring to the Hindu warriors, Amir Khusrau writes : 'There were Ahir Deo, Abar Deo, Amar Deo, demons upon demons, Narsih Sainsih, Barsih, Harmar, Bairimar, Parmar, all serpent-like and shouting *mar-mar* (strike, strike). The sandal-coloured robes on their bodies made the moist sandlewood dry with shame. All had wrapped themselves with a piece of silken cloth, ready to die, and felt proud of possessing bejewelled swords. Yet it is the custom with the Hindus that when they march out for battle, they wrap their heads with a kind of silken cloth called *baharaman*.... By tying the tail of cows on to their flags the Hindus associated hundreds of violence with the hairs of the cow's tail. Many of them had hog's teeth hanging from their necks, symbolizing their ferocity and suggesting that they were in no

[24] Rai Bunbal, Haider, Zirak as well as Kadar are not easily identifiable.

[25] Compare the celebration in the recent times of '*Monchon Ka Kunda.*'

[26] *Tughlaq-Nama*, 25.

[27] *Ibid.*, 86. Much more of such things are referred to in the *Ijaz-i-Khusrawi*, *Matta-ul-Anwar* and *Hasht-Bihisht*.

way inferior to tigers. The war Bhatts[28] (bards) of those worthless fellows were engaged with their sorcery to give them protection.' We need not consider the ensigns and emblems of the Tughlaq except that, unlike the Hindus, the distinguished mark of his flag was the peacock feather. As regards the Hindi words and phrases, a number of these have been aptly brought in. It would suffice to quote one very significant line in its original : 'Cho Bukshadand Tir-i-Be Khata ra-Bazari Guft' (*hai hai tir mara*).[29]

Before concluding, it seems necessary to say that Amir Khusrau's historical works have defects and merits of their own. His isolated fragments of historical continuum of about four decades, couched in a highly artificial, affected and obscure language and style cannot be put in comparison with the works of other medieval historians. His understanding of history did not centre upon records of historical occurrences systemetically and chronologically arranged, nor upon a set of ideas, but on persons and certain attractive themes. He does not always write in a straight forward manner, and seldom expresses his real sentiments lest that might offend and annoy those who were at the helm of affairs. He wrote with restraint about people whom he disliked for their character and conduct. He could not turn his eyes away from the atrocious deeds of Malik Kafur and Mubarak Khalji, but he had no hesitation in putting forward a lame excuse for the latter. He wrote in the *Ashiqa*[30] in the lifetime of that worthless son and successor of Ala-ud-Din : 'When the unkind or callous (*be mihr*) Sultan became cynical and surly (*tursh chihr*) and malicious towards his kith and kin, he saw it advisable for his state to shed their blood and thought them to be fit for the sharp sword. He decided to become vindictive and malignant so that the country should be freed

[28] Generally the Bhats were geneologist or family bards and not the enchanters or *afsungaran*.

[29] This 'hai, hai' is different from the auxiliary verb 'hai' of Khariboli. The text of the *diwan* of Hafiz, written or printed in India has this line which, if genuine, is very significant for those interested in linguistic studies. *Saqi agarat hawa-i-ma hai-juz bada mayar pesh-i-ma-shai.* The 15th century saint of Bihar, Qazi ola shuttari, puts this expression 'Khanda Hai Phanda Kahan' in the mouth of the 14th century Saint of Uchh, Makhdum Syed Jalal Bukhari (*Maadun-ul-Asrar*).

[30] According to some the addition in the *Ashiqa* came after the death of Mubarak Khalji, for Amir Khusrau could not afford to say anything disparaging of the Sultan in his life time.

from co-sharers. He secretly despatched some one to Khizir Khan and disclosed apologetically what he had in his heart (the evil thought) that he was nursing against him.' One should keep a balance in one's praise and blame and should not be unnecessarily severe and deprecatory in one's attitude. It would not be fair to judge the past with the yardstick of the present standard. It cannot be said that Amir Khusrau felt any animus towards those who were vicious and worthless, but it was dangerous to be out-spoken in public life. The favourite of Nizam-ud-Din Aulia, the great saint of Delhi, was not a *khiraqa-posh darwesh* (wearer of Sufi garments made up of patches), and we cannot expect him to have laid bare the character and motivation of the great ones of the time or to have disentangled the casual relations of human events. His primary concern was to demonstrate his literary ability and gain a lasting reputation, and also to get reward for his literary performances. Viewed favourably he was a historian. It has to be admitted that his works have great historical value and the contributions made by him to historical literature are in no way negligible.

3

Ziya-ud-Din Barani

'This is a work of solid worth', declares Barani, 'which combines several virtues. If you consider it a history, you will find in it an account of kings and *maliks*. If you search in this book for laws, government regulations and administrative affairs, you will not find it without them. If you want precepts and advice for kings and rulers, you will find them more plentiful and better presented in this book than in any other. And because everything I have written is true and correct, this history is worthy of credence. Also as I have put a lot of meaning in very few words, the example of mine deserves to be followed.'[1] This is Barani's own assessment of his *Tarikh-i-Firuz Shahi*. A modern writer has, however, to cross-examine him on a number of vital points before the historical value of his work can be objectively determined. What was Barani's idea of history ? How did he collect, assess and interpret his data ? What were the subjective elements in his thought and how did they influence his collection, selection and interpretation of facts ? How far was history a re-enactment of past experience for him ? What advantages, if any, did he seek to derive from his historical writings ? Barani's place amongst the medieval historians and his contribution to medieval Indian historiography rests on an answer to these questions.

As for Barani's idea of history and the advantages that accrue from its study, a fairly detailed discussion is available in his preface[2] to the *Tarikh-i-Firuz Shahi*. Like most medieval *'ulama'* he traced the origin of every science to the Quran. The development of the historical attitude amongst the Musalmans is also traced by him to those Quranic exhortations in which mankind has been asked to draw lessons from the fate of peoples and civilizations that once exercised

[1] Barani, *Tarikh-i-Firuz Shahi*, (Bib. Ind. 1860–62), 23.
[2] *Ibid.*, 1–23.

sway over the world, but have, since long, become tales of the past. The medieval system of Muslim education being theologically orientated, the source of this attitude is not difficult to trace. But its impact on his historical thinking cannot be emphasized beyond a point. The use of religious terminology is merely a literary convention with him and nothing more.

Barani looks upon history as a panorama of human activity unfolded before man to guide his faltering steps in life's journey.[3] Retrospect of the past, according to him, had a definite role to play in rectifying the present. What leads to the rise and fall of empires, dynasties and peoples should be clear to one who studies carefully the processes of historical change. History gives man a rare insight into human affairs and helps him in distinguishing between good and evil, vice and virtue, friend and foe. It makes man realistic in outlook as he learns from the experience of others. A ruler gets from its study the courage required to face difficulties and an insight needed to diagnose and treat the various ailments of the body politic[4]. He comes to know also how evil follows evil and good comes out of good. When an ordinary suffering individual, writes Barani, comes to know through his study of history that even prophets have not been spared trials and tribulations of life, it gives him immense power of endurance.[5] But unfortunately Barani's own knowledge of history could not come to his rescue during the days of his adversity.

Two other basic ideas of Barani with regard to history deserve to be noted : (1) The foundation of history, he says, rests on 'truthfulness.'[6] A historian should be exact in his statements and should avoid exaggerations or hyperboles which characterize the works of poets.[7] Incorrect statements lower the prestige of a historian and reduce the value of his work. Further, as a punishment for uttering lies, salvation is denied to him in the world hereafter[8] Thus Barani's sense of responsibility as a historian is conditioned both by pragmatic and religious considerations. (2) Barani considers History and the

[3] *Ibid.*, 1. See also 48, where, after describing the measures adopted by Balban in order to consolidate his power, he refers to the complete extinction of the family of Balban only 70 years after the latter's death.

[4] *Ibid.*, 11.

[5] *Ibid.*, 12.

[6] *Ibid.*, 12–13.

[7] *Ibid.*, 16.

[8] *Ibid.*

Ilm-i-Hadis as twins[9], and remarks that the study of history is necessary also because a scholar of Traditions, who is not an expert of history, cannot be a good scholar of his subject. The way Barani finds identity between the *Ilm-i-Hadis* and the *Ilm-i-Tarikh* has led Dr. Hardy to the conclusion that Barani's historical approach was theologically conditioned. But this is not so. What makes Barani bracket the study of history with the study of *ahadis*[10] is not the theological content of the *ahadis* but its *usul-i-asnad* which, in the words of Hitti, 'meets the most essential requirements of modern historiography.'[11] That an event should be traced to the person who actually participated in it or saw others participate in it, and that the veracity of all those persons who transmit that fact to others should be looked into through an investigation of their conduct, character, circumstances and background. This was the essence of the principles of critique evolved by the scholars of *ahadis*. Barani looks upon history and *hadis* as twins, and considers the principles of criticism applied to be the same in both.

It would, however, be a mistake to think that these abstract principles mentioned in the preface to his work contain all the basic postulates of Barani's thought or that it is possible to analyse the technique and tenor of the *Tarikh-i-Firuz Shahi* simply with reference to them. The *Tarikh-i-Firuz Shahi* is a much more complicated study which requires as much an examination of the basic categories of Barani's thought as an analysis of his fluctuating emotions. In this paper an attempt has been made to investigate the main tendencies of Barani's thought as it developed in a particular social background and the psychological reactions that his sensitive soul registered to different situations as they arose and conditioned his historical thinking and approach.

Barani belonged to an aristocratic family which had served three main dynasties of rulers during the Sultanate period—the Ilbarites, the Khaljis and the Tughluqs. His maternal grandfather Sipah Salar Husam-ud-Din was an important officer of Balban and performed the duties of *Wakil-i-dar Barbak Sultani*.[12] He enjoyed the

[9] *Ibid.*, 10–11.

[10] *Tarikh-i-Firuz-Shahi*, 10–11.

[11] Balazuri, *The Origins of the Islamic State*, trans., Hitti, (New York 1916), Intro., 3.

[12] *Ibid.*, 32, 41,

Sultan's confidence and was, therefore, appointed *Shahna* of Lakhnauti,[13] a very important assignment in view of the Sultan's concern for the consolidation of his power in Bengal after the Tughril revolt. Barani's father, Muwayyid-ul-Mulk, held the post of the *naib* of Arkali Khan[14] and lived in a palatial house at Kilugarhi,[15] the mosf aristocratic locality of medieval Delhi. His uncle Ala-ul-Mulk was a confidant of Ala-ud-Din Khalji from his Kara days. In fact he had helped Ala-ud-Din in his conspiracy against Jalal.[16] When Ala-ud-Din ascended the throne of Delhi, he first assigned to him Kara and Awadh,[17] and later on entrusted to him one of the most responsible duties of the Empire—the Kotwalship of Delhi[18]—and consulted him on almost every crucial matter—be it his personal religion[19] or a Mongol invasion.[20] Barani's father Muwayyid-ul-Mulk got the *niyabat* and *khwajgi* of Baran.[21] Barani himself joined the court during the reign of Muhammad bin Tughlaq and remained his *nadim* for more than 17 years[22]—an honour which a man with exceptional qualities of head and heart alone could enjoy. The Sultan consulted him very often[23] and recognized his knowledge of history.[24] When Firuz Shah Tughluq ascended the throne, Barani lost all influence at the court and his political career abruptly came to an end for reasons which will be discussed later. What happened to his family after that nobody can say, as the contemporary and later records are silent on this point. At a time when the complexion of the governing class was changing from dynasty to dynasty, his family had the political wisdom to maintain its position till the rise of Firuz Shah, when a political miscalculation by Barani was exploited by certain elements which had recently appeared in the political life of the country. Barani could never regain his lost prestige.

[13] *Ibid.*, 87.
[14] *Ibid.*, 209.
[15] *Ibid.*
[16] *Ibid.*, 222.
[17] *Ibid.*, 248.
[18] *Ibid.*, 250.
[19] *Ibid.*, 265–266.
[20] *Ibid.*, 255.
[21] *Ibid.*, 248.
[22] *Ibid.*, 504.
[23] *Ibid.*, 509–11; 516–17.
[24] *Ibid.*, 521.

Contact with the court apart, Barani and his family had occasions to move in the highest academic circles of the country and meet the finest intellects of the age. Some of the 46 scholars of the Alai period whom Barani considered as equals of Ghazzali and Razi, were amongst his teachers.[25] Amir Khusrau and Amir Hasan Sijzi were his close personal friends. 'They could not live without my company and I without theirs', says Barani.[26] In the highest circles of Delhi—both political and academic—Barani was known for his suavity of manners, great social charm and scintillating wit.[27] Family background and personal position thus made him a man of the higher strata of society. If at any point he came into touch with the common man, it was the *khanqah* of Shaikh Nizam-ud-Din Auliya. But there, too, it was in the closing years of his life—years of frustration and dismay as they were—that he turned in search of that peace of mind which his soul, deeply immersed in longings for material glory, could never attain.

Thus his own position in society conditioned his social outlook. His whole concept of society became coterminous with the life of the royalty and the upper classes. The ideological sustenance for this social attitude he derived from the Iranian ideals of historiography. He was never tired of referring to the Sassanid heroes of Persia as the ideals of kingship.[28] He looked upon the historical landscape from the foot of the royal throne focussing his attention on the royalty and the governing classes. For him history was their history and authority was their exclusive privilege. He failed to see greatness apart from or independent of kingship. Even the Prophet of Islam was *Sultan-i-Paighambaran*[29] in his eyes; and he found the greatness of his spiritual mentor Shaikh Nizam-ud-Din Auliya not in his God-conscious existence but in the externalia of his *khanqah*—the multitudes of people coming and going.[30] Even in the closing years of his life when he was dragging on his melancholy existence in a corner of Shaikh Nizam-ud-Din Auliya's *khanqah*, he could not get rid of his aristocratic complexes. It was a hangover of power

[25] *Ibid.*, 354.
[26] *Ibid.*, 166.
[27] Mirkhurd, *Siyar-ul-Auliya*, (Delhi, 1302 A.H.), 312.
[28] *Tarikh-i-Firuz Shahi*, 18, 20, etc.
[29] *Ibid.*, 2.
[30] *Ibid.*, 343–44.

which seared his soul. He never reconciled himself to his fate, and so the inner discontent grew apace. Humour changed into sarcasm, and buoyancy gave way to frustration. Had he been able to shake off his aristocratic complexes, he would have never thought of writing a history of the Sultans. He would have, on the other hand, written a history of the Chishti saints, who looked upon political power and authority with non-chalance and gave a wide berth to the government of the day.[31] Instead, he thought of compiling a *Tarikh*, a *Fatawa-i-Jahandari* and a *Hasrat-Nama*—all revealing the distress and anguish of a torn and frustrated personality desperately struggling to retrieve its position. He translated into Persian an Arabic account of the Barmeckides because he saw in their history an image of his own fate. He wrote a biography of the Prophet—*Sana-i-Muhammadi*[32]—at a time when, in his own words, he 'was not hopeful of being alive till the morning'—inspired not by any academic reasons but as an atonement for his past sins and in the hope of securing, through its spiritual benediction, his release from the prison of Bhatnir. 'Owing to the composition of this book', he writes, 'which is the protection, *pusht-wa-panah*, of my religious and wordly affairs, I feel a new strength in myself from time to time.' But adversity could not change his mentality. He died, as he was born, an aristocrat and continued to look upon humanity throughout his life through the aristocratic glasses.

This class-consciousness ultimately developed into a complex and embittered his attitude towards the lower sections of society. The source of this bitterness was political, not religious or social. When a new class of officers, consisting of man like Laddha, Najba, Manka, Shaikh Babu Naik, Peera etc.,[33] rose up under Muhammad bin Tughluq, Barani, with his grim political realism, heard the rumblings of a distant storm which in course of time was to sweep all the old families of administrators off their feet. Muhammad bin Tughlaq's love for history, his interest in literature and above all

[31] As two other contemporaries of Barani, Mir Khurd and Hamid Qalandar, had done.

[32] The only manuscript of this work is preserved in the Riza Library, Rampur.

[33] *Tarikh-i-Firuz Shahi*, 505. According to Barani all of them were low born; Najba, who was appointed malik and Gujarat, Multan and Badaun were assigned to him, was the son of a musician; Laddha was a gardener and Shaikh Babu Naik was the son of a weaver.

his affection for Barani, guaranteed the latter's position at the court, but Barani found himself an alien in that atmosphere in which plebians and upstarts rubbed shoulders with the old aristocracy. With the death of Muhammad bin Tughluq the mainstay of Barani's prestige collapsed, and events so rapidly moved against him that he slept a powerful *amir* but rose up a poverty stricken-pauper. A tactical blunder brought all this misfortune upon him. When Muhammad bin Tughluq died suddenly in Sindh, Khwaja Jahan placed on the throne of Delhi a boy of tender age. He was unaware that in Sindh Shaikh Nasir-ud-Din Chiragh and others had already raised Firuz to the throne. Barani gave his direct or indirect support to Khwaja Jahan's action, and thus cast his lot with an *amir* who was heading for the gallows. On Firuz's arrival in Delhi, the position of Khwaja Jahan and his Delhi group of supporters became extremely precarious. Left to himself Firuz would probably have forgiven these *amirs* who had acted in good faith but the new group, which had in the meantime filled the vacuum and attained pre-eminent position in the new set-up, forced Firuz Shah to deal sternly with them. Khwaja Jahan was killed and with him many others lost their heads, but Barani, despite the efforts of his enemies to the contrary,[34] succeeded in saving his skin. It was Firuz Shah's intervention which saved is life,[35] but he was deprived of his former position, status and property. 'God honoured me at the beginning and disgraced me at the end of my life,' he writes in great distress.[36] It was a most tragic position in which Barani was now placed. An *amir* of three generations, a *nadim* of the previous Sultan, reduced to a state of abject penury,[37] disowned by friends, neglected by relatives and dispised by enemies. In deep despair he remarks : 'Even the birds and fish are happy in their homes but I am not. Gloom and frustration consequently clouded his mind. The person who now dominated the political scene was Khan-i-Jahan Maqbul—an Indian by birth who had risen to high position shouldering out all old and distinguished families from their positions of power and authority. Barani's frustrated mind begins to develop a whole chain of causal connections. Khan-i-Jahan Maqbul would never have attained that position but for the policy of promoting low

[34] *Ibid.*, 556–57.
[35] *Ibid.*, 557.
[36] *Ibid.*, 166.
[37] *Ibid.*, 204–05.

born persons followed by some preceding Sultans. Muhammad bin Tughluq was an arch-criminal in this respect. He had broken the monopoly of the old and respectable families by introducing new elements in the aristocracy, primarily from the lower rungs of the society. The philosophers[38], who were constantly with him, were responsible for putting those ideas in his mind. These philosophers—mischief-mongers, enemies of stability and respectability—should be rooted out from society and philosophy should be tabooed[39] in the interest of stability. Education should be denied to the low born because it qualifies them for posts in the administration. They should be kept in a state of perpetual ignorance. Thus, one after the other, prejudices enter the texture of Barani's thought and colour his whole outlook and approach towards life and society. He begins to hate the low born and the philosophers, and opposes the extension of educational facilities to the common man. The development of this trend of thought was inherent in the situation he was placed in. A closer analysis shows that his prejudices did not emanate from his religious views but evolved out of the complications of his frustrated life. Conscious of the fact that this distinction of the low born and the high born could not be sustained in the light of Muslim religious concepts, he tries to convert it into a conflict between 'Faith' and 'Infidelity'. But many of these so called low born persons whom he was thus condemning under the mask of a principle, were converts to Islam. How could they be called 'infidels'? Here comes Barani's theory that conversion of the low born is always imperfect and incomplete. They are never genuine in their conversion; they are hypocrites. Then he tries to seek shelter in his theory of contradictions, as propounded in the *Fatawa-i-Jahandari*, but he never buttresses his point of view by a recourse to any religious authority. In fact he fully realized that distinctions based on birth had a *wordly* rather than a *religious* basis, and he makes this secret out in his estimate of Prince Muhammad.[40]

That much about the circumstances in which the basic categories of Barani's thought developed. Now a word about his approach to history. Barani sought in the history of the period the causes of

[38] *Ibid.*, 43, 464–65; Barani has particularly named the following philosophers : Sad, Ubaid, Najm Intishar, Maulana Najm-ud-Din.

[39] *Ibid.*, 43, 465.

[40] *Ibid.*, 68.

his own rise and fall, and this search introduced subtle threads of subjectivism in his narrative. He found the tragedy of his own life and its causes writ large in the actions and attitudes of the rulers and the maliks. He is writing about Balban. All of a sudden his mind finds some situation identical or inimical to his own and he starts talking about himself. 'I can', he says, 'compile two volumes regarding the atrocities perpetrated on me by the wretched and cruel sky.'[41] He describes the private assemblies of Jalal-ud-Din Khalji and he cannot help lamenting his own fate.[42] Such lamentations recur again and again. The historian seems to carry the weight of his own frustrated life on his shoulders throughout the work, and on the slightest provocation pours forth his heart, bursts into laments and starts questioning the historical data if it could explain the tragedy of his own life. 'The despair that is in my heart', he writes, 'flows in tears of blood from my eyes : a wave from river of blood pours out of my eyes, drips from my pen and stains the paper.'[43] A book produced in such a mental and emotional climate was bound to be soaked in irremediable subjectivity. It is interesting to trace these subjective threads in his narrative. He condemns Muhammad bin Tughluq for almost every one of his administrative actions and policies but when he comes to describe his death his heart begins to bleed.[44] Why ? There were Sultans who died under more tragic circumstances than Muhammad bin Tughluq but he did not express such feelings about them. Moreover, a sigh of relief rather than a mourning cry would have been more appropriate to the general attitude he had taken up towards the Sultan. But in the passing away of Muhammad bin Tughluq he heard the death-knell of his own life of prestige, power and position. He weeps as much for the Sultan as for his own self. His whole account of Muhammad bin Tughluq seems saturated with such vagaries of psychological moods. He showers encomiums on him and gives him a place in the Pantheon of Prophets and saints ; and then suddenly assumes another position and starts hurling invectives at him and finds in him the traits of Nimrod and Pharoah. This strange tribute of love and hatred, again, has its roots in Barani's own psychology. It was not so much the Sultan who was 'a

[41] *Ibid.*, 69.
[42] *Ibid.*, 200.
[43] *Ibid.*, 166.
[44] *Ibid.*, 525-26.

mass of inconsistencies' or a 'mixture of opposites' but the historian himself was a miserably torn personality. He projected his own psychological states in his assessment of the Sultan's character. It was due to his policy of throwing offices open to talent, his *kasrat-i-tehkimat-i-mujaddid*,[45] his recruitment of the promiscuous mass of people to the 'charmed' circle of nobles, his philosophic interests which led to the development of sceptic attitude in him towards the 'Revealed Books and the Traditions of the Prophets' (*kutub-i-samaki wa ahadis ambia*) which created confusion all around and made the position of the old and respectable families, like his own, absolutely untenable. He, therefore, deserved condemnation in the severest terms. And Barani starts disparaging the Sultan. But this mood does not last long. As soon as the historian returns from his mental incursion into the age of Muhammad bin Tughluq and suddenly becomes conscious of his present miserable plight, the direction of his emotions begins to change. 'I enjoyed status and position during the reign of Muhammad bin Tughluq.'[46] A patron and benefactor like him deserves to be praised and the historian starts extolling the Sultan to the skies. When Barani is in his *present*, he has love for Muhammad bin Tughluq ; when he is in his *past*, he has nothing but hatred for him. Love and hatred thus alternate with fluctuations in moods of the historian. The moment one succeeds in catching this subtle psychological mood of the historian, the entire data supplied by him neatly fits into the proper perspective.

No two persons could be more fundamentally different from one another in thought and outlook than Barani and Muhammad bin Tughluq. They were denizens of two different worlds—the Sultan, a revolutionary in politics and a rationalist in religion ; Barani, a hide bound reactionary in politics and a blind follower of tradition in religious matters. It is to the credit of Barani that in spite of this wide ideological gulf between him and the Sultan, he gives a complete picture of Muhammad bin Tughluq. Isami and Ibn Battuta, the other two contemporary historians supply valuable details about Muhammad bin Tughluq and help us considerably in fixing the chronology of his reign, but none comes up anywhere near Barani in his penetrating, graphic and comprehensive study of the Sultan. Ibn Battuta's Mohammad bin Tughluq is a man of scholarly temperament,

[45] *Ibid.*, 467.
[46] *Ibid.*

generous to a fault but essentially a tyrant; Isami's Sultan is an ill-guided, irreligious monarch, tyrannical and impulsive. It is in the pages of *Tarikh-i-Firuz Shahi* that the real and dynamic personality of the Sultan is revealed to us. Here and there one may find comments—harsh, bitter and uncharitable—but out of all these the thought and personality of the Sultan emerges in all its light and shade. This is due to the fact that Barani does not allow his subjectivity to gear his data to establish any particular hypothesis.[47] This may sound strange but is nevertheless true. A closer study of Barani shows that it is in his assessment of characters, not assortment of facts, that subjective elements play a part in his narrative.

Now, apart from his tendency to read the ups and downs of his own fate in the vicissitudes of history, Barani was, to all intents and purposes, a fairly honest historian. He did not suppress facts or distort them, however unpalatable they might have been to him or his family. He frankly confesses that he had not the courage to speak the truth before Muhammad bin Tughluq, and was, therefore, guilty of hypocrisy.[48] While describing Ala-ud-Din Khalji's conspiratorial activities at Kara—which he does not hesitate to condemn—he makes no attempt to withdraw his uncle Ala-ul-Mulk from the scene.[49] He recorded facts as they appeared on the screen of his mind and did not try to prove or disprove any hypothesis by accordingly selecting or rejecting the data. His senile mind often looses the chronological sequence of events. He records whatever he remembers, and he remembers whatever has left a deep impress on his mind. This is a serious shortcoming of Barani's work. A weak chronological framework is, doubtless, a blemish in a historical work. But what Barani aims at supplying to his readers is not a catalogue of events but a glimpse into the spirit of the age. He recreates the past and gets his

[47] To cite only two instances: (a) Barani has great respect and admiration for Jalal-ud-Din Khalji whom he calls *Sultan al-Halim* and is all condemnation for those who brought about his tragic end. But this does not prevent him from giving details which show that it was Jalal himself who rushed into the open jaws of death, ignoring all counsels of caution and preparation. (b) Barani refers to the episode of Sayyidi Maula and credulously establishes connection between the dust storm and the scarcity that occurred soon afterwards. He refers to his own visit to Sayyidi also. But his account leaves one in no doubt that his *khanqah* had become the refuge of discontented elements. Examples may be multiplied.

[48] *Tarikh-i-Firuz Shahi*, 516–17.

[49] *Ibid.*, 222.

reader involved in the life of the period. Barani is a historian whose real worth and value can be appreciated only when the chronological framework is available from other sources. Iltumish's life and activities have been dealt with in detail by Minhaj in his *Tabaqat-i-Nasiri* but in such a soulless manner that, except for a long and unbroken series of military campaigns, a reader's mind gathers no impression about the character or personality or even the problems of Iltutmish's period. Barani refers to him incidentally in connection with Balban, but the few references that he makes are so vital and significant that they light up the whole epoch. Minhaj describes the campaigns of Iltutmish against his rivals but his account tells us nothing as to how Iltutmish conciliated or crushed the large number of his quondom colleagues, the slave-officers of Muizz-ud-Din and Qutb-ud-Din. When Barani says that Iltutmish used to remark in his court : 'When I see these great nobles standing before me, I feel inclined to come down from the throne and kiss their hands and feet.' He tells us more about the situation than any other contemporary historian. It is a brief and incidental remark but shows how Iltutmish had to work in order to gain confidence and cooperation of his *maliks*. Minhaj's account of Iltutmish's patronage of saints and religious men is too general and vague to be of any particular value in understanding the character and personality of the Sultan. Barani's references present the Sultan's personality in the boldest relief. What different religious attitudes and opinions were presented before Iltutmish and how he reacted to them, Barani says more than Minhaj, and whatever he records brings us nearer to the spirit of the age, and we feel as if we have gained an insight into the problems of the age. Barani, in fact, had a better sense of history and its spirit than any other Persian chronicler of the early medieval period. Despite all his shortcomings no other historian of the period comes up anywhere near him. Minhaj, who has adhered so closely to the chronological sequence of events, has made history a dull, drab and insipid affair. His accounts are totally unrelated to the social and economic background of the period. No one can gather from the *Tabaqat-i-Nasiri* what social and cultural forces were at work when one of the greatest empires of the middle ages was being founded. How did the processes of adjustment and conciliation start and work ? How an alien administration succeeded in striking its roots in the soil ? These are questions which occur again and again in one's mind but no reply is found in Minhaj's pages. Barani had to deal with another significant development in medieval Indian history—the rise of Khalji Imperialism. He has succeeded in communicating its spirit to us in all its aspects—military, cultural and economic. His details about the actual battles fought by Ala-ud-Din Khalji may be inaccurate, but the total impression that he has been able to convey about the Khalji period is historically so significant that even Amir Khusrau does not come up to that level in his *Khazain-ul-Futuh*.

Dr. P. Hardy says that Barani treats history as a branch of theology and sees the past as a battleground between good and evil.[50] Unfortunately his view is not borne out by facts. Barani had a keen awareness of the changing phenomena of political life and his analysis of situations is basically and essentially political. One has to look into his accounts of Balban's *wasaya* regarding the consolidation of political authority[51] and his analysis of the characters and activities of Malik Nizam-ud-Din[52], Ahmad Chap[53], Almas Beg[54] and Malik Kafur[55] to be convinced of his understanding of the forces which lead to the decline and dismemberment of political authority. His intimate knowledge of administration and its problems extending over a number of years helped him in making a realistic appraisal of the factors and forces that worked in the life of the dynasties that controlled the contemporary political seene. Of all the medieval Muslim writers he alone posed the question whether the laws of the *shariat* could be meticulously enforced ? Despite his conservative and orthodox views he did not hesitate to declare that it had now become impossible to enforce the laws of the *shariat* in administration where the needs of the time necessitated a recourse to state laws (*zawabit*). Only one with a deep historical sense and awareness of the changes that had taken place in the Islamic polity through the centuries could state this opinion. An *alim*, no doubt, he was, but he cannot be bracketted with Sayyid Nur-ud-Din Mubarak or Qazi Mughis because he had a greater sense of realities. One other aspect of the problem also deserves consideration. His *Fatawa-i-Jahandari*

[50] Hardy, *Historians of Medieval India*, 39.
[51] *Tarikh-i-Firuz Shahi*, 77 *et seq*.
[52] *Ibid.*, 132 *et seq*.
[53] *Ibid.*, 184, 224 etc.
[54] *Ibid*, 229 *et seq*.
[55] *Ibid.*, 375 *et seq*.

in which he has expressed this opinion was written during the reign of Firuz Shah whose administration is generally believed to be religiously oriented. To say at that time that the enforcement of *shariat* laws had receded from the pale of practical politics is to give very accurate verdict on the actual nature and spirit of Firuz's administration. Professor Habib has correctly remarked that for Barani 'history was not a record or a chronicle or a story ; it was very definitely a science—the science of the social order and its basis was not religion or tradition but observation and experience.'[56]

Barani has dealt with nine rulers of Delhi, from Balban to Firuz Shah Tughluq. His account of Balban is based upon what he heard from his maternal grandfather, Sipah Salar Husam-ud-Din. Balban's reports about Sayyid Nur-ud-Din Mubarak Ghaznavi's discourses at the court of Iltutmish have been cited on his authority.[57] From the same source he obtained his information about the *wasaya* of Balban. Husam-ud-Din went to Lakhnauti with Balban who appointed him as *shahna* of that place after crushing the revolt of Tughril. His vivid account of the Lakhnauti campaign was probably based on his grandfather's reports. Besides, Shams Dabir whom Balban dictated the instructions for Bughra Khan, was a relation of Amir Hasan Sijizi, a friend of Barani. It was from Hasan and Khusrau that he learnt about the life and activities of Prince Muhammad. From the times of Jalal-ud-Din Khalji to the reign of Firuz Tughluq he writes on the basis of personal observation and personal experience. He has referred to very few contemporary authorities.[58] He considered an account of Khalji campaigns redundent as Taj-ud-Din had already covered that ground, and it was not Barani's habit to follow the beaten track. One of the determining factors in his selection of data was, therefore, the availability or otherwise of literature on that topic. If material was available, he would abstain from giving details; if not, he would give the necessary details with interest. He says about Malik Qutb-ud-Din Hasan, an important member of the *Turkan-i-Chehlgani*, that volumes have been written about him,[59] but his own account of the *malik* is brief, almost to the extent of being tantalizing. Though Barani does not mention

[56] Mohammad Habib, *The Political Theory of the Delhi Sultanate*, 125.

[57] *Tarikh-i-Firuz Shahi*, 41.

[58] He refers to Khwaja Zaki, Malik Qara Bek, Amir Khusrau and Amir Hasan as his informants. *Tarikh-i-Firuz Shahi*, 67, 114, 299, 118, 370.

[59] *Ibid.*, 113.

this, all this contemporary literature must have been studied by him some time in his earlier days.

Had Barani any records, notes or memoranda when he wrote his *Tarikh-i-Firuz Shahi* ? Professor Habib thinks that he had nothing but his memory and his pen, ink and paper.[60] This seems to be true with regard to the major portion of his work, but there are places in the *Tarikh-i-Firuz Shahi* where one is constrained to feel that Barani had some recorded data available to him e.g., the lists of principal officers, governors etc., prefixed to the account of each Sultan.[61] This could not obviously be a feat of his memory. Since these lists are not woven with the text, may be that he subsequently came to lay his hands on them and just put them at the proper places.

Was the *Tarikh-i-Firuz Shahi* written before or after the *Fatawa-i-Jahandari* ? The question is pertinent because on it depends the decision of the question if Barani was a political philosopher who took to history, or was he a historian who turned a philosopher—whether he cast history in the mould of his political thinking or his political ideas emanated from his knowledge of history. Internal evidences—style, structure and content—goes to prove that the *Fatawa-i-Jahandari* was compiled after the *Tarikh*.

What were Barani's motives in compiling the *Tarikh-i-Firuz Shahi* ? He wrote it because his frustrated soul found in it a satisfaction, a sense of self-realization and an opportunity to 'immortalize' his name and fame which seemed deserting him. It does not seem very correct to think that he wrote it in order to win Firuz Shah's favour. He says again and again in the *Tarikh* that it was his desire that Firuz Shah could glance at his *Tarikh*.[62] This was nothing more than a desire which developed when he started writing his book and not the real motive of compilation. Attention may be drawn to a problem in this respect. Barani condemns Muhammad bin Tughluq in harsh terms in this work. Firuz Shah, as we know from the *Futuhat* and other sources, had profound respect for him and used to refer to him as *Khudawand wali niamat* and *Makhdum wa murabbi i-man*.[63] How could Barani expect to win Firuz's favour through a work which found in his *makhdum* the traits of Nimrod

[60] *The Political Theory of the Delhi Sultanate*, 126.
[61] *Tarikh-i-Firuz Shahi*, 24, 126, 174, etc.
[62] *Ibid.*, 125.
[63] *Futuhat-i-Firuz Shahi*, 18–19.

and Pharoah ? Prabably Firuz Shah also did not see eye to eye with his distinguished predecessor and, despite his public professions of attachment with Muhammad bin Tughluq, he had no real respect or affection for him.

Here a probability may be considered. Probably the *Tarikh-i-Firuz Shahi* is not *one* but *two* books. It seems that the author intended to write two independent histories : one dealing with the early rulers from Balban to Muhammad bin Tughluq, and the other dealing exclusively with Firuz Shah Tughluq. He could not complete the second and decided to put them together under the title *Tarikh-i-Firuz Shahi*. Several factors deserve consideration in this connection: (1) Barani, it appears, had different plans of writing history in his mind. At one time he thought of writing a Universal History[64] but gave up the idea on two grounds ; regard for a much venerated predecessor Minhaj-us-Siraj and the general indifference of people towards history. (2) Barani's account of Kaiqubad leaves the impression that probably the historian wanted to write a separate monograph on that Sultan. (3) The two parts of the *Tarikh-i-Firuz Shahi*, the earlier one and the later one dealing with Firuz, are, structurally and from the point of view of approach, analysis and treatment entirely different. Barani is sharp, incisively critical and at places bitter in the first part ; he is a docile sychophant in the second. (4) Barani gives a list of themes which he proposed to deal with in his account of Firuz Shah. This list gives the impression of the planning of an independent work rather than being a chapter in a larger work.

The Barani of the last part of the *Tarikh-i-Firuz Shahi* is a shameless flatterer. He finds divine attributes in the person of Firuz Shah and considers his court as the Court of Allah, where *amirs* stand as Gabriel stands before *Arsh*.[65] While he extols Firuz to the skies, he condemns Khwaja Jahan in order to wash the earlier charge of being in league with him against Firuz Shah. Barani is condemned here by the canons he had himself formulated in the preface to his work. His reference to Khan-i-Jahan Maqbul is, however, significant. It is a praise which borders on a warning to Firuz Shah and reminds one of the observations of the author of *Rauzut-us-Safa* regarding the methods a historian should adopt to convey his real feelings. Barani remarks about him : 'For the last six years the *Wizarat* has been

[64] *Tarikh-i-Firuz Shahi*, 49.
[65] *Ibid.*, 578.

assigned to him. He has plenary and unrestricted authority in the *Diwan-i-wizarat* and has been made a despot. Whatever concessions the Emperor has been pleased to confer upon him are such that no earlier Sultan of Delhi has ever conferred upon a *Wazir*.'[66] There is praise and there is warning in what he says.

For an understanding of the *Tarikh-i-Firuz Shahi* it is necessary to comprehend the expression and terminology of Barani. Some of the terms used by him have their special connotation which is necessary to understand in order to follow Barani's thought. When he says that the Khaljis were not Turks,[67] he does not use the word Turk in its *racial* sense ; when he refers to Ala-ud-Din's harsh regulations against the *Hindus*,[68] he does not use the term *Hindu* in a *communal* sense ; when he talks about the enhancement of taxation by Muhammad bin Tughluq as an increase from one to ten[69] he does not use the expression in its *arithmetical* sense.

It is difficult to do justice to Barani in a single paper. Here attention has been drawn to some of the basic aspects of his thought and personality. Barani is one of those historians who refuse to enlighten a reader unless he has thoroughly familiarized himself with the basic categories of his thought and the Chief characteristics of his personality. The *Tarikh-i-Firuz Shahi* is, indeed, for one who knows Ziya-ud-Din Barani.

[66] *Ibid.*, 578–79.
[67] *Ibid.*, 176.
[68] *Ibid.*, 287.
[69] *Ibid.*, 473.

4

Writings in Medieval Kashmir

In this paper an attempt is made to deal with only Persian historical writing in Kashmir during the Sultanate period. It is now commonly accepted that Kashmir is the only part of India where historical writing flourished in pre-Muslim times. But although many chronicles were written, the only one which his survived is Kalhana's *Rajatarangini*, completed in A. D. 1148–49.[1] Two hundred years later, Jonaraja continued the narrative down to the reign of Sultan Zain-ul-Abidin and called it, like Kalhana, *Rajatarangini*. After the death of Jonaraja in 1459, his pupil Shrivara continued the history from where he had left off and brought it down to 1486. When Shrivara died Prajyabhatta composed his *Rajavalipataka*, which covered the period from 1517 to 1596.[2] This was the last Sanskrit chronicle to have been written in Kashmir.

Thus Kashmir had a strong tradition of historical writing and, in addition, with the establishment of the Sultanate, many learned men who came from Persia and Turkistan brought with them the Persian and Central Asian traditions. But it is strange that not a single historical work appears to have been written in Persian during the first eighty years of the Sultanate. The only explanation seems to be that during this period the court language was Sanskrit. It is only from the reign of Sultan Zain-ul-Abidin (1420–70), that Persian replaced Sanskrit as the language of court and learning, and histories in Persian began to be composed. Two of these were by Mulla Ahmad and Mulla Nadiri, the Sultan's court poets. But un-

[1] Kalhana, *Rajatarangini*, English trans. M. A. Stein, 2 Vols., London, 1900.

[2] The works of Jonaraja, Shrivara, Prajyabhatta and Shuka were edited by P. Peterson, Bombay, 1896. English trans. J. C. Dutt entitled *Kings of Kashmira*, 3 Vols., Calcutta, 1879–98,

fortunately none of them is extant. Nor is there any trace of the histories written by Qazi Ibrahim in the second reign of Sultan Fath Shah (1493–1505) and by Mulla Hasan Qari in the time of the Chak rulers (1566–88).[3] The only work composed in the pre-Mughal period that has survived is Sayyid Ali's *Tarikh-i-Kashmir*, written during Yusuf Shah's reign. All others, which are extent, were written during the Mughal period. Despite this they must be regarded as the works of the Sultanate period because their authors were born and brought up in Kashmir and lived through the later Shah Mir and Chak periods. Thus the histories of the Sultanate period are the *Tarikh-i-Kashmir* by Sayyid Ali completed in 1579[4]; the *Tarikh-i-Kashmir* by an anonymous writer (Aumer 287) written in 1590[5]; The *Baharistan-i-Shahi*, also anonymous, written in the time of Jahangir[6]; the *Tarikh-i-Kashmir* by Hasan b. Ali Kashmiri[7] also written in the time of Jahangir; the *Tarikh-i-Kashmir* by Haider Malik completed in 1620–21.[8] The other histories of Kashmir, besides being abridgements of the above works, were written in the eighteenth and nineteenth centuries and do not, therefore come within the purview of this study.

Among the above works the *Baharistan-i-Shahi* and Haider Malik's *Tarikh* are the most important. The others though useful in certain respects, are poor in chronology, give usually a summary of events and omit important historical episodes. Sayyid Ali's *Tarikh*, for example, is important only for Mirza Haidar Dughlat's career in Kashmir, which he wrote from personal observation, and for the religious history of the Sultanate period, which covers nearly one-third of the book. But it is very deficient in chronology and for the most part passes over the political history of the Sultanate. The *Tarikh-i-Kashmiri*—anonymous (Aumer 267) which covers the history of Kashmir up to the reign of Sultan Shams-ud-Din (1540), also gives few dates and leaves out important events like the arrival of Sayyid Ali Hamadani in the Valley. Moreover, it is at places confused and unreliable. Hasan b. Ali's *Tarikh* is a short history of

[3] Mohibbul Hasan, *Kashmir under the Sultans*, 1.

[4] Research and publication Department, Srinagar.

[5] *Tarikh-i-Kashmir* (K. Hof-Statsbibliothek Munich).

[6] *Baharistan-i-Shahi*, India Office, 509.

[7] Hasan b. Ali Kashmiri, *Tarikh-i-Kashmir*, Bodleian, 315.

[8] Haidar Malik, *Tarikh-i-Kashmir*, India Office, 509.

Kashmir written at the request of Jalal-ud-Din Malik, a Kashmiri noble, who wanted to preserve the record of the achievements of his ancestors. It claims to cover the period from the ancient times to 1616, but it actually does not go beyond Sultan Hasan Shah's reign (1472–84), except making only a casual reference to Yaqub Shah's submission to Akbar.

On the other hand, the *Baharistan-i-Shahi* and Haider Malik's *Tarikh* are more valuable both from the point of view of chronology and topography. Besides, they give a more detailed account of the period they cover than the other chronicles. Nothing is known of the author of the *Baharistan* except that he was, probably, in the service of the Baihaqi Sayyids[9] and wrote at their suggestion, for he gives much space in his work to their careers and bestows excessive praise on them. His sources are Kalhana's *Rajatarangini*, the chronicles of Jonaraja and Shrivara, the Persian histories of Mulla Ahmed, Mulla Nadiri, Qazi Ibrahim and Mulla Hasan Qari, which were extant in his time. As regards the later Shah Mirs and the Chaks, he wrote from personal experience or by gathering information from his contemporaries or near contemporaries.

Haider Malik wrote his *Tarikh* in order to preserve the memory and the great deeds of the kings of Kashmir and of his own ancestors who had played such an important role in the history of their country.[10] Haider Malik descended from Ramachandra, commander-in-chief of Suhadeva, the last Hindu king of Kashmir. He himself was a man of great attainments, being a soldier, a statesman, historian and an engineer. He served Yusuf Khan Chak for twenty four years and accompanied him in exile to Hindustan after the Mughal conquest of Kashmir. After the death of Yusuf Khan he entered the service of Jahangir who gave him the title of *Chaghatay* and *Rais-ul-Mulk*.[11] Haider Malik employed the same sources for his history

[9] The Baihaqi Sayyids came to Kashmir in the time of Sultan Sikandar. They married in the royal family, and played an important part in the political affairs of the valley. One of the Baihaqi Sayyids for a short period even wore the crown.

[10] Haidar Malik, *Tarikh-i-Kashmir*, f. 3a.

[11] The main reason why these titles were conferred upon Haidar Malik was that he, togather with his brother Ali Malik, saved the life and honour of Mehr-un-Nisa after Sher Afgan had been killed. (See my article 'A Note on the Assassination of Sher Afgan' in Dr. Yazdani Commemoration Volume, ed., H. K. Sherwani, 1966).

as the author of *the Baharistan-i-Shahi*. As regards the Chak Period, he was himself a witness to many events, being a young man at the time. In addition, he gathered information from his father and grandfather who held high offices in the government of the Sultanate.

It is difficult to point out to what extent the histories of Kashmir were influenced by the Kashmiri tradition of historiography as represented by Kalhana, Jonaraja or Shrivara. However, it is obvious from their study that they copied the tradition of historical writing in Hindustan and Persia with which they were in constant cultural contact. The Persian histories of Kashmir describe events in strict chronological sequence. Though sparing in dates they are compiled according to reigns, and describe rebellions, wars and conquests, rise and fall of dynasties. Episodes are interspersed with verses, carrying some moral, with anecdotes and with stories of miracles performed by the Sufis or of various other supernatural happenings in the rivers, springs, lakes and mountains of Kashmir.[12] They contain fairly good information about the spread of Islam in the Valley, but do not throw much light on the social and economic life of the people. Though mostly descriptive, they some-times try to explain why things happened. Thus while describing the overthrow of Mirza Haidar Dughlat, Haidar Malik explains that this was due to his trannical measures which antagonized the people of Kashmir and led to their revolt.[13] The author of the *Baharistan* is more explicit about this tyranny and says that Mirza Haidar was over thrown because of his persecution of the Shias, Shafis and Sufis.[14] Similarly these works attribute the Mughal conquest of Kashmir to Yusuf Shah's passing his time in ease and luxury and to his neglect of state affairs. They further attribute it to the neglect of the defences of the Valley by Yaqub Shah and to his persecution of Sunnis.[15]

One of the interesting features of the Persian histories of Kashmir is that they are written with a patriotic bias. The Kashmir historians love the green valleys of Kashmir, its high snow-capped

[12] There is a whole section devoted by Haidar Malik in his *Tarikh* to super-natural events happening in lakes, streams etc. of Kashmir.

[13] *Ibid.*, 146a.

[14] *Baharistan-i-Shahi*, ff. 111b–112b; 120a–b.

[15] Ḥaiḍar Malik, *Tarikh-i-Kashmir*, 192a–b; *Baharistan-i-Shahi*, ff. 181a–b.

mountains, its winding river Jhelum, its life-giving and sacred springs and its picturesque sceneries. They write with pride about the conquests of Sultan Shihab-ud-Din and of the cultural glories of the reign of Sultan Zain-ul-Abidin, and express admiration at the successful resistance offered by the Kashmiris to the Mughal invasions which began from 1527 onwards. They are critical of Yusuf Shah for having given up the struggle against the Mughals and surrendered to them, and admire his son Yaqub Shah for continuing the fight against heavy odds. And when finally Kashmir is conquered by the Mughals they are unhappy about it. Their grief at Kashmir's loss of independence is, of course, implied and becomes evident only after a careful study of the chronicles, for it must be remembered that they were written under the Mughals and their authors could not write openly anything which might displease their new masters.

Unlike most of important general histories of India and the histories of the provincial dynasties which ignore the pre-Islamic period of Indian history, the Persian histories of Kashmir commence with the legendary beginnings of the island and include the history of its ancient kings. This might be due to the fact that while no history of ancient India was available to the medieval historians to be drawn upon, there was ready to hand, so far as Kashmir was concerned, Kalhana's *Rajatarangini* of which a Persian translation had also been made in the time of Zain-ul-Abidin.

The *Baharistan-i-Shahi* is written in an ornate and verbose style, while Haider Malik's *Tarikh* is composed in a language which is simple and lucid. However, both write with considerable restraint and avoid strong language. They are, for example, not in the habit of sending non-Muslims to hell. They use words like *kufr* and *kafir*, but these are not employed in a derogatory sense; and although they describe at length the activities of Sayyid Ali Hamadani and his son Mohammad Hamadani in spreading Islam in the Valley, they do not write with the fanatic zeal of a Barani or Badauni. The Kashmir historians are, for the most part, tolerant and objective in their assessments. Thus the author of the *Baharistan*, though a Shia, disapproves of Yaqub Shah's intolerant policy towards Sunnis, and criticises the execution of Qazi Musa, which was ordered because of his refusal to recite the name of Ali in the *azan*.[16] Similarly, while

[16] *Ibid.*

both Haidar Malik and the author of the *Baharistan* describe the iconoclastic activities of Sultan Sikandar, they do not seem to disapprove of the measures taken by Sultan Zain-ul-Abidin and his successors to rehabilitate Hinduism in Kashmir and to treat Hindus liberally. The author of the *Baharistan* observes[17] :

> The temples destroyed during the time of Sultan Sikandar were rebuilt. Those Hindus who had fled to Jammu and Kishtawar were recalled. The learning of Hindus was encouraged. Hindus were given complete freedom of worship and freedom to perform their customs. They, therefore, began to celebrate their festivals on particular days of the year, Zain-ul-Abidin himself used to participate in them. He gave presents to singers and dancers and because of this he was very popular. The result of the revival of Hinduism under Zain-ul-Abidin was that Hindu rites and customs revived among the Muslims also. Even men of learning and the *ulema* practised them. This continued until the time of Shams-ud-Din Iraqi who took up arms against the idolatrous practices.

The source of these historians for the ancient history of Kashmir was Kalhana's *Rajataringini*, but unfortunately they never cared to adopt Kalhana' technique. In consequence, they did not consult inscriptions or deeds; nor is there any evidence to suggest that they utilised the archives which were maintained by the Sultans, or read the histories of the Sultanate of Delhi. Their only sources were the earlier Kashmiri works whose accounts were accepted uncritically. This failure to consult any other historical work, except those of Kashmir, is responsible for many inaccuracies in their accounts. For example, basing themselves mainly upon the histories of their predecessors, they have recorded that Shihab-ud-Din conquered Badakshan, Kabul, Ghazni and Qandahar, and then marched with a large army to conquer Delhi. He encamped on the banks of the Sutlej where he was opposed by Firuz Shah Tughlaq. Here a battle took place, but it was indecisive. In the end peace was made. It was agreed that all the territory from Sirhind to Kashmir was to belong to Shihab-ud-Din, while the rest lying to the east was to go to Firuz Shah. In addition to the territorial settlement, a marriage alliance was also entered into between the rulers of Delhi and

[17] *Ibid.*, ff. 48b.

Srinagar[18].

If the contemporary histories were to be studied, this account would be found to be spurious. In fact, if the Kashmir historians had cared to consult the histories of the Delhi Sultanate and Turkistan, they would not have fallen into these errors. But their uncritical approach added to their anxiety to magnify the achievements of a Kashmir Sultan. Their false sense of patriotism prevented them from sifting fact from fiction.

As I have already pointed out that all the Kashmir historians based themselves on common sources. The result is that there is sameness and monotony in their descriptions. Thus the accounts of the establishment of the Shah-Mir dynasty, of the conquests made by Sultan Shihab-ud-Din, of the activities of Sayyid Ali Hamdani and his son Muhammad Hamdani, and of the achievements of Sultan Zain-ul-Abidin read all alike in the chronicles. It is only when we come to the later Shah Mir and Chak periods that there appear variety and differences in the accounts. This is because there are no longer any common sources to draw upon.

[18] *Ibid.*, f. 20b; Haidar Malik, *Tarikh-i-Kashmir*, ff. 108b–109b.

5

Kalhana

Kalhana wrote his chronicle of the history of Kashmir which he entitled the *Rajatarangini* in the year 4224 of the Laukika Era, which works out to A.D. 1148–49. He is described as 'the son of the great Kashmiri minister, the illustrious Lord Campaka' in the colophon. It has been suggested that Campaka was the minister to King Harsha of Kashmir (A.D. 1089–1101).[1] This seems very likely as it would have given Kalhana the required access to matters political and bureaucratic upon which he evidently bases much of his historical analysis of the medieval history of Kashmir. Had he been a mere litterateur this analysis may have formed a minor part of the narrative or may have been omitted altogether, as frequently happened in the writings of some of his near contemporaries. The literary form of the chronicle is however that of the *kavya* (a poem).

The *Rajatarangini* is a long, narrative poem relating the history of Kashmir from earliest times to the twelfth century A.D.[2] It is based on traditions, legends, written records and inscriptions. Kalhana explains that he has painstakingly collected popular traditions associated with places of historical interest. He has also consulted major works written on the region such as, the *Nilamata-purana*, Kshemendra's *Nrpavali*, Helaraja's *Parthivavali*, the *Chavilla-kara*, etc. Of these the *Nilamatapurana* is easily the most important traditional source on the early history of Kashmir, although as an

[1] Stein, Introduction, 6.

[2] The standard edition of the *Rajatarangini* edited by Sir M. A. Stein has been used in this paper (Bombay, 1892). The references given are to the book number and the verse number of the original text. For the sake of consistency, where translations are given, they are from Stein's translation of the text in *Kalhana's Rajatarangini, a Chronicle of the Kings of Kashmir*, (Westminister, 1900).

accurate historical source it suffers from the same weaknesses as other Puranic sources. The *Mahatmyas* were another interesting source, being the handbooks of the family priests at various places of pilgrimage. The *Vitastamahatmya*, for example, mentions the important places of pilgrimage along the Vitasta or Jhelum river in Kashmir and relates the historical events (as handed down in the tradition) connected with these places.

Kalhana's use of inscriptions as source material is a strikingly original element in his historical writing. He refers to inscriptions found in temples, the *prashastis* (eulogies) on past kings, the inscriptions referring to grants, mainly of land or revenue, made by earlier rulers. The reference to inscriptions in itself is not what is so important as the fact that he uses the information they contain as a legitimate source of history.

Kalhana was aware of the functions of historical writing and declares that his purpose in writing the chronicle is multiple : to try and establish the true chronology and succession of the kings of Kashmir, to write a readable narrative on the past, and to provide a commentary on the past which would lead his readers to reflect on the nature and impermanence of life. In the last of these we find evidence of his philosophy of history.

Kalhana was deeply imbued with the idea of *dharma* and for him historical events were basically the unfolding of the whole system of *dharma* in its religious, social and even legal manifestations. It meant not only the adherence to the traditions of religion, but also the upholding of the social institutions as prescribed in the *shastras.* But fortunately Kalhana was not dogmatic on this point as we shall see. The theory of *karma* evidently also had its own role to play in history. The influence of previous births on the present life-time of a ruler frequently provided a comfortable way out of difficult explanations. It was often used by other contemporary writers as well to account for many actions on the part of kings and statesmen.[3] Linked to the idea of *karma* was the importance given to the role of Fate in human events. Kalhana does not resort to the interference of Fate all that often, but now and again it comes up. For instance, a number of reasons are given as to why king Harsha of Kashmir finally weakened and lost to his enemies, and the

[3] e.g Bilhana's *Vikramankadevacharita.*

power of Fate is one among these.[4] Associated with the above is the belief in Divine Retribution, especially in the case of evil kings. This attitude arises, in part, out of the inability of a people to overthrow a wicked king. But complementary to Divine Retribution is Divine Pleasure, which can be acquired through pious acts of merit, such as generous donations to brahmans. The use of witch-craft, particularly as a means of revenge, is not excluded amongst the many possible historical explanations of events.

Not surprisingly, Kalhana does not hesitate to draw moral lessons from the past. But at the same time it must be remembered that he was writing in a period of great stress, civil war and political confusion, when it was almost incumbent upon writers to point to the dangers that resulted from similar conditions in the past and warn against them even at the expense of being moralistic and didactic. It was, perhaps, also the fear of what might happen to the future of Kashmir, should be civil war continue that led to a lurking reliance on the supernatural.

Kalhana's ideas on the writing of history were directly influenced by two main streams of the Indian tradition which were concerned with recording the past : the Brahmanical and the Buddhist. Ideas relating to the brahmanical tradition can be culled from the epics, the *Puranas* and the historical biographies of the post-Gupta period, such as Bana's *Harshacharita*, etc. None of these works indicate a particularly sharp consciousness about time. The past extends back in a cosmological series of mystrical figures. Genealogies are carefully worked out but the overall concept of placing them accurately in the past in terms of time sequences, is not given the same attention. The historical sections in the *Puranas* are treated almost as a continuation of the mythological sections. The fact that they are written in the form of a prophecy when clearly they refer to events which have happened in the past, further detracts from their treatment as events of history. The idea of *dharma* provided the philosophical and social framework. If the system of *varna-ashrama-dharma* was observed then all events were explainable within this system. The emphasis was on the group—the family, the caste, the tribe, etc., and not on the individual.

The Buddhist tradition was significantly different. There is clear consciousness about time, which is related to and hinges

[4] VII. 1715.

around the central event of the Buddhist past—the *Mahaparinirvana*—which in historical terms is the date of the death of the Buddha. The reckoning in the two chronicles of Ceylon, the *Dipavamsa* and the *Mahavamsa* is based on this event. Although the idea of *karma* is accepted, the role of the individual's *karma* in his society is also considered. The past has both moral and social lessons to teach. The fact that Buddhism was an actively proselytising religion and missionaries were sent to various parts of Asia, required the keeping of accurate records of teachers and of missions. These in turn became the bases for much historical thinking and writing.

The influence of both these traditions of thinking on the writing of Kalhana can be seen in the gradual change which is noticeable in the *Rajatarangini.* The earlier part of the chronicle is not only based on brahmanical material but carries the impress of the same historical framework. The first three books are evidently based on semi-historical material, relying heavily on texts such as the *Nilamatapurana.* The fourth book covers the period of the Karkota dynasty and brings the narrative up to about the eighth century A. D. Clearly here, there was the additional use of the northern Buddhist tradition since the historical basis of the narrative becomes more marked. There is some evidence on this period of the history of Kashmir available in the Annals of the Tang Dynasty of China. (We are told for instance that Tchen-to-lo-pi-li, believed to be king Candrapida, asked for assistance against the Arab in c. 713, presumably when Sind was invaded by the latter and there was a threat to the regions around the upper reaches of the Indus). If communication with China was so close at this time (and there seems no good reason to doubt this), then perhaps some trickle of the Chinese emphasis on keeping records and dynastic chronicles may have found its way into the historical traditions of Kashmir. The next three books (five to seven) show a marked tendency towards trying to understand historical events in their context and seeking explanations other than the generally accepted explanations based on *dharma karma,* etc. A number of new causative factors are introduced (as we shall see) which suggest that the author wished to probe further into the historical past and not merely restrict himself to providing information. The maturity of Kalhana's historical thinking is made evident in the last book of the *Rajatarangini* (Book Eight) which is by far the lengthiest and deals with the period preceding his own, a period which obviously he was most familiar with. Not surprisingly the quality of analysis is significantly different from that in the earlier books.

The chronicle takes the reader right back to the beginnings of Kashmir to geological times when the valley of Kashmir was an inland lake. Finally it was dredged through the opening of a gorge above Baramula and this, in the traditional sources, is naturally ascribed to a supernatural agency. The earliest kings of Kashmir such as Gonada I, are associated with the epic heroes and traditional history as recorded in the *Puranas*. Thus Gonada I is related to Jarasandha and plays his part in the various battles of the *Mahabharata*. This is clearly based on the account in the *Nilamata-purana*, which would naturally try and link the traditional kings of Kashmir with the traditional history of the major *Puranas*. Again, Kashmir is brought into the orbit of the history of India by reference to the reign of Ashoka, the Mauryan emperor, as a ruler of Kashmir. Reference is made to his building *stupas* and to establishing the city of Srinagar. This is clearly based on accounts in Buddhist sources, since the *Puranas* merely list Ashoka as one of the Mauryan kings and say no more.

In the earlier books, supernatural causes are given an important role. Thus we are told that famine comes because of the will of the gods.[5] The queen prays to the gods and slowly the conditions of scarcity recede. Even more fantastic is the story of the resurrection of Sandhimata.[6] He is banished, then imprisoned and put to death by the king. The witches come and put his bones together into a skeleton and revive him, after which he becomes the successor to king Jayendra. Here it is not only the supernatural which is involved but also the power of Fate, since we are told that Sandhimata was fated to become king of Kashmir and to deliver the land from a number of evil practices. The timely death of king Vijayamalla, crushed by an avalanche just when he and the feudal lords were planning an attack on king Harsha, is another example of the interference of Fate.[7] The increasing popularity of Buddhism annoys both the brahmans and the Nagas (the local cult deities). In order to check this the Nagas send down excessive snow

[5] II. 17–55.
[6] II. 92.
[7] VII. 916–17.

at a particular time which the brahmans cleverly use against the Buddhists.[8] One of the more curious incidents is related in the fourth book. We are told that the king Lalitaditya was famous for the fact that he collected a number of wise men around him. One of them was the Tukhara (central Asian) called Cankuna. On a certain occasion he used a charm on the turbulent waters of a river of the Punjab, causing the waters to separate and leave a clear path in the middle for the army to cross.[9] One wonders whether an echo of the story of Moses and the Red Sea had found its way to Kashmir.

Human action, *karma* and the merit acquire from this and previous births, *punya*, are also seen as a part of the historical process. A king, no matter how good his intention, can be thwarted in his work by his own lack of *punya* or that of his subjects.[10] This does not necessarily suggest that the king should therefore be inactive, but rather it is an attempt to explain the obstacles which may beset the working out of a good intention.

The seventh and eighth books represent the latter phase of Kalhana's historical thinking. Here the supernatural element and the emphasis on the role of Fate are by no means denied, but owing to other causal explanations they tend to recede somewhat into the background. Historical events are now discussed from many points of view—the personalities involved and their ambitions, weaknesses and power; the emergence of feudatories and their relationship with the king; the role of the Damaras and the brahmans in Kashmiri politics; the economic conditions of Kashmir. In writing on the eleventh and twelfth centuries Kalhana was writing on his own period and was familiar with the multiple facets that go into the making of an historical situation. That he recognised the multiplicity of causes is all to his credit.

In reflecting on the decline of King Harsha, he mentions that the planets at his birth were ill-disposed towards him and consequently luck was not on his side.[11] But he adds that Harsha was weak because he avoided battles, and in those conditions battles were the obvious means of settling many problems. Furthermore he

[8] I. 179.
[9] IV. 248-51.
[10] I. 158.
[11] VII. 1715.

lacked independent judgement, particularly of men, and appointed the wrong kind of persons as ministers and then relied on their advice. Another source of weakness in a king, which is deplorable, is when he comes under the influence of a scheming woman.[12]

The medieval political history of Kashmir was dominated by two court factions, both of a military nature, the Tantrins and the Ekangas. In the first half of the tenth century, they made and unmade rulers. Their manipulation of court politics is carefully described.[13] In the succeeding century, the centres of power were no longer only the king and the ministers but included a number of Damaras. The word is peculiar to Kashmir and appears to have been a tribal name in origin. Judging by the description in the *Rajatarangini* they soon became feudal landowners.[14] They appear to have acquired their land through service tenures and gradually made themselves extremely powerful in the fertile parts of the valley. Their social status is apparent by the fact that they acquired wives from among the Rajputs or else often married into the royal family. They were evidently a serious source of opposition to the king and the history of Kashmir during this period is full of incidents relating to the Damaras.

When discussing administration, Kalhana totally disapproves of the activities of the *kayasthas*, to whom he attributes a large share of the misfortunes of the state. The *kayasthas* were the scribes and recorders and consequently the backbone of the administration of the state. The *kayasthas*, writes Kalhana, are not only responsible for much of the political intrigue[15] but even worse, they encourage the kings to oppress their subjects and thus cause disaffection throughout the land.[16] King Sankaravarman (in the ninth century) is described as 'the foremost among fools and sons of slaves' for heeding the advice of the *kayasthas*,[17] who suggest that he plunder the temples and oppress his subjects in order to extract more money from the land. The Damaras and *kayasthas* between them are bleeding the people dry.

[12] VII. 449.

[13] V. 248, V. 255, V. 259, VI. 121.

[14] VII. 494 sq.

[15] VIII. 258.

[16] IV. 621–31, VII. 1226, VIII, 89–94.

[17] V. 180–81.

Perhaps some of the venom directed against the *kayasthas* by Kalhana may have been due to professional jealousy. Many of the higher positions in administration were traditionally the preserve of the brahmans and possibly the entry of the *kayasthas* into these positions (such as collectors of revenue and treasurers) was resented. It must be said to Kalhana's credit that he was also critical (although not equally critical) of the official brahman organisations such as the *purohita parishads*. These were corporate groups formed by the *purohitas* attached to certain temples and places of pilgrimage. The group became the joint owner of all the property endowed to the temple and the income from donations. The members of such a *parishad* were, therefore, very well-off materially and were often very powerful politically.[18] Kalhana saw them as another source of interference in the running of the state. Yet his ire against the *purohita parishads* was somewhat softened by his unquestioning acceptance of the theory that a good king must liberally endow the brahman community in his land.[19]

Kalhana endorsed the role of the brahman as enunciated in traditional political theory at every level. He recognises as agents of revolt the Tantrins and Ekangas, the Damaras, the royal princes assisted by ministers and the brahmans. He does not approve of revolts by the first three of these as they are disruptive forces. Yet he acquiesces when it comes to references to brahmans using their traditional weapon against political power, the fast against a particular king or a minister,[20] on the assumption that the fast is always in a righteous cause, viz. the removal of an oppressive king or minister.

Kalhana early realised that there was a relationship between the political power of these various groups and their economic condition. A passage, which runs like a refrain through the second half of the chronicle, is that no village should be allowed to stock food in excess of a year's consumption, or keep oxen beyond the number required to till the fields, since the accumulation of wealth leads to the rise of the Damaras who, in the nature of things will disobey the king.[21] In addition, he lists as signs of trouble for a king the condi-

[18] II. 132, V. 465, VIII. 900.
[19] VIII. 76.
[20] VII. 13, VII. 400, VIII. 890–900, VIII. 2224.
[21] IV. 347–48.

tion when villages have the amenities of towns, when fortifications are not adequately guarded, when officials start inter-marrying and various other similar factors.

The oppression of the people by the king and his plundering of the temples is something which Kalhana regards with great horror. An oppressive king is not to be tolerated and this is the advice of the *shastras*. Sankaravarman's oppressive acts are listed at length, from plundering temples to the resumption of grants and the exaction of forced labour.[22] One of the reasons why Harsha lost power was because he plundered the temples and even went to the extent of appointing a *devotpatananayaka*, an officer for the uprooting of divine images.[23] The *shastric* injunction is that the king's primary duty is to protect his people and attend to their welfare. An oppressive king therefore deserves the misfortunes which surround him.

The latter part of the historical account in the chronicle shows an unusually modern understanding of what goes into the making of historical processes. This has led to Kalhana's writing being regarded as quite distinct from other historical works in the Sanskrit tradition. Histories of other regions were written at this time and historical biography became a frequent form of literary expression from the post-Gupta period onwards. *Vamshavalis* and geneological accounts of the various dynasties became increasingly frequent, and many of these have yet to be worked on by modern scholars. From the material available, it is clear that in this category of literature, the *Rajatarangini* holds a position of pre-eminence.

The question arises as to why medieval Kashmir gave rise to such historical writing. A number of reasons have already been suggested.[24] The geographical isolation of Kashmir—a valley surrounded by high mountains—led to a stronger sense of nationalism amongst its people. The persistence of Buddhism in Kashmir with its more definite sense of history than brahmanism, was another factor. Kashmir also came under the influence of a number of non-Indian cultures such as the Greek, the Chinese and possibly the Turkish, all of which again had definite historical traditions.

The geographical isolation of Kashmir was certainly a positive

[22] V. 165–77.

[23] VII. 1087–1091.

[24] A L. Basham, 'The Kashmir Chronicle' in *Historians of India, Pakistan and Ceylon* (ed C.H. Philips), 57 ff.

factor. Yet Kashmir was not totally isolated. The material remains of the culture of Kashmir shows close contacts with Gandhara and northern India, central Asia and even China.[25] To the fact of geographical isolation should be added the corollary that the period when Kalhana wrote was one of intense regional loyalties throughout northern India. There was ample patronage available in the proliferating courts of the small kingdoms and inevitably there was a concern with local culture, local problems and local events. Each kingdom saw itself as a great kingdom in exaggerated terms but in fact the area of reference was a parochial one. This had the advantage that it permitted the thinkers of the time to concentrate on a small canvass and work on it more intensively. The Damaras were the concern of the kings of Kashmir and not of the rest of India, and Kalhana was content to leave it at that.

The impact of Buddhism was probably a sub-conscious impact on Kalhana. The text makes it clear that he was no supporter of the Buddhist religion, but instead regarded it with great suspicion.[26] But he must have had to consult many Buddhist texts on certain sections of the history of Kashmir. The recording of some of these traditions in Kashmir itself (at the monastic centres) must also have contributed to creating a more real sense of the past. Similarly the influence of the Greek, the Chinese and the Islamic (as available via the central Asian Turks) historical tradition need not have come through a direct knowledge of Greek, Chinese and Turkish historical writing, but rather through a familiarity with the cultural ethos which produced such writing, both as something of the past (the Greek) and something contemporary (the Chinese and the Turkish). Kalhaṇa nowhere indicates familiarity with any of these languages or their literatures, so the influence must have come about through a process of cultural osmosis.

Credit must also be given to the man himself, writing as he was at a particular time in history. None of the earlier accounts of Kashmir which Kalhana used as sources, nor for that matter the post-Kalhana chronicles, show evidence of the same historical understanding as does the *Rajatarangini* The later historians and chroniclers such as Jonaraja, Shrivara, Prajnyabhatta and Shuka, who were

[25] The Neolithic site of Burzahoma, the Buddhist site of Harwan and temple of Martanda, are all indicative of such contacts.

[26] I. 177.

subject to the same influences, do not reveal the same grasp of historical processes. Kalhana was obviously a man with an analytical mind, which the later writers were not. He was writing the history of a state which at that time was passing through its moments of decline, which in itself must have given rise to considerable interospection and questioning in the mind of a sensitiveand thoughtful person. Kalhana himself belonged to a ministerial family which had once held power but had gradually lost it. He was thus familiar with the forces which go into the making of politics and history but was not a part of them. He could look upon the situation with the perspective of an outsider, but at the same time retaining the insights of one who is a part of the situation. Having once decided not to write a sycophant's history, he could afford to probe impersonally into many of the existing conditions.

Finally, perhaps the greatest advantage that regions such as Kashmir derived from being opened up to Buddhist, Greek, Chinese and Turkish influences was that in the Indian tradition these were non-orthodox or foreign influences and could therefore nurture non-orthodox thinking. This is not to suggest that Kalhana wrote his history because he was a non-conformist. He was not. As we have seen there are many aspects of his writing which adhere closely to orthodox thinking on the subject. It is rather to suggest that Kalhana was not a man with a closed mind, and this after all, is an essential qualification for a good historian.

6

Shaikh Sikandar

The *Mirat-i-Sikandari* of Sikandar bin Manjhu has the rather unenviable or probably enviable distinction of having blanketted its predecessors and successors. It has come to be recognised as a handy reference work for the history of Gujarat, to be more particular, for the history of the Sultans of Gujarat. The eighteenth century Mughal historian, the author of an equally or even more celebrated history of Mughal Gujarat, did little more than to summarise the earlier *Mirat* in the few pages he devoted to the Sultanate; subsequent writers, even the British ones, went hardly further when they dealt cursorily with the same period. It was not until Sir Denison Ross chanced to discover the equally valuable, equally copious *Zafar-ul-Walih*, the only secular history, so far as I know, to be written in Arabic in this country, did it come to be recognised that the *Mirat* had compeers of equal value—that the pedestal on which it had been placed did little justice either to itself or to those whom it had served to supplant. For one of the consequences of this oblivion to which other histories had been consigned was that, while the *Mirat's* own copies had proliferated in libraries, both Indian and foreign, the copies of other works had become scarce to the point of vanishing—and one of the most valuable had vanished altogether.

Yet, Gujarat had been well-served by its historians. Right from the time of the first Sultan, histories, chronicles and, let us also admit, fulsome eulogies had begun to be composed. It is not my purpose here to list these or to recount their historical worth : that I have done elsewhere and it has also been done by other writers.[1] I

[1] A full discussion of the sources of the *Mirat*, period of composition has been made in the Introduction to the Baroda edition of the work and is not repeated here. It also contains a full bibliography of the literature on this work. (The *Mirat-i-Sikandari* of Shaikh Sikandar ibn Muhammad *urf*

wish only to suggest that 'official' history writing was patronised by the Sultans from the very start, and that Sikandar was very true, though not very charitable, when he asserted that these historians, writing in the age of those whose acts they recorded, preferred discretion to truth by failing to include prejudicial items.[2]

It is unfortunate that all but two or three of the histories used by Sikandar, have not come down to us or have not so far been discovered, and, therefore, we are not in a position to judge his verdict. Nevertheless, to an extent evaluation is possible, it cannot be denied that these historians had all the failings and all the excellences of 'court' historians—though not in all cases. Hulwi Shirazi's versified *Tarikh-i-Ahmad Shahi* seems to have sacrificed matter for form, at least in the rather stilted verses quoted in the *Mirat*. Thus, the English translations have lost nothing by omitting these profuse fulminations. Possibly, in his more 'prosaic' moments, which Sikandar did not think worth quoting, Hulwi did contribute something—but if internal evidence is any guide, it does not seem likely.

More valuable and more ambitious are the annalistic, universal histories which have fortunately come down to us, all belonging to the reign of Sultan Mahmud Shah popularly called 'Begado' in Gujarat. The earliest appears to be *Tarikh-i-Mahmud Shahi*, whose authorship is in doubt; the next probably is *Tabaqat-i-Mahmud Shahi* by Abdul Karim Nimdihi continued in the *Zamima i-Mahmud Shahi*. The third, again a universal history, *Tarikh-i-Sadar Jahan*, which is hardly a history of India at all. Undoubtedly a monument of extensive learning, its major value in the present context is to indicate the pattern of scholarship flourishing in the court of Ahmedabad—or to be found in the cloisters of Patan where, as I was told, scholars held history in disdain while pursuing the elevated disciplines, *hadith* and *fiqh*.

Manjhu ibn Akbar : edited by S. C. Misra and M. L. Rehman : Baroda, the M. S. University of Baroda, 1961. Introduction, 1–56 : Bibliography, 53–56).

I should like to refer to two important articles which have appeared since this bibliography was prepared. They are : Z. A. Desai, *Mirat-i-Sikandari* as a source for the study of cultural and social conditions of Gujarat under the Sultanate (1403–1572), *Journal of the Oriental Institute*, Baroda, Vol. X, No. 3 (March 1961); and Jean Aubin. The Secretary of Mahmud Gawan and his lost chronicle, *Journal of Research Society of Pakistan*, Vol. I, Part II (October 1964), 9–13.

[2] *Mirat-i-Sikandari*, Baroda text (MS), 2.

I have not yet had the opportunity to go through the *Tabaqat-i-Mahmud Shahi,* though I am given on good authority that it 'has not so great a value as could be expected.'[3] Probably, its flowery style obscures some of its descriptions. Even a greater limitation can be said to be the annalistic form which the author imposed upon himself and which, valuable from the point of view of chronology, permits little latitude for reflection, the essence of historiography. Finally, it was probably never completed, and both of its manuscripts are the 'very incomplete draft of an incomplete text.'[4] The *Tarikh-i-Mahmud Shahi* is more rewarding for the historian of Gujarat, but it was on this work that Sikandar directed his barbs. In his opinion the author has used his ample talents in camouflaging the truth.

Court histories or histories written to order or written to please as these two histories are may be detailed, may be meticulous and, of course, florid and verbose—but they rarely, if at all, tell the whole truth and nothing but the truth. This tendency to varnish the rough surface is uppermost in a contemporary history of Malwa, the *Maathir-i-Mahmud Shahi* of al-Kirmani, whose tortuous and convoluted prose meanders through nearly eight hundred pages of high-flown epithets.

It was to sift the truth from the chaff of such verbiage and downright adulteration that Sikandar took up the pen. These strictures on his predecessors which Sikandar passes and his own apologia deserve quotation :

'And it is evident that whichsoever of these writers hoped for reward or patronage from these rulers, owing to this reason, abstained from including full and true description of events in the aforesaid histories; so, nothing is included in these pages which is not the praise of these patrons, although man is not free from faults or virtues.....

'And in the account of the Sultans of Gujarat of just dealings, I have not thought it proper to refer to only their good acts and to leave the others in ambiguity; for, after weighing, their good deeds were found to be more than their bad ones and, in some, even non-existent. In any case, whatever bad or good has been heard from trustworthy persons or gleaned from scanning histories, has been reduced to writing so that it might be known to the readers, as to

[3] Aubin, *op. cit.*, 11.
[4] *Ibid.*

what extent goodness emanated from them and how far they abstained from evil; and, what means they adopted for conquest (*Jahangiri*) and what for rulership (*Jahanbani*). Consequently, the compendium has been entitled that *Mirror of Sikandar* so that the totality of the event may be reflected in it without dimunition or addition....'

Sikandar was sincere in his apologia for bringing a new article in an already well-supplied market. In his opinion, even when the whole truth was told, his cherished images would not be tarnished; rather they would gain, for at least the worst would have been said and the ambiguity removed.

It may be doubted if this alone was the reason which, despite his numerous difficulties, made Sikandar 'put his hand to pen and paper.' It was obvious that the age of the Sultans had already passed into oblivion; he could expect no reward, no patronage for his labours except probably a well-earned reputation. Several other imperatives which moved Sikandar in the evening of his life to undertake this difficult, and not too rewarding, task may also be discovered.

That Sikandar loved his region and had a nostalgia for the past should not, however, in any case, not be overlooked. To him, the Gujarat of the Mughals could not hold a candle to the Gujarat of the Sultans. 'Blessed be Allah' he bewails of the fled glories of Champanir, was it this Champanir—now the abode of tiger and the lion ? Its buildings are ruined, its inhabitants have given their property to the winds of destruction, even its waters are poisoned.... Even the Koranic saying has been here realized : 'Every thing on earth shall perish except the Face of the Glorious and Gracious Lord.'

Elsewhere too, for instance, when he speaks of the prowess of the Sultans against the Portuguese and the relative weakness of the Mughals, Sikandar's comparison is always in favour of the bygone age. Sorath, the country which combined in itself the excellences of Malwa, Khandesh and Gujarat and whose ports supplied Gujarat with merchandise—the same country has been ruined 'on account of the constant change of its governors and has become the land of marauding free-booters, swindling merchants, charlatanic priests, grasping land-owners and ragged soldiers.'[6]

This is evidently not wholly true; the Gujarat of Akbar and

[5] MS , 2.

[6] MS., 137 : Translation (Fazulullah Lutfullah, Dharampore n. d.), 68.

Jahangir, it may be doubted, was really less prosperous than the Gujarat of Mahmud Shah Begada and Muzaffar Shah. It sounds like the wail of an old man always seeing his own age and earlier ones in a halo. But is there something more to it ?

Sikandar, it will be recalled, was two generations old in Gujarat. His father entered Gujarat with Humayun and presumably stayed on in the service of the highly venerated and princely Sayyids of Batwa. It was in this service that Miyan Manjhu, Sikandar's father, attained to some distinction and it was with him and his son, Sayyid Mirar, and grandson, Sayyid Hamid, that Sikandar first underwent his adult experiences. Throughout the age of Akbar and till the 5th year of Jahangir's reign, when he entered the Imperial service, he remained with the Sayyids.[7]

Sikandar consequently acquired the dual character of a foreign 'elite'—in Gujarat he was a member of an essentially foreign community which borrowed its culture from the North, but among their compeers elsewhere the members of this community had become sufficiently indigenised to the land of their adoption, to be termed as its denizens. Sikandar's basic orientation was to this foreign, ruling aristocracy, and to them he was concerned in proving the greatness of the land to which he and they belonged, the heritage which it had. He was not concerned with the shadowy past; even the Gujarat of the Delhi Sultans did not interest him as it hardly contributed to the glory of Gujarat in itself. But with the Sultans it was a different story; probably, Sikandar would not have been averse to the statement that of all the Mughal *subas*. Gujarat had the most glorious past.

I should like to suggest that this feeling which acculturised a foreign bureaucracy to the land of its adoption and makes it take pride in its own achievements there—it is akin to the embryonic nationalism which sprouted in a pre-industrial society. It did not go deep among the people, for the responses there were to different stimuli, and the patterns of thought which Sikandar expresses had not seeped through to them. Consequently, it was hardly pervasive, paper-thin, limited to the surface alone; but it did provide an identification and a cognitive we and non-we framework to the ruling strata.

The present consequently, a commonly shared heritage was not

[7] M.S., 115-16 : Translation, 52.

so bright to Sikandar as the past which distinguished Gujarat and the Gujaratis among the Mughal aristocracy. It is therefore at the hands of that section of the Mughal aristocracy which hailed from Gujarat—and not the least of whom were the Sayyids of Batwa—that Sikandar expected recognition and praise if not more material rewards. And, it could also drive home to other nobles occupying exalted positions, more exalted than probably held by Gujarat-origin nobles, the value of the heritage of Gujarat and its people. The fact that Sikandar presented a copy of his work personally to Itimad-ud-Daula, probably journeying to Agra for this purpose, indicates, not merely a desire to gain mundane ends but also a pride of an author in his book and its subject[8].

To some extent, I think this trait was shared by all regional aristocracies, though about Gujarat we are better informed because of its richer historiographic and literary tradition—and also probably because, next to the Gangetic Heartland and Bengal, it was materially the most prosperous of the Mughal *subas*. Its sea-coast also permitted a more frequent association with the Arabic and Persian tradition, leading to the birth of an indigenous Muslim tradition, developed by the local Muslim communities, some of them regarded as heretical by the official classes. How deep was the Gujarat 'mark' and how it differed from the stamp imprinted by other regions, it is obviously difficult to say. But that it was, that it served to differentiate and probably to categorise the ruling strata at its several levels, and that it inculcated a sense of pride and belonging to their regions, seems to be fairly clear.

I have referred earlier to Sikandar's service under the Sayyids of Batwa and to his father's rise under them and his own lifelong association with them. While Sikandar's admiration for the Sultans of Gujarat is obvious, his respect and veneration for his patron's family and their forbears was probably even greater. The Sultanate of Gujarat was the gift of Hazrat Makhdum Jahanyan to Zafar Khan; his successor in Gujarat Sayyid Burhan-ud-Din provided Zafar Khan's successor, Qutb-ud-Din Shah the means with which he saved himself against Mahmud Shah, the Sultan of Malwa. It was when Qutb-ud-Din Shah turned against this allegiance that he perished : his successor, the greatest of the Sultans of Gujarat, was brought up in the household of Shah Alam, the greatest of the Sayyids, who,

[8] MS., Introduction, 46-48.

incidentally is still venerated in Gujarat.[9]

Examples like these can be multiplied, for Sikandar's history is replete with them. In fact, Sikandar's bias or favour becomes apparent when his history is seen together with either the *Tabaqat-i-Akbari* or the *Gulshan-i-Ibrahimi.* Neither of these writers give the same pre-eminence to the Sayyids, as Sikandar does in his pages. It might even be plausibly argued that Sikandar is using the Sultans as a convenient frame to put his patrons on a pedestal.

This would, nevertheless, be hardly fair to Sikandar. Sikandar visualised no dichotomy between these who appeared to him to be the temporal and the religious upholders of the realm. Rather, the temporal rulers, while supreme in their own sphere, had the obligation to bow to the superior authority, denoted by orthodoxy, by spiritual heritage and by personal eminence in the religious field. Simultaneously, the spiritual pillars of the kingdom had the obligation to come to the rescue of the ruler when in difficulty and the kingdom prospered when the balance was kept. It was Sikandar's deep regret that the unwritten agreement was not always observed, and he holds the Sultans, not the Sayyids, responsible for this.

Underlying this position is the medieval assumption of cause and effect..... the widely accepted fact of a supernatural agency interfering to alter the usual course of events. Like almost all other men in his age, Sikandar believed in the prowess conferred by spiritual discipline, by austerity and, it would seem, by voluntary self-humiliation.[10] Virtue therefore was not just an spiritual enhancement of personality but, also, a means through which environment could be changed or at least affected. It was thus to be cultivated by those so gifted; by others such men were to be respected.

Obviously, Sikandar saw these values in the context of the conservative orthodox framework of his age. Both the rulers and the saints were seen by him to have the primary duty to uphold the faith, to uproot heresy, and also to maintain proper order in the realm, to foster sanctioned virtues. Conflicts between Muslim rulers were to be avoided as far as possible—but it was not always possible, for rulers too, were, more often than not, fallible men. Thus, it may

[9] Poona Text of the *Mirat* : superscription on the title page : MS Introduction, 1, 46.

[10] MS., 10-11, 71-77, 80-81, 90-91 *et seq.* For Shah Alam also see 123, *et. seq.* and for Shaikh Jiu, see 170-71, 228-30 *et seq.*

be noted that Sikandar does not hold the rulers of Gujarat responsible for the duel with Malwa; he is 'patriotic' enough to lay the blame on the Malwa Sultans, though this may not always be historically accurate.

Given this framework, it is not surprising that Sikandar, convinced of the spiritual attainment and the exalted status of the Sayyids of Batwa, particularly of Shah Alam and his successors, should have viewed the inevitable tension between Ahmedabad and Batwa as something of a deplorable turpitude on the part of the Sultans. History to him, as he wrote in the introduction of his book, is teaching by example; the actions of the great in the past are lessons for the present[11]. The history of the Sayyids of Batwa was to him at rich as that of the Sultans in this respect.

It seems to me that what appears to us as deliberate exaltation was to Sikandar the proper perspective. In placing Makhdum Jahaniyan, Sayyid Burhan and Shah Alam on a pedestal, he was reflecting a current and widely felt sentiment in Gujarat. With their collateral branch at Dholkah, he had personal experience. And since nearly a third of his history was devoted to the last forty years of the Sultanate preceding Mughal conquest—a period of politics sometimes by means other than diplomacy among the nobles, in which Sayyid Mubarak and his sons took active part, Sikandar recounts this in detail.

It is understandable that Sikandar betrays a partiality to the part played by his father in the service of Sayyid Mubarak. Much of the information for this period which he describes in great detail was derived from his father and elder brother, Shaikh Yusuf[12]. It may, therefore, be that it is not filial affection alone which has placed this aspect rather out of proportion : the source material itself dictated it, helped as it was by a sympathetic *rancoteur*.

However, it is at this place that Sikandar reveals some of his less pleasant attitude, traits which are not uncommon in those who seek the favour of essentially capricious masters. Thus, he goes out of the way to run down a work written for Sayyid Mubarak by a fellow 'scribe'—Aram Kashmiri, also in the same employ. It would appear that Aram Kashmiri and Sikandar were rivals and

[11] For instance the story of Malik Muhammad Ikhtiyar and Dawar-ul-Mulk, MS., 161 *et seq*.

[12] MS., 361, 438.

there was little love lost between them—or probably, Sikandar's father and this author had been colleagues. In any case, Aram's history has not come down to us, but Sikandar's rather unfair remark has.[13] It does not leave the impression, taken with the paragraph which follows it, in which Sikandar quotes the authority of his father and brother, that this interpolation is rather uncalled for and not quite in the best of taste.

Likewise, Sikandar has been less than fair to his earlier predecessors. His diatribe on them has already been quoted and, from what we know, they deserved it—but with at least one exception, the *Tarikh-i-Bahadur Shahi.*

From what we know, Sikandar derived the bulk of his information from this work, celebrated as it must have been in his days. In fact, Sikandar's historiography is at its best when he is following this author; in later pages, where he relied upon 'trustworthy persons' he is prone to indulge in lengthy anecdotes and to collate information rather than to sift it. But it is surprising that though Sikandar must have had this work almost constantly by this side, must have known in detail about it and its author, he never cites him by name. It is not through the Mirat but by *Zafar-ul-Walih* that we are able to identify Husam Khan as the author.

In fact, the omission of any direct reference to the author by name is so glaring that Sir Denison Ross termed it as a 'conspiracy of silence'.[14] It does not seem fair to accuse Sikandar of deliberate suppression; at one point he does go out of his way to point out a high noble of Mahmud Shah Begada as the 'forbear of the author of *Tarikh-i-Bahadur Shahi*'.[15] But Sikandar's initial reference to 'a person (*shakhs*) as being the author of this work when he *should* have known the name, the title, and the designation of the person concerned, the total absence of Husam Khan's very name in Sikandar's history and, finally, Sikandar's slighting reference to the work he so largely depended upon—they indicate a person, who to say the least cantakerous and niggardly in acknowledging due indebtedness.[16]

[13] MS., 361.

[14] E. Denison Ross, (ed.), *An Arabic History of Gujarat, Zafar-ul-walih bi Muzaffar wa-Alih* of 'Aballah Muhammad bin Omar al-Makki, al-Asafi, Ulughkhani also known as Hajji ad-Dabir. Indian Texts Series (3 volumes, London, John Murray for Government of India, 1910, 1921 and 1928) Vol. II. Introduction, XXVIII.

[15] MS., 126.

[16] MS., 1-2.

Sikandar's work, like other creative writing, is an epitome of his personality, a reflection of his *weltanschauung*. He belonged to a class which primarily depended on landed aristocracy for its livelihood, and which was inclined not so much towards the profession of arms as to civil occupations. To his category belonged probably the *diwans*, *naib-diwans* and a host of other functionaries who administered the *jagirs* of Mughal nobles and looked after their other interests during their long absences. In other and parallel spheres, men of his class and ability functioned in the numerous civil and judicial positions opened up by the Mughal administration as *qazis*, as *muhtasibs*, and *amins* and a host of other posts.

Therefore, it is not surprising to find in him traits and attitudes of this class. He had prodigious learning, an ability to write the language with clarity and a degree of elegance and, in his own way, the capacity to sift evidence. He had his limitations; he could not see below the surface of events because, for him, history meant the recording of events with moral overtones—not their analysis or dissection to discover their inner logic. He had his prejudices, his jealousies which he could not succeed in keeping away from his work. He had also his beliefs which necessarily formed the infrastructure of his history.

Essentially, Sikandar appears to me as a typical Mughal intellectual—conservative, learned, opinionated but veracious, unimaginative and highly responsive to the sanctioned social and religious attitudes. One of the chief qualities which his history possesses is that it mirrors these traits—and has thus become an excellent specimen of the age in which it was written.

7

Mirza Nathan*

The discovery of the *Baharistan*[1] was hailed as an 'epoch-making achievement for the reconstruction of the history of North-Eastern India' by Dr. Borah who edited and translated the full manuscript.[2] Prior to its discovery the contemporary sources of information on the history of Bengal and Assam were of a limited utility. They contained very little about the details of the political and social history of the area. The debt which the history of the region owes to Mirza Nathan is indeed great, and it has been acknowledged by the discoverer of the work, Dr. J. N. Sarkar, in the following words, 'No period of the history of Medieval Bengal is now known even in half such fulness and accuracy of detail...as the reign of Jahangir (1601–1627).'[3] This aspect of the work has rightly been emphasised by all the writers who have noticed it since its discovery.[4] But the

* A re-examination of the nature and contents of the *Baharistan-i-Ghaibi.*

[1] The original manuscript belongs to the Bibliotheque Nationale, Paris; Gentil-42. Supplement 252. It was first brought into public notice by Dr. J.N. Sarkar, who published some articles on it in the Bengali monthly journal *Prabasi.* Later, he wrote an article in the JBORS, 1921, giving an account of its discovery and a full table of contents.

[2] Published by the Government of Assam, in the Department of Historical and Antiquarian Studies, 1936. My article is based on this edited text. Dr. Borah used a rotograph of the manuscript which belonged to the Dacca University. Apart from a transcript and a rotograph which Dr. Sarkar got done for his use, no other copy of the Persian text is available in the country. The Sarkar transcript is now in the National Library, Calcutta, but I have not been able to use it.

[3] History of Bengal, Vol. II, Preface, p.x., ed. J.N. Sarkar, Dacca, 1948.

[4] S.R. Sharma's articles, entitled *Bengal under Jahangir, JIH,* Vols. XI, XIII–XIV, and *Prince Shahjahan in Bengal,* IHQ, Vol. XI. Also see S.N. Bhattacharya's article, entitled *Rebellion of Shahjahan and his career in Bengal,* IHQ, Vol. X and his book, *A History of Mughal North-East Frontier Policy,* Introduction.

pre-occupation with only one aspect of the work has resulted in a neglect of its basic nature and parts of its content.

The *Baharistan* is essentially a memoir of Ala-ud-Din Isfahani (alias Mirza Nathan), entitled Shitab Khan. It has the format of formal Persian chronicles with its division into four *Daftars* each with its headings and sub-headings.[5] But the central character of the whole work, like all good memoirs—is the writer himself. It is around his activities that the whole story is woven. The main purpose of the book is to narrate a part of the memoirist's career. The details of the provincial history and the military expeditions come in secondarily, as parts incidental to the expounding of the careers of the memoirist and his father.

The author begins the work in the usual style of formal chronicles. 'As it occured to the mind of this most insignificant one that if a small portion of the events of Bengal which took place during the prosperous reign of...Jahangir Badshah...be put into writing (then) the imprint of that writing will remain on the pages of time.... Therefore...it has been written with the hope that if it comes before the scrutinising eyes of the scholars...they will adorn it with the pen of correction and incorporate its contents into the history of Jahangir.'

But a close perusal of its contents shows that they are more like the entries of a personal diary. Events and incidents are not described in their entirety at one place, but are scattered over different pages[6] (perhaps as they happened or as the author recalled them).

The book is divided into four *Daftars*, three of them relating to the events of three *Subadars* of Bengal, Islam Khan, Qasim Khan and Ibrahim Khan. The fourth contains an account of the events in Bengal and Bihar during the rebellion of Shahjahan. *Daftars* I and III are dedicated to the respective *Subadars* and named after them. The real link between the three *Subadars* is Mirza Nathan himself. The period has not been selected because of any intrinsic merit or historical importance, but because it coincides with the active

[5] Not all the headings and sub-headings as present in the printed text are from the original; some were added by the editor. But the four *Daftars*, their titles and dedications are as in the original.

[6] *Baharistan-i-Ghaybi*, tr. M. I. Borah (Gauhati, 1936), Vol. I, 282–87, 294–95 ; *Ibid.*, 741, 777, etc. Henceforth quoted as *Baharistan*.

military career of the memoirist himself. The first *Daftar* begins with the appointment of Islam Khan as the *Subadar* of Bengal, but that is about all. Thereafter the chief topic is the appointment of Ihtimam Khan, father of Mirza Nathan, as the *Mir Bahr* and his journey towards Bengal. Even the story of the suppression of the provincial chiefs is told more in terms of the exploits of Mirza Nathan and his father. Minor events of disagreements between the *Subadar* and Mirza Nathan and his father are described in disproportionate lengths (pp. 33–34, 115, 147, 154, 156, etc.). The importance of the memoirist and his father in these minor disputes is exaggerated much—after all they were the subordinate officers of the *Subadar*, but one is made to feel as if the disputes related to important matters of state policy between officers of equal rank. The same is true of the other *Daftars*. If someone statistically inclined took up the checking of the space alloted in each of the *Daftar* to the *Subadar*, on the one hand, and the memoirist and his father, on the other, he may well find the ratio at 1 : 2, or even more.

The discoverer of the manuscript Dr. Sarkar also refers to this point. 'The *Baharistan*', he writes, 'professes to be a history of Bengal and Orissa under the three *Subadars*...but it is as much a very detailed record of the doings of the Shitab Khan and of his father Ihtimam Khan as a history of the *Subadars*, and nearly half of the book can be better styled 'the Memoirs of Shitab Khan'. But he goes on to add that its real value lies in the 'full details which it supplies of the complete subjugation of the Bengal and Orissa zamindars...and of the long and endless wars of the Mughal empire with the Mongoloid Kingdom on its eastern border.'[7]

Prof. Sharma, who examined the work at some length, puts it under the section of Provincial Histories in his *Bibliography of Mughal India*, although it has a Section on Memoirs too. He criticises the 'vaingloriousness' of the writer—'he is one of the most vainglorious writers of history, whose one aim seems to have been to exalt his own services...whenever the Mughals win a victory he is the mainspring thereof ; whenever a disaster befalls them it is due to the jealousy of his superiors.'[8] The egocentricity, and even boastfulness, of the author is quite evident, but the point is that it is in keeping with the basic nature of the work– a memoir. All memoirists tend

[7] JBORS, *op. cit.*, 3.

[8] Sharma, *Bibliography of Mughal India*, 69-70.

to see things from their own angles and to emphasise the crucial importance of themselves in shaping the events. But while good memoirists are able to guide and control the projection of their images, Shitab Khan sometimes makes himself appear ludicrous. This is a defect common to many memoirists but is in keeping with the nature of the work.

Attention may also be drawn in this connection to the informal style and the personalised nature of some of the entries and to the intimate portrayals of the rebel-prince (pp. 763, 769, 772, 775–76) and other high dignitaries (pp. 115–16, 155–56). The vivid sketch of a defeated, harried and hungry Shahjahan sleeping under a tree with his quiver as his pillow and breakfasting on the roasted meat of a goat caught in the jungle near Sasaram (p. 763); of Shahjahan walking upto Mirza Nathan and picking up the letter he was writing to his family (p. 772); of the young prince Aurangzeb (the stern puritan Emperor of the future) surreptitiously eating some of the Martaban bananas kept aside for Mirza Nathan by Shahjahan (p. 780), are in refreshing contrast to the conventionalised character portrayals in the official chronicles.

Another daring and vivid sketch is that of Islam Khan, the great *Subadar*, getting annoyed with his son, Hushang, over some trifling matter and beating him up in the presence of all the courtiers. "Before the whip was brought, he put his head below his knees and taking hold of an ewer, began to beat him with it...an order was given to Khwaja Danish to beat him with the bamboos of the canopy. When he began to cry saying—'You beat me yourself; please do not allow the Khwaja to strike me with the sticks' he ordered the attendants to beat him." The *Diwan* and some other officers who tried to save him also 'received several blows'. (pp. 155–56). Entries like this are more fitting to a personal diary than to provincial history.

A peculiar feature of the work is its rather stilted style. Unlike all other memoirs, the narrative is, in many parts, not in the first person, which makes some of the entries appear affected and artificial. The author frequently refers to himself simply as Nathan or uses the customary humble epithets about himself. In the concluding portion he uses the title of Shitab Khan. If one did not know about his title or alias one might feel that the author is writing about someone else.

In fact there is a marked dichotomy of style throughout the work. It is a curious mixture of affected formal passages along with informal intimate pieces.

The end of the work is also noteworthy. It is abrupt and quite unlike that of a formally prepared work. The story begins somewhere in the middle and ends much before the logical conclusion. One feels as if a cinema reel has been snapped in the middle. Even the story of Shahjahan's rebellion, which is the main topic of *Daftar* IV has not been narrated to its full extent.

Dr. Borah feels confident that the work, as it was found, is complete. However, there are sufficient grounds to doubt whether the extant copy is complete or whether it represents the finished form. It appears more likely that the present copy is an incomplete[9] draft copy based on some casual notes which Shitab Khan maintained ; and he, subsequently, tried to convert it into a formal history. He made some preliminary arrangement of the assorted materials (*viz.*, the division into *Daftars*, the Introductions to the different *Daftars* and their dedication to the *Subadars*, etc.), but could not complete the work.

As pointed out by Prof. Sharma[10], the table of contents attached to the manuscript contains summaries of chapters.[11] But the summaries are not reliable—'the author not infrequently taking the wish for the deed, and thus mentioning many things in the summaries of the chapters which he probably intended to put therein but ultimately decided otherwise.' This also lends credence to the doubts about the extant copy being a tentative draft. As remarked ealier, the pre-occupation with only one aspect of the work has resulted not only in the neglect of its basic nature but in the non-utilisation of a lot of other materials scattered in its pages. Apart from the account of the expansion of Mughal rule in the area, which has already been closely examined, there is good deal of information about adminis-

[9] No definite assertion can be made on this point in the absence of more positive information. But this suggestion is supported by internal evidences.

[10] *Journal of Indian History*, Vol. XI. 334.

[11] Surprisingly, Dr. Borah does not refer at all to this table in the manuscript. Prof. Sharma consulted the rotograph copy of Dr. Sarkar and must have seen it. Dr. Sarkar himself published a full table of contents in his article in the JBORS but does not specifically state that it is based on the one attached to the manuscript itself.

trative, military and social matters which deserve our attention. The instances mentioned below are by no means exhaustive. They have been selected only to illustrate the point.

Prof. Sharma, too, refers to the 'manifold interest' of the work. But many of the instances, noticed here, are not included in the summary abstracts published by him or passed over briefly without comments.

ADMINISTRATIVE MATTERS

At the end of the first *Daftar*, while describing the consequential official changes, following the death of Islam Khan, the author mentions a significant administrative point. He writes, 'It was laid down in the imperial regulations that when the *Subadar* of Bengal died, the highest imperial officer who stayed at Monghyr was to take charge of that office.... If there be no man of this position at Monghyr, then the *Subadar* of Bihar should go to Bengal.' This order of precedence has not been mentioned in any *Dastur-ul-Amal* or official history. It raises many questions. What was the idea behind this rule? Obviously, the *Subadar* of Bihar was a man of much higher rank than the highest imperial officer who stayed at Monghyr. Why then should the latter claim precedence in succession to the *Subadari* of Bengal? Was it because the latter was in a position to reach Dacca more quickly and thus obviate the dangers which a long gap could cause to the stability of the *Suba*? If so, was it a rule applicable only to Bihar and Bengal? Or were there similar rules in regard to the other *Subas*? Even though the work does not give any answer to these questions it is important because it enables us to raise them.

Nathan goes on to add that Zafar Khan, the *Subadar* of Bihar, in his eagerness to succeed the *Subadari* of Bengal, violated this rule, and bypassing the claims of Qasim Khan, the brother of Islam Khan, who was then at Monghyr, went to Dacca to assume charge. However, the *Diwan*, the *Bakhshi* and the Newswriter of the Suba informed the Emperor that Zafar Khan was then engaged in besieging the Raja of Kukradesh (modern Chotanagpur area), and that if he had persisted with the siege for sometime more he could have secured from the Raja 'diamonds weighing thirty two *misqāls* as *peshkash*.' The Emperor got annoyed and ordered Zafar Khan to finish his incompleted task and appointed Qasim Khan (who was entitled under the rules) as *Subadar* of Bengal. The incident shows that the rule was observed. It also shows that the subordinate provincial officers, particularly the Newswriters, did sometime report on the violations of rules and regulations by the *Subadar*. They must have enjoyed adequate departmental security to enable them to work fearlessly.

We get another instance which amply illustrates the fearlessness and ingenuity of the Provincial Newswriters. During the interval after the departure of Islam Khan's son to Agra and the arrival of Qasim Khan at Dacca, the men of Mirza Husain Beg, the Provincial *Diwan*, took over control of some of the market-places, formerly under the charge of the *Kotwal* of Islam Khan. The control of market places being a lucrative charge, Qasim Khan after his arrival appointed his own Kotwal of markets, and he tried to take possession from the *Diwan*'s men. It led to a fracas between the *Diwan*'s sons and their armed men and the *Subadar*'s contingents. The former were suppressed, beaten and arrested, and their properties were confiscated.

Khwaja Yaghma, the Newswriter, was in a fix as to how to report the matter to the Emperor. Qasim Khan controlled the frontiers so tightly that 'even a bird cannot fly from this side to Upper India (Hindusthan) without his knowledge and orders, not to speak of letters of the Khans and the reports of the chroniclers.' At the same time if he failed to report the incident and the Emperor learnt about it from some other source, 'how shall I stand an enquiry ?' So he thought of a good device. He got two of his runners disguised as *jogis* and sent them to Anirai Singh Dalan, a close attendant of Jahangir. They were to present themselves along with the Rai, under the *Jharoka-i-Darshan* and to report the matter to the Emperor. The runners 'with many false pretences' went all the way from Dacca to Agra and did as instructed. The Emperor took cognizance of the matter and deputed an officer, Saadat Khan, to enquire into it. Qasim was warned that 'in consideration of the services of the Chishti family and our own favours to them we do not desire to ruin his career.' He was ordered to pacify the *Diwan*, obtain a letter of satisfaction from him and send it through Saadat Khan. Qasim Khan pacified the *Diwan* and his sons by various favours. He gave them one lakh of rupees and also the *pargana* of Madhopur Bhagwan, which belonged to his personal *jagir*. Over all these the Imperial enquiring officer took a public attestation of the whole incident with the seals of the nobles. He also took the representation of the aggrieved *Diwan* and submitted the documents to the Emperor.

Thus we have a full account of the incident which shows that the Newswriter's report were not just filed, but looked into and that the departmental machinery worked it out to its successful conclusion.[12]

Attention may also be drawn to the episode of the deputation of an Imperial Officer with *Farmans* and oral instructions regarding the respective duties of the *Subadar* and the other provincial officers. The instructions, described within quotation marks, are valuable as administrative documents.[13]

OVER-ASSESSMENT OF REVENUES

The variations between the actual and nominal revenue yields (*jama*) of most of the *parganas* and areas was a crying evil of land revenue administration under the Mughals. The official *jama* statistics, *jama-i-raqmi* as they were called, of Akbar's reign had been inherited from the Sur regime and were found to be grossly inflated. As a result many of the officers found their *jagirs* yielding much less revenue than their official estimate and it caused much dissatisfaction among the *jagirdars* and *mansabdars*. The problem constantly engaged the attention of Akbar and he made several attempts, first with the help of *Qanungoes* and then through directly supervised surveys of land to collect a more reliable estimate of revenue. Some improvement was effected by these but the malady was never fully removed. In fact variation between official and actual estimates was accepted as an unavoidable evil. Dr. Irfan Habib shows on the basis of a large number of 17th century documents, that a new method of month-ratio was developed in the reign of Shahjahan to overcome this evil. Under it the *jagirs* were classified into different categories, depending on the ratio between their actual and nominal yields. Thus in a first class *jagir* the revenue yield corresponded fully with the official estimate, and it was known as *dwazdamaha* jagir; one whose ratio was 50% was known as *sashmaha* and so on. Dr.

[12] *Baharistan*, Vol. I, 282–87, 294–95, 298.
[13] *Ibid.*, 309–10. See also 213.

Habib mentions an example of this system from the reign of Jahangir but goes on to remark that it came into general use in the reign of Shahjahan.[14] Mirza Nathan also mentions a case which appears like another instance of this system.[15] The case is significant because it belong to a period before the practice came into general use.

Sher Khan Fath Jung, an important Officer of Shahjahan while he was in rebellion, was granted a *Jagir* in Tajpur—Purnea, but he had some doubts about the assessment of its revenue. Mirza Nathan, who was then practically the *Faujdar* of Akbarnagar, was ordered to enquire into the correctness of the estimate. Accordingly, an Afghan officer and Khaja Todarmal, the *Mir-i-Saman* of Shitab Khan, were deputed to make a thorough enquiry so that 'neither the ryots and the jagirdars may be put to hardship nor the imperial revenues fall short.' They were warned that they must be strictly honest, for Shitab Khan might 'send another party to make secret enquiries about the real state of affairs' or he might go there personally.[16] They were to prepare a correct register of revenues.... with the consent of the ryots, the signature of the *Qanungoes* and the deed of the agreement (*Qabuliyat* of the *Chawdhuris*, verified by the agent of Shir Khan (the grantee).[17] The officers ascertained the revenues of the *pargana* as Rs. 1,20,000, and 'it was assigned to Shir Khan in lieu of his salary of Rs. 2,40,000 as a grant for six months.'[18]

The concluding portion of *Daftar* II is also valuable. It relates to an important point of provincial administration— viz., the difficul-

[14] Irfan Habib, *Agrarian System of Mughal India : 1556–1707*, (Aligarh, 1963), 264–65, footnote 30.

[15] *Baharistan*, Vol. II, 741–42, 777. As explained at the outset (*viz.* footnote No. 2) this article is based on the published English translation of the text. The translation of this passage does not exactly support my interpretation. But a close perusal of the episode makes one suspect that actually it is a case of month-ratio grant of Habib's description.

[16] It is a typical case of the Mughal system of double checking, prevalent in the different branches of administration. While it may be argued that the practice shows the prevailing state of corruption among officers, it may also be taken to indicate the painstaking efforts of the Government to know the real state of affairs and to collect correct information.

[17] The details illustrate the procedure by which the system worked.

[18] This is how Dr. Borah translates it. But I suspect that what has been translated as salary for six months actually means the month-ratio system.

ties which sometimes occurred during the period between the departure of a dismissed *Subadar* and the arrival of the next one. The disloyal and fraudulent activities of the outgoing *subadar* put the other subordinate provincial officers, particularly the personal officers of the *subadar*, in a difficult situation. It severely tested their loyalty to the State, on the one hand, and their immediate employer, on the other. The whole problem is typified in the conduct of Qasim Khan after his dismissal.[19]

Also of interest are the doings of Mir Safi, the *Diwan* and *Bakhshi* of the territory of Kamrup. He made changes in the assessment of revenues in the *parganas*. He started the innovation of charging the allowances for the archers on the rent-roll of the ryots. He divided the *parganas* in two classes, one portion entrusted to the *Karories* (under direct Government administration ?) and the other to *mustajirs* (revenue-framers) who enhanced the assessment for their 'own benefit and expenses'. All this caused much dissatisfaction and unrest and the Diwan was removed to 'counteract the sedition which had its origin in the enhancement of taxes on account of the paiks and arches.'[20]

MILITARY MATTERS

The book is particularly rich in military details—construction of forts, method of siege, instruments of war, categories of war-boats, etc. The author was a naval officer and a participant in most of the encounters described by him. As such his descriptions of the various naval engagements are not only vivid (viz., the pursuit by river of the defeating rebel, Udayaditya, and his hair-breadth escape by jumping from his heavy *mahalgiri* boat into the lighter and swifter *kusa*, Vol. I, p. 129) but also very informative. The Navy was the blind spot of the Mughals and information on the topic is scarce in Persian chronicles.

One instance showing the engineering skill of the author and illustrative of some of the problems of naval wars in the area is particularly significant. During the expedition of Islam Khan to Bhati, Ihtimam Khan was ordered to follow him with the fleet. It was to sail up the Kudia Canal to Siyalgarh, but the canal was

[19] *Baharistan*, Vol. I, 421–40.

[20] *Ibid.*, 289.

found to be very shallow. A quick decision on whether or not to sail up the canal was necessary, for the canal might dry up further and then the fleet would have been stranded. Mirza Nathan was sent up-stream to check the depth. In the meantime 'bunds of earth and straw' were constructed to stop the outflow of the water. Nathan found that it was impossible to go up the canal but luckily, he discovered two *jallas* or large sheets of water and a *daha* or deep marsh, situated at some distance from the canal. He got 10,000 boatmen to dig a deep channel 'as deep as the height of a man' to connect the waters with the canal. Another 25,000 boatmen were ordered to build an embarkment at the mouth of the canal to stop its water flowing into the Karatoya river. Thus, sufficient water was collected in the canal for the fleet to move up.[21]

The description of a review of the fleet is more valuable. The different categories of the boats are named—*katari*, *maniki*, *bathila*, *piara*, *kusa*, *balia*, *pal*, *ghurab* (floating battery, gun boat) *machua*, *pashta*, *jaliya*, etc. The manner in which large cannons were mounted on the war boats, screened by a line of wagons or *thatari*, which could be lowered down at the time of firing the cannon, is thus described, 'the big boats, which contained large cannons and *zabarzangs* (field pieces), were arrayed like battlements. On the gangway of each of these boats he arrayed (a line of) wagons called *thatari* and on them he arrayed a series of towers and on each of those towers a red flag was hoisted. Tigers' and leopards' skin were spread over the wagons and on each of the distinguished cannon, skins of tigers were laid. Every boat was covered with a gold embroidered canopy...if it was desired to discharge the artillery, these wagons, which stood like the wall of a fort on the boats extending from one side of the river to the other, could all at once be made to lie flat on the boats and when the dreadful cannon were discharged, by the time their smoke disappeared, these wagons could be raised to their former position. There follows a description of a floating bridge 'as has never been done by any leader at any time' made by grouping tying the boats in such a way that the whole structure could be made to sail straight or turn sidewise as desired. The sailors were dressed in steel uniform.'[22]

The details of land-warfare are no less valuable. Bamboo

[21] *Ibid.*, 45-47.
[22] *Ibid.*, 48-49.

stockades were a common means of defence and fortifications. Elephants (which were commonly found in the area) were used in pulling down such fortifications. Sometimes *bildars* (sappers) were sent ahead, under protective artillery fire, to undermine the walls before the elephants charged. They used to charge under the cover of a heavy protective screen, mounted on wheels, known as *thatari* or *gardun kalan.* It must have been a heavy contraption because on one occasion, when it had to be moved, Mirza Nathan himself and a number of soldiers had to be engaged in pulling it.[23] Individual elephant combats have also been vividly described.[24]

There was a peculiar method of constructing raised platforms in front of a besieged fort and raising it to a height overlooking the remparts, and then bombarding the garrison from the commanding height. *Paiks* and common labourers were used in large numbers to cut grass in the day and pile it up; in the night the heaps were plastered with mud to harden the surface. Such structures were raised either storywise or gradually extended towards the besieged fort. But it sometimes boomeranged upon the besiegers for the enemy would make a sally, 'rush forward with burning thatches tied to long bamboo poles...set fire to the heaps of grass and before the perplexed water carriers could think of bringing water the fire caught on and in the twinkling of an eye all the bundles of grass were burnt to ashes...and the enemy became triumphant.'

SOCIAL MATTERS

The whole story revolves around wars. This leaves little occasion or scope for dwelling upon matters of social interest. But even in the midst of marches, sieges and campaigns one gets glimpses of matters of social interests—festive and funerary ceremonies, superstitious beliefs,[25] taking of auguries (p. 487),[26] practising of witchcraft.[27] prevalence of slavery, practice of *jawhar* ceremony among Muslims, etc.

Of particular interest is the description of a grand feast given

[23] *Ibid.*, 235–37.
[24] *Ibid.*, 181–82, 238.
[25] *Ibid.*, 168.
[26] *Ibid.*, 487.
[27] *Ibid.*, 273, and Vol. II, 626.

by Mirza Nathan on the occasion of the expiry of six months after the death of his father, which marked the end of the period of mourning. It fell on a Friday, the day of the congregational prayers. Islam Khan himself attended the prayers, and it was proclaimed that those who would abstain from the prayers will be fined. Many of the participants wanted to leave but Nathan persuaded them to stay on by saying that 'if you are thinking of the fine, then I hold myself responsible for it.' The guests stayed on. As the party warmed up the guests began drinking heavily so much so that when Islam Khan came there 'the comrades who were heavily drunk did not come near Islam Khan and they dispersed in every direction through corners of the house of Mirza Nathan. The servants of Mirza poured on their dress rose water and aroma of orange flowers and sprinkled scents of ambergris in the air in such a way that the room which was stinking with the smell of wine assumed the fragrance of paradise.' The party went on for seven days and nights and Nathan himself remarks that 'it was such a convivial meeting that it deserved to be noted in the histories of the world.'[28]

There is an interesting case of the performance of *jawhar* by the members of Nathan's family themselves. Surprisingly, this important event has been passed over not only by Borah but by all other writers of the work. In the war against the Assamese the forces of Mirza Nathan had suffered a severe set back and their fort was in danger of being captured. Nathan wanted to send away the ladies of his harem on some elephants, but as the imperial artillery was loaded on the elephants only one was available. The ladies were sent away with a trusted servant with instructions that he should kill them after hearing about Mirza's death. As the *khidmatgaran* of the harem could not be sent due to shortage of elephants, they were ordered to perform *jawhar*, and 'fifty to eighty persons of Mirza's *mahal* performed *jawhar* and many of the men of the army, who thought that they would lose their honour, also performed *jawhar*.'[29] Even though Dr. Borah's explanation about the prevalence of this awful and un-Islamic rite may be partly true, it is significant that these two rare examples should come from the outlying eastern area. It is likely that some of Nathan's wives also belonged to the area where he lived for so long. The performance of *jawhar* by

[28] *Ibid.*, I, 215–16.
[29] *Ibid.*, Vol. II, 598–99.

them is more significant.

MISCELLANEOUS MATTERS

References are available to the hazards of transmitting the Bengal revenues to the capital.[30] These relate to the 18th century when the Bengal revenue was one of the substantial sources of income left to the Emperor. The *Baharistan* mentions another incident which not only illustrates the difficulties but also shows how they were sometimes overcome.

Shitab Khan was appointed by Shahjahan as the officer in charge of Akbarnagar. One of his important assignments was to transmit regularly the revenues and the strategic war materials (he despatched during this period 4,000 maunds of gun-powder, 8,000 maunds of lead, iron and stone hots on boats with loading capacities of 500–1000 maunds). On one occasion a sum of Rs. 7,C0,000 had to be sent but as it was the height of rainy season, the roads were inundated and the only way was by river. This too was subject to the danger of floods or the boats getting sunk. Shitab Khan therefore thought of the following novel way. He first calculated that at no point would the depth of the river be more than 600 ft. He then got one hundred ropes, each 600 ft. long and of the width of the middle finger. He also procured 500 small gourds used for practising swimming. The first instalment of Rs. 1,00,000 was divided into 100 bags each containing 1,000 rupees. One end of the rope was tied to each of the money-bags, while the other was tied to a gourd. The money-bags instead of being put in chests, as was the usual practice, were put on wooden planks with which the boats were covered. To complete the precautions some fishing boats were deputed to sail alongside with expert divers 'who could dive to a depth of two hundred yards.' The whole idea was this : If any of the boats got sunk the gourds tied to the money bags would be floating like so many signals and the fishermen would simply pull up the bags of money 'like buckets'. If perchance the bags got entangled in any object in the bed of the river the divers would dive down and extract them.[31]

Shahjahan the Magnificant, the builder of the Taj and a host

[30] Wilson, C. R., *Early Annals of the English in Bengal*, Vol. II, 24–26.
[31] *Baharistan*, Vol. II, 739–41.

of other exquisite buildings is well-known. The *Baharistan* provides evidence of his architectural interests since his earlier days. Even when he reached Akbarnagar in a distracted condition with the Imperialists in pursuit, he found time to enquire about the completion of a royal mansion he had earlier ordered to be built. He remembered even minute details of the proposed layout and called for explanations for the slightest changes made. He got annoyed with *Daragha-i-Imarat* and ordered him to be given sixty stripes. He ordered new changes and immediate improvisations were made for the construction of a special bedroom. The *Jharokha* and the *Ghusul-khana* buildings were made. What is more important, all the 36 workshops of furniture—*Karkhanajat-i-Rakhwati*—which were in use were set in order—Shitab Khan contributing Rs. 17,000 for it from his private purse.[32]

A distinguishing feature of the Mughal period is the abundance of contemporary and near-contemporary chronicles. Most of these are not only Court-oriented, but they deal mainly with important personalities and major political events. This has led to a rather lop-sided view about many things of that period. The two royal memoirs of Babar and Jahangir are in a class by themselves and represent a refreshing contrast. But being the memoirs of emperors their view-points are, naturally, limited to a particular high social level. The *Baharistan* is the memoir of a provincial military officer. His observations and descriptions present a view of a quite different level. But for a correct over-all idea of the period such works are also essential. The *Baharistan* does contain some descriptions that are credulous, even trifling. However, they contribute to its value, as correcting our perspective on many points. We could do well with a lot more of such works.

[32] *Ibid.*, 769–72.

8

Histories of the Qutb Shahi Dynasty

There is such a dearth of scholars actively interested in the history of this vast sector called the Deccan that it is to be expected that very little should be known regarding the sources of the history of a part of the region called Golkonda or, as I put it, Tilang-Andhra. It may seem strange to scholars that an eminent historian has ascribed to Ferishta the abridged translation of the book by an 'Anonymous Writer' which Briggs has appended to the third volume of his *Rise and Fall of the Mohommedan Power in India.* Again we seem so much indebted to Elliot and Dowson that the only thing we know about Abd-ur-Razzaq's book the *Matla-us-Sadain,* is his description of the City of Vijayanagar which he visited as the accredited envoy of the king of Hirat to the court of the Raya.

There is such an enormous historical data about the history of the Qutb Shahi dynasty that it is impossible to analyse it in a short paper. I, therefore, propose to limit myself here only to the contemporary works written in the Deccan.

For the purpose of clarification the paper is divided into the following sections :

Section 1 : Contemporary Indo-Persian histories written in the Deccan in prose, including certain letters written by Abdullah Qutb Shah and others.

Section 2 : Contemporary Indo-Persian histories written in the Deccan in verse.

Section 3 : Telugu poems with a bearing on the history of the Qutb Shahi dynasty.

I

CONTEMPORARY INDO-PERSIAN HISTORIES IN PROSE

1. *Burhan-i-Maasir*

It is noteworthy that *Burhan-i-Maasir* is the first Indo-Persian chronicle bearing on the history of the Qutb Shahi dynasty compiled in the Deccan. The author, Sayyid Ali b. Azizulla Tabatabai, came to India from Iraq and entered the service of Ibrahim Qutb Shah (1550–80). He was present at the siege of Naldrug, which started in the reign of Ibrahim in September 1581 and continued to the first months of the reign of his successor, Muhammad-Quli, in January 1582. But it was probably not long after this that he quitted Qutb Shahi service and entered the service of the Nizam Shahis. It was Burhan Nizam Shah II (1591–95) who commissioned him to compile the chronicle which has been named after him. The title of the work, *Burhan-i-Maasir,* is a chronogram and answers to 1000/1592 (which, incidentally, is the year of the foundation of Haidarabad) and this may be regarded as the date of the commencent of the compilation. The author says that he completed the work on 14th Rabi II, 1003/17.11.1594, but the narrative is continued right up to the prolonged Peace Conference between Chand Bibi Sultan and Prince Murad, which was concluded on 27th Rajab 1004/14.3.1596. There is an interesting colophon at the end of the Cambridge manuscript from which the printed edition has been copied, saying that the manuscript was copied by the author's own son, Abu Talib, on 22 Muharram, 1038/11.9.1628.

The chronicle is divided into three *Tabaqat* or Sections of unequal size. The first Section deals with the Bahmanis of Gulbarga, the second with the Bahmanis of Bidar and the third, with the Sultans of Ahmadnagar as the central theme, up to the peace treaty of March 14, 1596. The first Section is the shortest, covering barely 52 pages in print, the second covers 115 pages, while the last covers nearly 470 pages and gives a detailed account of the Nizam Shahi kings up to the reign of Burhan II. As the author was in Qutb Shahi service before he migrated to Ahmadnagar, he pays special attention to the history of Golkonda—Haidarabad. He deals with the reigns of Sultan-Quli Qutb-ul-Mulk, his son Jamshid, but he practically skips over the short reign of his son Subhan (whom he does not name) and passes on to the reigns of Ibrahim Qutb Shah and Muhammad Quli Qutb Shah. He describes the reign of the last two monarchs with some interest, though he does so only in connection with the events of the Nizam Shahi kingdom. He is full of useful details about the Qutb Shahi dynasty, while he refers to the rulers of Berar as simply İmad-ul-Mulk and the second of the line as

Shaikh Ala-ud-Din Imad-ul-Mulk, perhaps because the Imad Shahi's were at daggers drawn with the Nizam Shahis.

As has been mentioned elsewhere (Sherwani, *Bahmanis of the Deccan : an objective study*), Burhan provides correctives to Ferishta so far as the Bahmanis are concerned. In the case of the post-Bahmani period, Tabatabai was an eye-witness to many events of his day, while his information about past history may also be regarded as fairly trustworthy. He was present at the two sieges, one of Naldrug, where he was in service of Muhammad-Quli Qutb Shah, and the other of Ahmadnagar, where he appears as a high dignitary in the entourage of Chand Sultana. Moreover he gives such a vivid account of the Peace Conference, which ended the Ahmadnagar-Mughal conflict for the time being, that one may surmise that he was personally present at the Conference itself.

The first two *tabaqas* were translated and abridged by J. S. King and published in 1900 as '*The History of the Bahmani Dynasty*,' while the third *tabaqa* was likewise abridged and translated by Sir Wolseley Haig and published in 1923 as *The History of the Nizam Shahis of Ahmadnagar*.

2. *Gulshan-i-Ibrahimi*, generally called *Tarikh-i-Ferishta*

Muhammad Qasim Hindu Shah, surnamed Ferishta, was born at Astrabad in Iran in 1552 and died at Bijapur in 1623. He was brought to Ahmadnagar when still a child and remained there till 1591, when he joined service at the court of Ibrahim Adil Shah II of Bijapur.

His monumental work, the *Gulshan-i-Ibrahimi* or *Nauras Nama*, generally known as *Tarikh-i-Ferishta*, was presented to the king in 1606 in a complete form, though subsequently the author enlarged it, bringing it to 1606. It is certainly one of the most important chronicles relating to the medieval period of Indian history. Its importance is such that the chronicles compiled after it may be regarded either as supplementary to the respective themes or else mere copies of Ferishta dealing with specified areas.

In his Introduction the author has given a list of thirty two works on which he has drawn for his information, but not one of these was a history of the Qutb Shahi dynasty. In the very brief section 4 of volume 2 (Lucknow edition) devoted to *Rulers of Tilang* he only refers to one work, the *Waqai Qutbshahiya*, which was supposed to have been written by Shah Khurshah of Iraq in the time of Ibrahim Qutb Shah (1550–80), but he confesses that he did not have recourse even to that work. As a matter of fact no such work by Shah Khurshah exists. There is a fine copy of *Tarikh Ilchi Nizam Shah* (by Khurshah b. Qubad-al-Husaini) prepared for the royal library of Abdullah Qutb Shah in 1038/1628–29 (Salar Jung Museum, Haidarabad, Mss. No. 118 B), in which the author describes the history of the world right up to the Bahmanis of the Deccan, including the Turkoman ancestors of the Qutb Shahis. But when he comes to Muhammad Shah Lashkari (1463–82) and the disintegration of the Bahmani Empire, he stops there and promises to write later detailed histories of the Bahmani Succession States, namely, the states ruled by Nizam-ul-Mulk, Adil Khan, Qutb-ul-Mulk, Imad-ul-Mulk and Qasim Barid. Even if he did write a history of the Qutb Shahis we are not aware of it and at least Ferishta did not have recourse to it.

In the Lucknow edition of Ferishta barely five pages are devoted to the Qutb Shahis, while 92 pages have been taken up by the Adil Shahis and 74 by the Nizam Shahis. Even in these five pages the author has made certain palpable mistakes due to his ignorance of facts. A few instances of his *faux pas* may suffice : (1) He says that Muhammad-Quli ascended the throne in 989/1581 at the age of 12, although he himself says that he was born on 1st Ramazan 973. (2) Writing in 1018/1609–10 he says that the Persian envoy, Aghuzlu Sultan, was still in the Deccan waiting for the acceptance of the proposal for the marriage of the son of Shah Abbas II of Iran to the Sultan's daughter, Hayat Bakhshi Begum ; although her marriage with the Sultan's nephew, who later became Sultan Muhammad Qutb Shah, had already taken place two years earlier. (3) *Ferishta* is so much interested in the supposed romance of Muhammad-Quli with the '*zan-i-fahishah*', Bhagmati, that he calls the newly founded capital 'Bhagnagar' in 1018/1609–10, when we have a number of coins struck at 'Dar-us-Saltanat Haidarabad' in 1012/1603. He forgets his own theory when he says categorically that the Qutb Shahi army, which had been sent to Ahmadnagar in 1005/1597, was routed by the Mughals and fled back to 'Haidarabad'.

Thus, so far as the Qutb Shahi dynasty is concerned it cannot be said that Ferishta's *Gulshan-i-Ibrahimi* is to be relied upon.

3. *Tazkirat-ul-Muluk*

Mir Rafi-ul-Din Ibrahim bin Nuru-ud-Din Taufiq Shirazi was born about 947/1510–11. He came to Bijapur with his father as a merchant in the time of Mahmud Shah Bahmani, but gyrated into government service in the time of Ali Adil Shah (1557/79) apparently as a *Khwan Salar* or Steward of the Royal Household. He rose step by step till Ibrahim Adil Shah II (1579–1626) sent him on an important mission to Ahmadnagar in 1005/1596–97. He also served as governor of Bijapur for some time.

Rafi-ud-Din began writing the *Tazkirat-ul-Muluk* on 19th Ramazan 1017/17.12.1608 and completed it at Nauraspur, a suburb of Bijapur (which, he says, was renamed Bidyapur), on 6th Jamadi II, 1024/23rd June 1615. The *Tazkira* is primarily a chronicle of the Adil Shahis of Bijapur, prefaced by a chapter on the Bahmanis and ending with two chapters on the Mughals from Amir Timur to Akbar. The remaining seven chapters are taken over by the history of the Adil Shahis right up to Ibrahim Adil Shah II. But the politics of the Bahmani Succession States were so much intertwined with each other that a detailed history of the Adil Shahis was bound to have a fairly important niche for the Qutb Shahis as well. It is interesting to note that the author calls the first four rulers of the Adil Shahi dynasty by their names without the suffix of Shah, thus denoting that they did not proclaim their kingship. It should, however, be noted that there are certain inscriptions of the fourth ruler, Ibrahim Adil, dated 945/1538–39, in which he is called Ibrahim Adil Shah. It is also interesting that he traces the geneology of Yusuf Adil Khan to Mahmud Beg of Sawah in Central Asia, and not to Mahmud I or II, Sultans of Turkey as is sometimes asserted.

The author devotes considerable attention and space to the Qutb Shahis. He is all praise for Ibrahim Qutb Shah, and gives some very useful information about the foundation of the new capital Haidarabad. He describes its *raison d'etre*, its general lay-out, the details of the part of the royal palace and the position which men of learning and wisdom occupied in the State. On the whole the book is a fairly good authority for the earlier period of the Qutb Shahi dynasty.

4. *Tarikh-i-Muhammad Qutb Shah.*

5. *Maasir-i-Qutb Shahi*

The *Tarikh* is a comprehensive and detailed history of the Qutb

Shahi dynasty. It was compiled under the order of Sultan Muhammad Qutb Shah in 1025/1616. The author, who chooses to be anonymous, says in his Introduction that he had before him a larger history 'by one of the servants (Chakiran) of His Majesty' which he has condensed and added on certain other facts which have a bearing on the history of the period. As a history of the dynasty with an official hallmark, it begins with a description of the Qara Quvinlu background of Sultan-Quli's family before he and his uncle Allah-Quli first came to India, and goes on to the history of the dynasty in all its aspects. The book is divided into four 'Accounts' and an Epilogue as follows :

(1) Account of Sultan-Quli Qutb-ul-Mulk.
(2) Account of 'Jamshid Qutb-ul-Mulk' and his son 'known as Subhan-Quli'.
(3) Account of the life and reign of Ibrahim Qutb-Shah.
(4) Account of the life and reign of Sultan Muhammad-Quli Qutb Shah.
(5) Epilogue : Account of 'some of the events' of the reign of Sultan Muhammad Qutb Shah.

The book not merely describes the events at the court, the campaigns undertaken and the conquests made, but also surveys the public works of the Qutb Shahis, their patronage of literature and their constructions. He gives the *raison d'etre* of the foundation of Haidarabad, the scheme of its lay-out, various edifices and roads which went to and from the new capital, the relative importance of Golkonda and Haidarabad and numerous facts not found elsewhere. He is very punctilious about dates, and his survey of facts is chronologically correct to a large extent. The author completed the work in Shaban 1026/July-August 1617.

Another author, Mahmud b. Abdulla Nishapuri, has brought the narrative to 1038 in his *Maasir-i-Qutb Shahi*. He entered the service of Muhammad-Quli Qutb Shah in 995/1587 and compiled the book between 1033/1624 and 1038/1629. It was originally in three volumes but was 'several times altered and enlarged.' The only portion extant today is the one in the India Office Library and even that is defective at the end. Apart from the history of the Qutb Shahi dynasty up to the year of Muhammad-Qutb Shah's death in 1035/1626, he deals in some detail with the history of his home country Iran, and stops at the death of Shah Abbas II in 1038/1629.

6. *Hadiqat-us-Salatin*

Hadiqat-us-Salatin is a volumnious history of the first nineteen years (not 16 as in story) of the reign of Abdullah Qutb Shah (1626–72) written by Mirza Nizam-ud-Din Ahmad at the instance of the well-known Peshwa or Prime Minister of the kingdom, Shaikh Muhammad bin Khatun. It purports to be a day to day chronicle of Abdullah's life from his birth on November 21, 1614, to January 1, 1644. The period was one of extreme decline of the political power of the Qutb Shahi kingdom. It had become a virtual protectorate of the Mughal Empire by the fateful 'Deed of Submission' of January 1636, and whenever a Mughal envoy arrived at the capital the king received him at the farther end of the bund on the Hussain Sagar, five miles from the royal palace. He was forced to mint money with Shahjahan's name and to have the *khutba* read on Fridays with prayers for the long life and prosperity of the Emperor and for the success of his arms. The Sultan had to seek favour from those in power at Imperial capital and to write abject letters to Dara Shikoh, Prince Aurangzeb and Imperial ministers and envoys, such as no independent sovereign would ever care to write (*Makatib-i-Sultan Abdullah Qutb Shah*, for which see later). And yet the author of the *Hadiqat* represents him as the most mighty monarch, and relates that when he was born astrologers predicted that 'he would be like Alexander and Solomon, and issue orders to all the kings of the world.' He describes him with great bombast and details the various functions connected with the celebration of various festivals 'when flowers abounded, casks of scent distributed, lakhs of lamps lit and thousands and thousands of *huns* distributed.' The progress of the king to the east coast is described in words which would put the Field of the Cloth of Gold to shame. And just then Mir Jumla was conquering the Rayalsima with his centre at Gandikota and unfurling the Qutb Shahi flag on eminences south of St. Thomas' Mount and preparing for the day when he would cross over to the Mughal camp and put the Court to shame.

Hadiqat-us-Salatin is like a diary of the Qutb Shahi Court in which not merely the pomp and merriment are described but also the way the country was administered, the ways of the great lords, the duties and functions of the Peshwa and other ministers, the etablishment of the *Majlis-i-Diwandari* or Privy Council, the administration of justice and even the day to day posting of various high civil and military officers. It gives a fairly correct picture of the social life of the people, their superstitions, their rites and ceremonies, and what is significant, of the cordial relations which existed between the different sections of the population, chiefly the Hindus and the Muslims. Finally we can glean from it the international set-up, the position which foreign *hajibs* or envoys, both permanent and extra-ordinary, occupied in the capital. The diction of the book is such that in spite of the wealth of facts the book contains the reader is not bored, and in fact his interest increases with almost every page.

7. *Hadaiq-us-Salatin*

The full name of the book is *Hadaiq-us-Salatin fi Kalami'l-Khawaqin* or 'The Gardens of the Sultans and the Poetic Compositions of Kings'. The author, Ali ibn Taifur al-Bustami, says that he was a pupil of Muhammad ibn Khatun, and it was at the instance of Sultan Abul Hasan Qutb Shah (1672–87) that he completed this work in 1092/1681. The *Hadaiq* is not a book on history but is a compendium of Persian poetry and some letters written by the Kings of Iran and of India as well as of some of their ministers and learned men. Although it was barely six years before the fall of the dynasty and the life-incarceration of the last of the Qutb Shahis at Daulatabad, the author ends his narrative with a prayer that the power and prestige of the king should last for ever !

The book is divided into three *Hadiqas* or Gardens and each divided into a number of *Tabaqas* or Sections :

(*i*) Pre-Islamic Iranian Kings from the Pishdadis to 30/650–51.

(*ii*) Muslim Kings and Emperors of Iran, Central Asia and India, including Ghoris, Seljuqis, Khwarizm Shahis, Turkish Sultans, the Mughals from Timur to Jahangir, the Qaraquyinlus, Safawis, Bahmanis, of whom only 'Mahmud Shah' (meaning Muhammad I) and Firmoz are mentioned the Adil Shahis and finally the Qutb Shahis, of whom only 'Sultan-Quli known as Bara Malik' Jamshid Muhammad-Quli Qutb Shah and Sultan Muhammad Qutb Shah's reigns are touched. It is strange that Abdullah Qutb Shah and Abul Hasan Qutb Shah do not appear as poets or patrons of poetry at all.

(*iii*) The life histories, poems and some letters of certain ministers, amirs, judges and learned men. These include more than thirty names, but north India is represented only by Abd-ur-Rahim Khan Khan-i-Khanan, Ali Quli Khan, Faizi and Abul Fazl, while the Deccan is represented by Mahmud Gawan, Mirza Amin Isfahani Mir Jumla of Muhammad-Quli Qutb Shah, and Riza-Quli Beg entitled Neknam Khan.

The subject matter of the book is mainly poetry and the poet as the name of the book itself connotes, but the life history of each of them gives certain historical data, though, as the author himself admits, culled from Indo-Persian and other chronicles. Out of more than 200 folios only about 20 have a bearing on the history of Golkonda-Haidarabad, but even here certain new facts are mentioned which bring the *Hadaiq* into line with the source books of Qutb Shahi history. It must, however, by stated that the standard of the work is definitely inferior to the standard maintained by such histories *Tarikh-i-Muhammad Qutb Shah*, and considering the steep downward political trends of the region, it was only natural that it should be so.

8. Letters of Abdullah Qutb Shah.

(1) *Makatib Sultan Abdullah Qutb Shah ba nam Dara Shikoh waghairah.* (MSS. Salar Jung Library, Adab, Nasr Farsi, No. 295).

(2) *Araiz wa Ittihad Namajat wa Faramin Abdullah Qutb Shah* (MSS. Anjuman Taraqqi Urdu, Karachi, No. 7/27).

(3) *Insha-i-Abdul Ali Khan Taliqani* (MSS. Salar Jung Library Adab, Nasr Farsi, No. 15).

These three collections of letters and *farmans* of Abdullah Qutb Shah and certain other important personages of his reign give us important data regarding the political position of the kingdom after the fateful Deed of Submission signed by the king after the defection of Muhammad Said Mir Jumla to the Mughal camp. The manuscript in the Karachi collection is virtually a copy of the MSS. Salar Jung Library, No. 295 with certain additions and deletions which are not of a very great importance. The last actual date mentioned in the collection is Rajab 1072/February-March 1662, being the date of the marriage of the king's third daughter to Mirza Abul Hasan who was destined to be the last ruler of the Qutb Shahi dynasty. The third book, *Insha-i-Taliqani* is obviously meant to be a collection of certain choice letters illustrating the Persian diction in vogue in the Deccan of the seventeenth century, and contains not only some letters common to the other two collections, but also other letters which have no bearing on the history of the period.

The letters in the first two collections roughly cover the period from Mir Jumla's treason in 1065/1654 up to 1072/1662. Most of the letters are undated, some have only the month and the year while a few have the full dates. There are letters of Abdullah Qutb Shah addressed to Shah Abbas II of Iran, to Shahjahan, Dara Shikoh, Prince Aurangzeb, Shahjahan's daughter (may be Jahanara), to Ali Adil Shah to Abd-us-Samad Dabir-ul-Mulk, Qutb Shahi envoy to the Mughal Court, Haji Nasir, Qutb Shahi envoy to Bijapur and many other personages.

The range of these interesting letters, some of which are very important, is such that they throw a flood of light not merely on the complete dependence of Abdullah's Haidarabad on the Mughal power, but also the utter despondency of the King who stooped low to complain of his plight to the Shah of Iran and his own brother-in-law of Bijapur. The first letter in all these collections is to Shah Abbas II in which Abdullah bitterly complains to him of Mir Jumla's treason and the 'faithlessness of Sultan Khurram.' On the other hand his 'Petitions' not merely to the Emperor but also to Prince Dara and Aurangzeb are couched in the most abject terms. Thus, whenever he mentions the Emperor's name it is with a profusion of laudatory epithets running sometimes to many lines, while he says that these petitions are 'entreaties'. He calls Prince Aurangzeb 'the Pearl of the Great Caliphate'. Even when he sends a *farman* to his envoy at Delhi he refers to his letters to the Emperor as '*arz dashts*' and the Emperor himself as 'the Abode of the Refuge of the Khilafat'.

The letters, therefore, are valuable for they furnish us a correct estimate of the foreign, diplomatic and, to a certain extent, of the domestic policy in the later part of Abdullah's reign.

II

CONTEMPORARY INDO-PERSIAN HISTORIES, WRITTEN IN THE DECCAN, IN VERSE

(1) *Nisbat Nama-i-Shahryari*,

(2) *Nasab Nama-i-Qutb Shahi,*
(3) *Tawarikh-i-Qutb Shahi* (London),
(4) *Tawarikh-i-Qutb Shahi* (Haidarabad).

The *Nisbat Nama-i-Shahryari* was compiled by Husain Ali Shah Furshi who completed it in 1016/1607, and it was copied at Lahore in 1019/1610. The name, *Tawarikh-i-Qutb Shahi,* occurs in one of the lines at the commencement of the book. It is divided into 4 cantos and 'appears to be an abstract of the *Nasab-nama.*' The *takhallus* of Fursi appears on page 5, but the book is ascribed to Hiralal Khushdil, Secretary (Munshi) of Haidar-Quli Khan, and the *takhallus,* 'Khushdil' appears in one of the odes in the book.

There are two copies of the name *Nasab Nama-i-Qutb Shahi* in the collection of the Asiatic Society of Bengal (Ivonow, 690 and 691) both ending at the beginning of the rule of Muhammad Quli Qutb Shah (1580–1611).

The book is divided into four *Maqalas* or Theses; namely

(i) Introduction and the early history of the dynasty ending in the death of Mahmud Shah Bahmani (1518).
(ii) Decline of the Bahmanis and the rise of Bare Malik.
(iii) Inter-statal wars of the Deccan Sultanates, up to the death of Ibrahim Qutb Shah, with odes in honour of Ibrahim and his son Muhammad-Quli Qutb Shah.
(iv) The first year of the reign of Muhammad-Quli Qutb Shah up to the celebration of the King's marriage with Mir Shah Mir's daughter.

The book contains three fine vignettes. The first part was copied from the library of Muhammad Qutb Shah by Ali b. Abi Muhammad and completed on 22 Shawwal 1022/25.11.1613, while the remaining parts were copied by Said-ud-Din Isfahani. Ivonow says that the word 'Lahore' has been added as it is in a more modern hand.

The narrative goes on to the first year of the reign of Muhammad-Quli Qutb Shah before the king's father-in-law was deposed from his office and ordered to leave the kingdom; but it seems to have been copied down in the first year of the reign of Sultan Muhammad Qutb Shah, in 1021/1613, not in the reign of his predecessor Muhammad-Quli as Ivonow would have it.

The other book also called *Nasab Nama-i-Qutb Shahi* by Ivonow (No. 691), is 'a poem of the same content but half its size', while the name of the author, 'Fursi' appears in a number of places.

Tawarikh-i-Qutb Shahi (Ethe, No. 1486). This book is similar to the two books described above, and it was likewise dedicated to the reigning Sultan, Muhammad-Quli Qutb Shah. The author 'who conceals his name', was engaged in this compilation for ten years, It is also divided into 4 parts, namely.

Part 1 : Geneology of the Qutb Shahi family up to the birth of 'Sultan-Quli Qutb Shah'.

Part 2 : Reign of 'Malik Sultan-Quli Qutb Shahi' and of Jamshid.

Part 3 : Reign of Ibrahim Qutb Shah.

Part 4 : Reign of Muhammad-Quli Qutb Shah,

As in the case of other books the frontispiece is illuminated in gold. There are 137 folios, *i. e.*, 274 pages written in clear *nastaliq.*

Tawarikh-i-Qutb Shahi (Salar Jung Library, Adab, Nazm-i-Farsi, No. 1101). The work which is, like the above three books, a history of the early Qutb Shahs in verse, and was compiled in the reign of Muhammad-Quli Qutb Shah as the author indicates in the beginning. It covers barely 55 folios with 21 lines to a page and is a beautifully gold illuminated book written in fine *nastaliq* and an embellished frontispiece in gold. It traces the history of the dynasty from its inception and deals with certain events in great detail, some of which may have been the product of the fertile imagination of the author. There are blank spaces left for vignettes on folios 9 (a), 30 (b) and 35 (b). The manuscript is incomplete, for while it was written in the time of Muhammad-Quli Qutb Shah, it ends the narrative with his accession in 1580. Evidently the last few folios of the manuscript have been lost.

Although it is not so mentioned, the book is virtually divided into four sections, each beginning with the praise of God, a device which ends a narrative and begins another with *aghaz-i-dastan* or 'Beginning of the Story'. The four sections are as follows :

(1) The reign or rule of Sultan-Quli Qutb-ul-Mulk to the successful campaign of Kovilkonda and the death of Ismail Adil Shah of Bijapur;

(2) From the accession of Mallu to the Bijapur throne to the murder of Sultan-Quli Qutb-ul-Mulk;

(3) From the accession of 'Jamshid Khan' to his return from Sholapur;

(4) The remaining period of Jamshid's rule, Subhan's interlude and Ibrahim's reign.

The work contains certain useful data which is not found in any other work. Thus the interesting episode of Jamshid going to pray at the grave of his martyred father, the search for his father's murderer and his execution shed some light on the problem of the complicity or otherwise of Jamshid in his father's murder. There are also some interesting details of the battle 'on the banks of the Krishna' of January 1565. These and certain other episodes described in the manuscript are both interesting and useful. As has been mentioned above the book has not been listed in any of the Catalogues published so far.

III

TELUGU POEMS WITH A BEARING ON THE HISTORY OF THE QUTB SHAHI DYNASTY

1. *Long Poem* : There is no history proper of the Qutb Shahis in Telugu. Apart from inscriptions, with which we are not concerned here, there are some long poems which throw some light on certain aspects of Qutb Shahi political and social history. Thus, Addanki Gangadhara Kavi's *Tapati Sambaranamu* describes the extent of the conquests of Sultan Quli Qutb-ul-Mulk and praises his character as a king. He also gives an account of Ibrahim Qutb Shah's campaigns against Rajahmundri and Srikakulum and further up to the confines of Orissa as well as a full pen-picture of Ibrahim's court. Similarly, the anonymous writer of the long poem *Chatupadyamanimanyari* describes in some detail the patronage accorded to Telugu by Ibrahim. The third important Telugu work which has a bearing on the social set-up is *Yayaticharitramu Ponnaganti Telegannarya*. It is a mythological poem consisting of the story of Yayati who was descended from the Moon and from whom all the Chandravansis were supposed to be descended. It is a poem in *atsa* or pure Telugu without any *tatsam* Sanskrit word, and is dedicated to Amin Khan of Patancheru. From the historical point of view we are more concerned with the dedicatory introduction than with the story, for in it the author gives a fairly long account of Amin Khan's family, its position in the field of diplomacy and public service and the general

set-up of the village society. Although the three books mentioned are not books dealing with history as such, they give us the Telugu view point of the events mainly of the time of the early Qutb Shahs.

2. A very interesting set of compositions in Telugu are long laudatory odes sung generally every morning at the courts of the kings and other feudal rulers. They are compositions of the bards of varying knowledge, capacity of understanding, and are therefore of a heterogeneous variety. The most famous of these are the *Velugotivari Vamsavali* and *Chikkadevaraya Vamsavali* which describe the deeds of valour of the members of the families in question. There is also the *Ramarajavijayam* containing odes in praise of the Aravidu family of Vijayanagar. All these are just family chronicles, and when they ostensibly sing praises for the subjects of their adoration, we should expect the description to be one-sided and at times exaggerated. Moreover, as no dates are mentioned we have to draw from other chronicles for the chronological sequence.

3. *The Mackenzie Collection*: We have a mass of village accounts called *Kaifiyats*. These originated in the *dandakaviles* or *kaviles* which were kept by the village *karnam* or revenue officer (*patwari*), and contained information about the political, religious, social and economic conditions of the village, including an account of the contemporary events which had bearing on the locality. Entries were made by each *karnam* during his incumbency, who then passed them on to his successor. It was Col. Mackenzie who realized the value of these village *kaviles*, literally hundreds in number, and tried to collect them or have their copies prepared. But the *karnams* as well as the clerks who were sent to copy the documents thought that it was futile to copy down the long accounts fully, and made their gists according to their predilictions. It is these gists which are called *kaifiyats* or 'Narratives' and they are collectively known as the 'Mackenzie Manuscripts' or 'Mackenzie Collection'.

These *kaifiyats* are 'an admixture of legend and history—the legendary element preponderates in the account of the early period, but it leaves the later period free. The research worker, therefore, must use them with great caution especially as the *karnams* were sometimes ignorant of even elementary facts. The most important of these *kaifiyats* from our point of view are those of Chittiveli, Cuddapah, Hanamkonda, Kondavidu, Nandyala, Sara, Siddhavatam (Siddhout) and Tadpatri.

Included in the Mackenzie Collection is *Ramarajna Bakhair* which is supposed to give an account of the decisive battle wrongly called the Battle of Talikota. The *Bakhair* furnishes us with a bewildering mass of statistics regarding the battle. Among other things it says that 'Akhabara Jaladin Mogal Padusaha', the lord of 'Jahalnapura' took part in it, and the army which he contributed to the joint forces included 2½ crores of foot-soldiers, a lakh of elephants, two lakh camels, 5 lakh archers, about 12,000 guns and 12,000 riderless horses. That was only 'Akhabara's contribution. On the other side Rama Raja's resources included 65,50,000 horses, nearly 19 lakh camels, about 20,000 elephants, 9,87,76,413 maunds gun-powder and 9,87,65,43,21,00,000 cannon balls ! On the basis of such a data one of the foremost of modern historian thinks that 'this chronicle furnishes us with the Hindu version of the great battle and enables us to investigate the problem afresh.'

9

Babur

'From the eleventh year of my age till now', Babur wrote in 1527, 'I had never spent two festivals of the Ramazan in the same place. Last year's festival I had spent in Agra. In order to keep up the usage, on Sunday night, the thirtieth, I proceeded to Sikri to keep the feast there.'[1] This was the man who never claimed to be a historian, and yet the testimony of his Memoirs has not only been accepted as sufficient proof, as Lane Poole says,[2] but all the later historians, whether contemporary, British or modern, seem to have treated the *Babur-nama* as an indispensable source material. Mirza Haider Dughlat's *Tarikh-i-Rashidi* and Gulbadan Begam's *Humayun-nama* do throw some light on the lacunae occurring in Babur's Memoirs, but whatever he has recorded himself, with a very few exception,[3] has stood the test of time as well as criticism, Beveridge has said : 'His autobiography is one of those priceless records which are for all time and is fit to rank with the confessions of St. Augustine and Rousseau and the Memoirs of Gibbon and Newton. In Asia it stands almost alone.'[4] Babur was quite conscious of his standing. He knew that his records would be scrutinised by posterity. He writes : 'I have no intention, by what I have written, to reflect on anyone ; all that I have said is only the plain truth...I have only spoken of things as they happened. In all that I have written, down to the present moment, I have in every word most scrupulously followed the truth. I have spoken of occurrences precisely as they

[1] *Memoirs of Zahir-ed-Din Muhammed Babur*, tr. Leyden and Erskine (London, 1921) Vol. II, 316–17. Henceforth referred to as Memoirs.

[2] Stanley Lane-Poole, *Rulers of India—Babur*, 13.

[3] The most important one being his attitude towards Shaibani, and his efforts to gloss over the fact of his sister being given over to the same formidable adversary, 157

[4] H. Beveridge, *Calcutta Review*, 1897.

really passed; I have consequently described every good or bad act, were it of my father or elder brother, just as it occurred and have set forth the merit or demerit of every man, whether friend or stranger, with the most perfect impartiality. Let the reader therefore excuse me, and let not the hearer judge with too much severity.'[5]

Babur was proud of his imperial heritage. His ambition was to follow Timur in his military exploits and in compiling a Memoir. If, on the one hand, Babur wanted to become a Padishah in deed, on the other hand he wanted to leave a record of everything he did. In fact, it was expected of all the Timurid princes that they would use the pen and the sword with equal skill, and they were judged by the same standards. Babur writes about one of his uncles, Sultan Husain Baykara : 'No person of the race of Taimur Beg ever equalled Sultan Husain Mirza in the use of the scimitar. He had a turn for poetry and composed a *diwan*. He wrote in Turki. His poetical name was Hussaini. Many of his verses are far from being bad, but the whole of Mirza's *diwan* is in the same measure.'[6] Mirza Haidar wrote about Babur that 'in the composition of Turki poetry he was second only to Amir Ali Shir. He wrote in Turki and invented a style of verse called Mubaiyan.'

Babur seems to have been in the habit of noting down all the occurrences, although it is not known when he sat down to write his Memoirs, the first portion of which he could clad in a fine literary style, subtle prose sprinkled with verses in Turki and Persian, while the latter remains in the original form of a diary which perhaps he had no time to re-write. For this inference he gives us one clue, and that is of his notes and papers being blown away in a violent storm on his return journey from the eastern provinces in 1529. 'That same night after the *tarawih* prayers...the clouds of the rainy season broke and there was suddenly such a tempest, and the wind rose so high that most of the tents were blown down. I was writing in the middle of my pavilion, and so suddenly did the storm come on that I had no time to gather up my papers and the loose sheets that were written, before it blew down the pavilion, with the screen that surrounded it, on my head.... The books and sheets of paper were drenched and wet, but were gathered again with much trouble, folded in a bed cover of scarlet wool, and placed on the throne over which

[5] Memoirs, Vol. II, 32-33.

[6] *Ibid.*, Vol. I, 288.

carpets were thrown. The storm abated in two garis. We...... kindled a fire with much difficulty and did not sleep till morning, being busily employed all the while in drying the leaves and papers.'[7]

The historical truth presented by Babur in his Memoirs is mixed up in an almost inextricable manner with his own opinions, sentiments, judgements and his philosophy of life. His predilections colour all his observations, and while reading his Memoirs we seem to live with him, to think with him, move with the hectic speed that was peculiarly his, and yet stop to reflect on the surroundings. Babur combined chronology with a deep knowledge of geography. This formed a definite corollary to historical events and helped him in forming the estimate of the resources, the climate, and the habits of the people of a particular place. Farghana, according to him, was 'situated in the fifth climate......Farghana is a country of small extent, but abounding in grain and fruits.'[8] The same was the case with Samarkand. It was pleasantly situated in the fifth climate in lat. 39° 37′, and long. 90° 16′. But Babur could not stop there, as he had the mathematician's bent of mind always ready to make calculations. 'I directed its wall to be paced round the rampart and found that it was ten thousand six hundred paces in circumference.'[9] After this he writes about its people. 'The inhabitants are all orthodox Sunnis, observant of the law, and religious' and then proceeds to describe the eminent theologians of Mawera-un-Nahr. Then he comes to its boundaries, rivers, fruits, public buildings, bazars, its bakers and cooks, and finally he says : 'The best paper in the world comes from Samarkand......Another production of Samarkand is Kermezi (or crimson velvet), which is exported to all quarters.'[10] The meadows are not overlooked either. It was one of his passions to alight from his horse and sit down to relax in the meadow threaded by a stream. Yuret-Khan was one of such meadows. 'The river winds round the Yuret-Khan in such a manner as to leave room within for an army to encamp......Perceiving the excellence of this position, I encamped here for some time during the siege.'[11] He

[7] *Ibid.*, Vol. II, 408–09.
[8] *Ibid.*, Vol. I, 1.
[9] *Ibid.*, 76.
[10] *Ibid.*, 83.
[11] *Ibid.*, 84.

completes his observations by giving a description of the provinces and tumans. Does this not resemble the modern gazetteer ? Information of every kind can be gleaned from his pages. When he goes to Kabul he turns eloquent again, saying 'From Kabul you may in a single day go to a place where snow never falls, and in the space of two astronomical hours, you may reach a spot where snow lies always.......'[12] And then follows the usual description of the place, animals and fruits, birds and the manner of fishing and catching water fowl.

Then he proceeded to Hindustan. A man of his calibre could not rest content with the kingdom of Kabul. It did not even justify his title of Padishah for which he gambled with his life, his convictions, his belief. The target was to become King of Kings, on the one hand, and to become the custodian of his heritage on the other. Uzbeks and Persians had deprived him of both in the land of his own people. His generosity had taken toll of Badakhshan, which he had given away to the grandson of Shah-begam. His knowledge of history must have pointed out the plains of Hindustan, which once Timur had conquered. And he crossed the hurdles of Afghans who, he says, 'are provokingly rude and studid'[13] to come to the country that could satisfy the political and economic dreams of this student of the *Shah-Nama*. He reflects in his Memoirs : 'Sultan Mahmud, at the time when he conquered Hindustan, occupied the throne of Khorasan, and had absolute power and dominion over the Sultans of Khawarizm and the surrounding chiefs (Transoxiana). The king of Samarkand, too, was subject to him.'[14] When Babur became Padishah, he was indeed exultant with joy. 'This success I do not describe to my own strength, nor did this good fortune flow from my own efforts, but from the fountain of the favour and mercy of God.'[15]

After the fall of Panipat he reflected on the inherent weakness of India. 'All Hindustan was not at that period subject to a single Emperior : every Raja set up for a monarch on his own account, in his own petty territories.'[16] He makes a study of the different

[12] *Ibid.*, 220.
[13] *Ibid.*, Vol. II, 178.
[14] *Ibid*, 193.
[15] *Ibid.*, 195.
[16] *Ibid.*, 194.

petty kingdoms, Muslim as well as non-Muslim, and then proceeds to his favourite subject, the geography of the country. 'Hindustan is situated in the first, second and third climate. No part of it is in the fourth....Its hills and rivers, its forests and plains, its animals and plants, its inhabitants and their languages, its winds and rains, are all of a different nature.'[17]

The plains of India could not satisfy the aesthetic sense of Babur which was rooted deep in his personality. He always ventured to look for the pure pleasures of nature which had always soothed his ruffled mind. The vast stretch of the Indo-Gangetic plain could not yield any such pleasure for him. He has referred to the perennial problem of the people who never had any inclination to pay the taxes, and whenever it suited them could and did rise in revolts.[18] His observation about the cities being completely abandoned within a single day or a day and a half symbolises the standard of living of the people. Obviously the masses did not have much to pack up. They did not use much of clothing. He writes : 'Their peasants and the lower classes all go about naked. They tie on a thing which they call a *langoti*......The women, too, have a *lang*—one end of it they tie about their waist, and the other they throw over their head.'[19] The rich people must have been very few. The nobility aided by soldiers did the fighting and the zamindars lived in their own mud forts with their army of disaffected peasantry, and had to be reduced one by one, if the ruler was strong enough to do so. Otherwise they were an open challenge to him and increased their power at the cost of his authority. 'The peasantry and soldiers of the country avoided and fled from my men. Afterwards, everywhere except only in Delhi and Agra, the inhabitants fortified different posts, while the governors of the towns put their fortifications in a posture of defence, and refused to submit or obey.'[20]

Indian society was caste-ridden and any kind of social intercourse could not have existed. But it was not possible for him to understand the complexities of the caste system. The man who was used to the drinking parties of his father, the display of friendliness and ceremonial gatherings of the Khans, and who had been holding

[17] *Ibid.*, 201.
[18] *Ibid.*, 208.
[19] *Ibid.*, 242.
[20] *Ibid.*, II, 247.

such parties himself, could only sit back and think as to what was amiss, and state his conclusion that the people of India 'have no idea of the charms of friendly society, of frankly mixing together or of familar intercourse.'[21] The only good thing he could say about the caste system or whatever he understood of it was that there was an abundance of work people. 'The workmen of every profession and trade are innumerable and without end. For any work, or any employment, there is always a set ready, to whom the same employment and trade have descended from father to son for ages.'[22] He has touched upon the aspect of administration also when he says that the countries from Bhera to Bihar yielded a 'revenue of fifty two krores, as will appear from the particular and detailed statement.'[23] The parganawise revenue has been given by him, but Babur throughout his life had been too much of a soldier to be a good revenue administrator. And one does not find any permanent settlement of any kind made by him. He seems to have been conscious of the fact that his could not be the last word in the description of Hindustan. He had written whatever came to his knowledge and whatever he had been able to verify. He adds : 'Hereafter, if I observe any thing worthy of being described I shall take notice of it; and if I hear anything worth repeating, I will insert it.'[24]

Though he may have ignored or disregarded certain injunctions, Babur was a deeply religious man. This attitude he had inherited from his father. 'He (Umar Shaikh) never neglected the five regular and stated prayers and during his whole life he rigidly performed the *kaza* (or retributory prayers and fasts). He devoted much of his time to reading the Koran. He was extremely attached to Khwaja Obeidullah, whose disciple he was, and whose society he greatly affected.'[25] Two main trends of Islamic religious thought were obvious in his character. He was orthodox in the performance of his prayers in the prescribed manner, and nothing short of serious illness perhaps prevented his performance of religious duties. 'It was wonderfully cold,' he writes, 'and the wind of Ha-derwish had lost none of its violence, and blew keen......I required to bathe on

[21] *Ibid.*, 248.
[22] *Ibid.*, 241.
[23] *Ibid.*, 244.
[24] *Ibid.*, 245.
[25] *Ibid.*, I, 11.

account of my religious purifications, and went down for that purpose to a rivulet, which was frozen on the banks but not in the middle, from the rapidity of the current. I plunged myself into the water and dived sixteen times. The extreme chillness of the water quite penetrated me.'[26] He did not even think twice when on his way to India he ordered the tomb of a heretic *Qalandar*, Shahbaz, situated at the hill of Mukam to be pulled down.[27] On the other hand we find him translating the *Risala-i-Walidiyah* of Khwaja Ubaidullah Ahrar in the hope of an early recovery from his illness.[28] But he was not blindly superstitious and believed in exerting himself in order to achieve his ends. In his letter to Humayun he had written :

> Ambition admits not of inaction;
> The world is his who exerts himself,
> In wisdom's eye, every condition
> May find repose, but royalty alone.[29]

The philosophy of his life was action with a tenacity of purpose. He could proclaim a *jehad* and build towers of human skulls, or leave the Hindu temples untouched as the situation demanded.

Babur, the Great Mughal, could never think of India as his home or of the Indians as his people. His dream of Samarkand and its 'Garden Palace' with its minarets being reflected in the aqueducts could not be realised in India. When he wanted to build a palace and a garden at Agra, he felt that the whole place was 'ugly and detestable.'[30] However, he accomplished all that he wanted, although the manner of working was not up to the standards. 'In this way, going on without neatness and without order, in the Hindu fashion, I however produced edifices and gardens which possessed considerable regularity......In every garden I sowed roses and narcissuses regularly and in beds corresponding to each other.'[31] Till his end he cherished a desire to go back. He wrote to Khwaja Kalan on the

[26] *Ibid*, 161.
[27] *Ibid.*, Vol. II, 90.
[28] *Ibid*, 347.
[29] *Ibid.*, 352.
[30] *Ibid.*, 257.
[31] *Ibid.*, 257–58.

11th February, 1529 : 'As soon as matters are brought into that state (i.e., completely settled), I shall, God willing, set out for your quarter without losing a moment's time. How is it possible that the delights of those lands should ever be erased from the heart ?...... They very recently brought me a single musk-melon. While cutting it up I felt myself affected with a strong felling of loneliness, and a sense of my exile from my native country; and I could not help shedding tears while I was eating it.'[32] No Indian fruit had risen to the standard of a musk-melon. He wrote : 'Many praise the mango so highly as to give it the preferences to every kind of fruit, the musk-melon excepted; but it does not appear to me to justify their praise.'[33] Incidentally, Jahangir, Babur's great grandson, who had all his associations with India only, had observed in Kabul : 'Notwithstanding the sweetness of the Kabul fruits, not one of them has, to my taste, the flavour of the mango.'[34] Much before Jahangir's time, Babur's descendants had made India their home, and there was no thought of returning to their ancestral lands. Still, Babur remained the ideal, and the utmost desire of every prince and reigning sovereign was to follow him in word and spirit.

[32] *Ibid.*, 372.
[33] *Ibid.*, 225.
[34] *Memoirs of Jahangir*, Vol. I, 116.

10

Badauni

'I am not concerned with those who are not bound by the *sharia*, and who disown it in principle and in detail,'[1] Badauni says in the short introductory statement to his work, 'for such persons do not deserve to be addressed in this way. They are not fit to be included among the trustworthy, among those possessing vision and mastery of affairs.'[2] He has stated a little earlier : 'We must realise...that the reading and study of this branch of knowledge'—that is, history—'has been a cause of deviation from the straight path of the illustrious *shariat* of Muhammad...for those of weak faith, who are filled with suspicion and doubt. It has landed them in different positions and in the turbid ways of caprice and innovation, and has therefore become a source of disappointment. Such people as are by nature not disposed towards faith become hardened and suffer abiding loss (even) when they read the Eternal World...How could they attain to a true knowledge of history ?[3]

Why, then, did Badauni write at all ? History is too important to be ignored. 'How can one deny absolutely the value of a branch of knowledge, which is one-seventh of the Seven Sections and is the foundation for the strengthening of faith and certainty ?' 'History is in itself a noble branch of knowledge and a refined art, as it is a means of warning to those who are aware and a source of experience for those who have intelligence and insight.'[4] And, after all, not everybody is predisposed to error. So Badauni could say : 'I address myself to those people who have a healthy nature, a keen

[1] Badauni, *Muntakhab-ut-Tawarikh*, ed. Lees (Calcutta, 1865), Vol. I, 3.
[2] *Ibid.*, 3–4.
[3] *Ibid.*, 3.
[4] *Ibid.*, 2–3.

mind and the habit of judging justly,'[5] and proceed to write what he wanted, and as he wanted.

He was very fortunate indeed, in the time during which he lived. He was born in 1540. The fate of the Mahdavi leaders hung in the balance, and hardly anyone could get educated without becoming aware of the deep rift among the *ulama* caused by the teachings of Syed Muhammad of Jaunpur and being affected by the personalities and opinions of the different parties to the conflict. There were among the *sufis* those who possessed and enjoyed as well as those who despised wealth and influence, and both types had admirers and followers. The struggle for power between Afghans and Mughals put the loyalties of many to the test and must have made many more reflect on the nature and value of loyalty itself. And finally, by the time Badauni was qualified and mature enough to undertake literary work, Akbar's intellectual curiosity was demanding satisfaction, and he was collecting men, ideas and books. After a period of necessary apprenticeship in the households of government officers, Badauni was presented before Akbar by Jamal Khan Qurchi and Hakim Ain-ul-Mulk. Abul Fazl found his way to the court about the same time. Shaikh Abd-un-Nabi was the *sadr*, and Akbar was uneasy under his dominance and that of other *ulama*. 'As learning was merchandise much in demand,' Badauni says, 'I had the privilege of being addressed (by His Majesty) as soon as I reached (his presence). I was included among the members of the assembly and was thrown into the discussion with the *ulama* who blew the trumpet of profundity and thought nothing of anybody.... By the grace of God, the power of my mind, the sensitiveness of my intelligence and that boldness which is a natural quality of youth I often proved myself the superior.'[6] For now on Badauni was in the thick of the battle. He was fighting for the *shariat*, and anyone who got hurt was the enemy ; Akbar, Faizi, Abul Fazl, all intellectuals, all infidels, all accursed Shias, all fanatical Sunnis, all impostors. Could one want better hunting ground and more varied game ?

But let us try to understand him. He received his education at the hands of persons like Miyan Hatim of Sambhal who, even if they cannot be called liberal in our sense of the term, were men of goodwill and free from fanaticism and the conceit of the learned.

[5] *Ibid.*, 3.
[6] *Ibid.*, Vol. II, 172.

He seems to have studied also under Shaikh Mubarak of Nagor, the father of Faizi and Abul Fazl and a supporter of the Mahdavis. His father took him round to visit *sufis* and devout persons, and seems to have cultivated in him an attitude of reverence. His was learned enough in theology and jurisprudence to be able to meet the *ulama* on their own ground and emerge victorious. In fact, he found favour with Akbar because of his literary ability and his success in argument against the *ulama* of the court. He was willing to join in the fight because he was angered by the conceit, the fanaticism, the intellectual crudity and the bad manners of these *ulama.* What he writes of Maulana Abdullah Sultanpuri and Shaikh Abd-un-Nabi, and even more his sympathetic account of the Mahdavi leaders, Miyan Abdullah Niyazi and Shaikh Alai, should convince us that he was orthodox, but not insensitive or narrow-minded. He is sarcastic and contemptuous in his treatment of impostors exploiting the good name of the *sufis* to win favours from kings and courtiers ; he shows no respect for *sufis* who amassed wealth. But he makes no adverse comments on *sufis* whose life and conduct was obviously idiosyncratic and could easily be construed as heretical. He always speaks of Shaikh Mubarak of Nagor with respect, although the Shaikh was the originator of the idea of the superiority of the *Imam-i-Adil* over the *ulama* and himself drafted the *fatwa,* and although the Shaikh said on one occasion to Bir Bal—whom Badauni disliked intensely—in the presence of the Emperor that there were interpolations in the books of the Hindus, and many accretions also in our religion (of Islam) and one could not trust anything.[7] His chronogram for the date of the Shaikh's death is 'The perfect Shaikh,'[8] which means that his reverence for him lasted till the very end.

Badauni is fairly proud of his literary competence and his ability as a disputationist, but he has no illusions about his own piety. We may disregard as purely formal his frequent references to his own sinfulness, but he mentions, without trying to extenuate his own folly, an incident when he was wounded, and might easily have been killed by rowdies for making love to the wrong woman in the wrong place. If his sense of truthfulness is perverted, it spares him as little as anyone else. He seems to be aware that while others have their faults, he himself is bold and blunt and cannot resist the impulse

[7] *Ibid.*, 312.
[8] *Ibid.*, 388.

to be mischievous.

Why is it, then, that Akbar and Badauni changed their opinions about each other, and while Akbar began to suspect that Badauni was at bottom a fanatic, Badauni became severely and maliciously critical of Akbar, his ideas and policies. Badauni relates how once Akbar asked him to come forward and then said to Abul Fazl : 'I thought this young man had attained the state of annihilation and followed the path of the *sufis*, but he has turned out to be such a fanatical theologian that no sword could cut through the jugular vein of his fanaticism.'[9] Akbar had misunderstood the purport of a verse which Badauni had inserted in a translation of the *Mahabharata*, and Badauni was able, with Abul Fazl's support, to clarify his position. But Akbar's suspicion would seem to indicate, as Badauni continuously affirms, that his own attitude had somewhat hardened, and he was not inclined in principle, even if he was in practice, to allow a wide latitude to his Muslim courtiers and favourites in the matter of belief. We must not, therefore, dismiss Badauni's bitter criticism of Akbar's favourites and his reforms as deriving from fanaticism, ingratitude or sheer perversity.

We know what Badauni thought of Shaikh Abd-un-Nabi, Maulana Abdullah Sultanpuri and in general of all the *ulama* who frequented courts, whether Akbar's or Islam Shah's. But was this a valid reason for condemning all the *ulama* and denying the value of theological study ? Was it at all a plausible reason turning away from the *shariat* ? If the nature and conduct of particular *ulama* could serve as an argument against the *ulama* as such, what about the courtiers, in particular those who were close to Akbar ? Badauni could have felt that they did not deserve lenient treatment if, fault for fault, they where no better than the official *ulama*. Both in their own ways offended against the *shariat*, which for Badauni was the final criterion of judgement.

But could the *shariat* itself be defined precisely enough to serve as a criterion ? That is Badauni's weak point. How can one choose between wicked fools who claim to represent the *shariat* and wily intellectuals, poets and courtiers who make a fashion of deriding it ? Badauni is vexed enough to lose his balance, and he touches the depths of meanness in the aspersions he casts on Faizi and Abul Fazl, his benefactors throughout his career at the court. But he

Ibid., 399.

was not really mean. He seems to have felt, like many educated Indian Muslims towards the close of the nineteenth and the beginning of the twentieth century, that while the *ulama* could not be defended and a liberalisation of the Indian Muslim way of life was essential, respect for the *shariat* must be maintained at all costs. And not Indian Muslims only. I remember Dr. Behdjet Wahbi of Egypt, who came to lecture at the Jamia Millia in 1934, saying that if one did not pray, one should admit it was something wrong, not make a principle out of not praying. Badauni saw in his time the righteous *ulama* being persecuted, the wicked in the seat of judgement, and he must have felt that if, in such a contingency, the example and the influence of the court reinforced the general sentiment against the official *ulama* and their enforcement of the *shariat*, the *shariat* itself, which was the mainstay of Muslim life, would be destroyed. Therefore, he utilises his command over language to vent his spleen on those who were impudent and supercilious in their attitude towards the *shariat* and who ultimately succeeded in eradicating all reverence for it from the heart of the Emperor.

Badauni had no taste for investigation and research, no desire to add to existing historical knowledge. He states quite ingenuously that for the period beginning with the establishment of the Delhi Sultanate up to his own time his account is just a selection from the *Tarikh-i-Mubarakshahi* and the work of Nizam-ud-Din Ahmad Bakhshi, which he calls the *Nizam-ul Tawarikh* and also the *Tabaqat-i-Akbari*. But he has 'added something of his own.'[10] When we examine this 'something of his own,' we find that Badauni was not interested in political history. Indeed, his lack of interest is much more than is indicated by his remark in the introductory statement that he would briefly relate something about each king. Not only do we find his narrative interspersed with verses, quatrains, *qasidas* and chronograms; he seems to think the production of poetry of equal if not greater importance as compared to political events. He discusses a poet and quotes his poems in between the accession of Razia and an account of her reign, and of the two, the poet seems to be the far more significant personage. Nasir-ud-Din's reign occupies four pages as against thirty-one allotted to *qasidas* written during his reign. The death of Balban's crown-prince, Sultan Muhammad, provides opportunity for inserting long elegies. What he thinks of

[10] *Ibid.*, 6.

political ideas and policies is evident from his passing over the advice given by Balban to his son by saying that it has been mentioned in the histories of Delhi, and from his giving more space to Kaiqubad than to Balban. His values do not change when he is writing of his own time. Momentous administrative decisions are thought worthy of only this brief reference : 'And in this year His Majesty ordered the institution of branding and muster under the guidance of Shahbaz Khan Kamboh, the appointment of *Karoris* in all the territory under control and the reversion at one stroke of all land to Khalsa.'[11]

The 'something more' which Badauni has added to his selection of events from his two sources includes also continuous references to *sufis* and poets. The references are not particularly helpful, except perhaps in fixing dates, for hardly has anyone's death been mentioned without a chronogram being given. Badauni was also found of relating anecdotes. He has not the rambling imagination of a story-teller, and he would have regarded telling stories a frivolity. He has no taste for the supernatural. In the account he gives of natural portents and calamities that followed the killing of Sidi Maula by Firuz Khalji he is quite restrained as compared to Barani, and he qualifies his statement about the drought by saying that it may have been due to natural causes. But anecdotes do enrich his narrative. There is the story of slave-girl of a Iltutmish who is found to be his sister. There is the romance of Sayyid Musa and Mohini, the goldsmith's daughter. This is something that happened in his own time. Badauni interrupts his narrative to tell this story at length; one feels that here, at last, he has stopped looking at persons and actions through the glasses of the *shariat* and has identified himself completely with the persons whose fate he describes. The story is a literary masterpiece.

But most characteristic of Badauni are his epigrams and sarcastic remarks. It would not be easy to find a more accurate and incisive summing up to Muhammad Tughluq's reign than Badauni's : 'The sultan was relieved of the people and the people were relieved of the sultan.'[12] The following are typical examples of naughtiness.

'And in this year the Scholars of the Age, Mir Murtaza Sharifi Shirazi, departed from this inn of unreality. First, he was buried at

[11] *Ibid.*, 173.
[12] *Ibid.*, 238.

Delhi, in the neighbourhood of the grave of Amir Khusrau (May God have mercy on him). Then, because the *Sadr* and the *Qazi* and the *Shaikh-ul-Islam* represented (to His Majesty) that Amir Khusrau was an Indian and a Sunni and Mir Murtaza an Iraqi and a *rafizi*, there was no doubt that Amir Khusrau would find his company a torture.... His Majesty commanded that his body should be removed and buried elsewhere.'[13]

'And in this year Shaikh Ibrahim Chishti died a natural death at Fatehpur. He bid farewell to mountains of gold and rendered his account to the Creator of life. Out of his wealth twenty-five crores in cash, in addition to elephants, horses and other goods were taken into the treasury, the rest fell to the share of his enemies—his sons and representatives.'[14]

'Makhdum-ul-Mulk died at Ahmadabad in the year 990/A. H. Qazi Ali was sent from Fatehpur to Lahore to make an inventory of his property. He uncovered so much wealth and buried treasure that one could not open its lock with the key of the imagination. A part of the treasure found in the family grave-yard of Makhdum-ul-Mulk were boxes filled with gold bricks, which had been buried under the pretence that they were corpses. What was apparent to the eyes of men was so much that only God the Creator could make a reckoning. All those bricks, along with the books, which counted for no more than mere bricks were confiscated to the Treasury.'[15]

There are chronograms which are not only naughty but nasty, such as 'the miserly Shaikh'[16] for Shaikh Ibrahim Chishti and 'carcase of a swine'[17] for Shaikh Gadai.

It goes without sayiny that Badauni's *Muntakhab-ul-Tawarikh* is obviously and intensely subjective. It belongs to the category of Memoirs rather than histories, and indeed often reminds one of the Memoirs of St. Simon. But perhaps the value of Badauni's work lies just in this. He wears no disguise; he writes as he feels. He has no affiliations of class or interest, he is a free-lance. He has no idea of pleasing anyone, and no conception of the historian's function that can make him diffident. If we agree that he means by the

[13] *Ibid.*, 99.
[14] *Ibid.*, 374.
[15] *Ibid*, 311.
[16] *Ibid.*, 374.
[17] *Ibid.*, 119.

shariat only an attitude of reverence for God, the Prophet, the revelation, we shall realise that he has allowed himself and would allow to others latitude for difference of opinion and for living as one liked. We may still sometimes feel irritated, but we shall also feel that here is someone who enjoys looking at life from all sides, who writes with relish and writes well, who has not searched for facts that were obscure or had escaped the notice of others but has given us something live and vibrant, reflecting him and his age.

11

Tarikh-i-Alfi

The significance of the millennium did not remain a subject for dicussion confined to the theologians and *sufis*, but had been a subject of popular speculation for many centuries, so much so that even poets loved to recite verses on the above theme. Shaikh Abul Fazl has quoted the following quatrain composed by *Khaqani* (d. 582/1186) in his *Akbar-nama*.

> They say that after every thousand years of the world,
> There comes into existence a true man,
> He came before this, ere we were born from nothingness,
> He will come after this when we have departed in sorrow.

Elsewhere the same poet wrote :

> Every now and then, the world is saturated with wretches,
> Then a shining soul comes down out of the sky,
> Khaqani ! Seek not in this age for such a thing,
> Sit, not by the way for the Caravan will come late.[1]

In India, the Mahdavi movement was already on the wane in Akbar's reign, but there did exist an increasing tension among the Muslims as the completion of one thousand years after the Prophet Muhammad's death brew near. It was in about 1573–74 that Mulla Abdul Qadir Badauni visited Shaikh Daud (died 982/1574–57) and informed him through one of the Shaikh's favourites, Miyan Abdul Wahhab, that the *mashaikh* of Hindustan were planning to start an uprising under a decendant of Sultan Ala-ud-Din bin Muhammad Shah bin Mubarak Shah bin Khizr Khan, the last Sultan of the Sayyid

[1] Abul Fazl : *Akbar-nama*, trans. Beveridge, (Calcutta, 1897–1921) Vol. I, 142.

dynasty. They professed to have received directions from Ghaus-i-Azam Shaikh Abdul Qadir Jilani. Some *amirs* of the frontiers had also joined them.[2] The proposed uprising did not materialise, but the political adventurers were too ready to exploit the hopes and fears of people to their own advantage. Akbar was not seemingly disturbed by these movements. He is said to have observed : 'Although I am the master of so vast a kingdom, and all the appliances of the government are to my hand, yet since true greatness consists in doing the will of God, my mind is not at ease in this diversity of sects and creeds; and apart from this outward pomp of circumstances, with what satisfaction in my despondency, can I undertake the sway of empire ? I wait the coming of some discreet man of principle, who will resolve the difficulties of my conscience.'[3]

He, however, ordered to commemorate the millennium of the Islamic era by getting the 'Era of the Thousand' stamped on the coins and a *Tarikh-i-Alfi*, commencing with the death of the Prophet, written. The orders in no way sought to proclaim the end of Islam or to flout its ordinances as the following account[4] of Mulla Abdul Qadir Badauni tends to indicate. 'And since, in his Majesty's opinion, it was a settled fact, that the 1000 years since the time of the mission of the Prophet (peace be upon him !), which was to be the period of the continuance of the faith of Islam, were now completed, no hindrance remained to the promulgation of those secret designs, which he nursed in his heart. And so, considering any further respect or regard for the Shaikhs and Ulama (who were unbending and uncompromising) to be unnecessary, he felt at liberty to embark fearlessly on his design of annulling the statutes and ordinances of Islam, and of establishing his own cherished pernicious belief (in their stead).'[5] However, Badauni, after giving a brief account of some of the ordinances of Akbar's reign, which according to him were issued in 990/1582–83, again observed in a rather sober style : 'The year 1,000 of the *Hijrah* era, which is in general use, being new on the point of completion, the Emperor ordered a history of all the kings of Islam to be written, which should in reality supersede all other histories, and directed that such a name should

[2] Badauni, *Muntakhab-ut-Tawarikh*, (Calcutta, 1864–69), Vol. III, 35.
[3] Abul Fazl : *Ain-i-Akbari*, trans. Jarret, Vol. III, 380.
[4] *Muntakhab-ut-Tawarikh*, Vol. III, 301.
[5] *Muntakhab-ut-Tawarikh*, trans. Lowe, Vol. II, 310.

be given to the work as to denote the year of its composition. It was for this reason that the work was entitled *Alfi*.'[6]

The work was intended to serve the same broadly based motives with which a sort of translation bureau was established. Asaf Khan (Jafar Beg)[7], who after the death of Mulla Ahmad Tattawi completed the *Tarikh-i-Alfi*, after extolling the high sense of justice which Akbar sought to dispense, observed in a short preface to the portions written by him that the Emperor always made strenuous efforts to mobilize his energies in making every one acquainted with 'perfect knowledge' and in making the followers of different religions and diverse faiths realise the truth underlying each religion and faith and give up their innate bigotry. It was with this view that the Emperor ordered that the principles of different religions, which were based on reason, should be translated in different languages.[8] He also ordered that as far as possible the rose garden of the principles of traditional knowledge of every religion should be cleaned out of the thorns of bigotry, for in India innovations had been contrived in every religion and thousands of undesirable regulations had been carved out. *Azan* was quoted by him to substantiate the thesis. It was pointed out that *azan* was being regularly repeated for five times since the days of Prophet Muhammad, but the Sunnis and Shias, on the basis of the traditions of their own faiths, sharply differed from each other on the mode of its calling. Similarly people of nefarious designs found a wider scope for giving vent to their peculiar feelings and sentiments in the narration of the events

[6] *Ibid.*, 327.

[7] Mirza Qiwam-ud-Din Jafar Beg of Mirza Badi-uz-Zaman Qazwini reached India in 985/1577 and was presented to Akbar by Mirza Ghiyas-ud-Din Ali Asif Khan Bakhshi, his uncle. He was a scholar of considerable eminence and a free thinker. He died in 1021/1612.

[8] Abul Fazl wrote in his preface to the Persian translation of the *Mahabharat*: 'Akbar was anxious to introduce reforms among all classes of his subjects and did not discriminate between a friend and a foe. As he found that there were exceedingly great differences amongst Hindus and Muslims, and there was no end to the polemics and refutations of each other, he decided to get the reliable books of both the religions translated in the language of their apponents, so that shaking off their enmity they should try to search for truth. However, having been acquainted with their respective weaknesses, they should try to reform themselves. Secondly, in every religion there were a number of ignorant ones who always thought themselves to be great scholars and misrepresented the original works of the masters. Common people took

relating to the past rulers and their policies.[9]

A board of seven scholars was originally constituted to undertake the compilation of the *Tarikh-i-Alfi* which was commenced in 993/1585. The account of the first year was assigned to Naqid Khan[10], of the second to Shah Fathullah,[11] of the third to Hakim Humam,[12] of the fourth to Hakim Ali,[13] of the fifth to Haji Ibrahim Sarhindi,[14] of the sixth to Nizam-ud-Din Ahmad[15] and of the seventh

these misrepresentations for the real religion and were often misled. Akbar thought it essential to protect the people from becoming a victim to the nefarious designs of such custodians of faith and came to the decision that if the books of different religions could be translated into a simple language, the common people would be able to know the truth themselves. (Abul Fazl, Preface to the Persian Translation of the *Mahabharat*, Lytton Collection, Maulana Azad Library, Aligarh Muslim University), f. 9b.

[9] *Tarikh-i-Alfi* (Bodleian 99/Ousely 341), f. 333a.

[10] Mir Ghyas-ud-Din Ali bin Abdul Latif Qazwini, the grandson of Mir Yahya Qazwini (died 962/1555), the author of *Lubb-ut-Tawarikh*, arrived with his father in India, when Akbar after his accession had not yet left the Punjab. (*Akbar-nama*, Vol. II, 230). He soon became a personal friend of the Emperor. He generally read out the books to the Emperor and supervised the translation of Sanskrit works into Persian. He excelled in the art of writing history and was said to have committed all the seven volumes of *Rauzat-us-Safa* of Mir Khwand to memory, Jahangir also highly extolled the virtues of Naqib Khan.

[11] Mir Fathullah Shirazi, after his arrival in India, served Ali Adil Shah I (1557–80), fifth king of the Adil Shahi dynasty of Bijapur. He was an eminent Mathematician and Scientist. He reached Akbar's court at the Emperor's invitation in 991/1583–84. His name is associated with many inventions in the field of mechanics. He died in Kashmir in 997/1588–89.

[12] Hakim Human, son of Mir Abd-ur-Razzaq Gilani, left Iran after 974/1566–67 and reached Akbar's court with his brother Hakim Abdul Fath in the 20th year of the Emperor's reign. He was very intimate with Akbar, and was sent with Sadr Jahan to Turan as an ambassador in the 31st year of the Emperor's reign. He died on 6 Rabi I, 1005/9 November 1595.

[13] Hakim Ali Gilani reached India from Iran in Akbar's reign. He soon acquired a high position by the dint of proficiency in medicine. In the 39th year of the Emperor's reign be constructed a wounderful reservoir ; was raised to the command of 700 and given the title of Jalinus-us-Zaman. He attended Akbar in his last illness. He died in 1018/1609.

[14] Haji Ibrahim Sarhindi was one of the leading theologians of Akbar's court. He had an immense influence over the Emperor in the early part of his reign and was a keen debator. Later on he was required to collaborate with the scholars who were ordered to translate Sanskrit works into Persian. He died at Ranthambor in 994/1586.

[15] Nizam-ud-Din Ahmad son of Muhammad Muqim Harawai was

to Mulla Abdul Qadir Badauni.[16] The board comprised the scholars of all shades of opinion. Indeed, Akbar had ordered that a very high degree of objectivity and perfection should be reached in the compilation of the *Tarikh-i-Alfi*. The account of the first thirty-five years after Prophet Muhammad's death was distributed for compilation to the members of the above board. Akbar himself supervised the progress of the work, Mulla Abdul Qadir Badauni says : 'During the time that I was compiling the events of the seventh year, and was engaged on the life of the second true Khalifa (may God be propitious to him !) one night, when the Emperor heard the account of the foundation of Kufa, and the building and destruction of Qasr-ul-Imarat, which was narrated in detail together with the cause of its destruction, and the marriage of *Umm-i-Kulsum*, daughter of the Amir-ul-Muminin Ali (God be propitious to them both !) as well as the institution of five stated times for prayer, the fall of the city of Nasibin, and the scorpions as big as cocks, which were made use of to effect its capture, he raised great objections and would not accept the truth of it. Asaf Khan Salis, who is the same as Mirza Jafar, helped me but in a poor way, but Shaikh Abul Fazl and Ghazi Khan Badakshi, on the other hand, confirmed my assertions. When I was asked whence I got this information, I replied that I had seen it in books, and had written accordingly, and that it was not my own invention. Immediately, the *Rauzat-ul-Ahbab* and other historical books were called for from the library, and given to Naqib Khan to verify the accuracy of the statement, which by God's grace being found correct, I was relieved from the charge of invention.'[17]

It seems that the board could not get on with the work satisfactorily and Mulla Ahmad bin Nasrullah Dai-buli Tattawi was ordered to undertake the compilation of the work from the thirty-sixth year, at the recommendation of Hakim Abul Fath. He was asked to write in a simple and easy language, and was ordered that

---

appointed Bakhshi of Gujarat in the 37th year of Akbar's reign and died on 23 Safar 1003/6 November 1594. He was the author of *Tabaqat-i-Akbari* which he completed in 1001/1592-93 but subsequently brought down the account of Akbar's reign to 1002/1593-94.

[16] Abdul Qadir 'Qadiri' bin Muluk Shah bin Hamid Badauni, the celebrated author of *Muntakhab-ut-Tawarikh* was an active member of Akbar's translation bureau and was associated with the compilation and translation of a number of works.

[17] *Muntakhab-ut-Tawarikh*, trans. Lowe, Vol. II, 328.

on introducing the founder of an empire, an account of his ancestors and of the manner in which he rose to power should invariably be given.[18] Mulla Ahmad brought down the account to 693/1294 (683 Rihlat) within three years. He was murdered by Mirza Faulad Beg Barlas in 994/1588 and Asaf Khan Jafar Beg was ordered to complete the work. He commenced the compilation with the reign of Ghazan Khan (694/1295 to 713/1304) and added a brief preface comprising a short account of the motives of Akbar in getting the work compiled, a brief reference to the murder of Mulla Ahmad, the punishment awarded to the murderer and his being commissioned to complete the work.[19] He must have brought down the account to 1000/1591–92, but none of the existing manuscripts exceed beyond 997/1588–89. Mulla Abdul Qadir Badauni was subsequently ordered to revise and collate the work in collaboration with Mustafa Katib of Lahore. He seems to have hurriedly revised the first volume of the work and his labours were duly recognised. He was then ordered to revise the second volume for, according to him, it comprised highly biased material. Badauni says : 'In the course of one year I sufficiently collated it, but on account of my own taint of bigotry I did not interfere with the book, except as regards the order of the years, and did not alter the original, but laid the blame on my state of health; and may it not, God grant ! be a cause of any further injury. My condition with regard to these books was like that of one who eats dates together with the stones, and another says to him, 'Why don't you throw away the stones ?' and he answers, 'They have apportioned me only just this amount.'[20]

The work was originally divided into three volumes. The first two volumes, written by Mulla Ahmad, brought down the account to Ghazan Khan, while the third volume was completed by Asaf Khan.[21] Badauni seems to have confused Ghazan Khan with Chingiz Khan. The existing manuscripts do not strictly adhere to the original plan, and the copyists, binders and owners of the manuscripts have divided the volumes according to their whims and

[18] *Tarikh-i-Alfi*, (British Museum) Riu 118b–119a, Or. 142 f. 498a.

[19] *Tarikh-i-Alfi*, (Bodleian 99), ff. 332b–33a ; British Museum, Or. 465, f. 97a.

[20] *Muntakhab-ut-Tawarikh*, trans., Lowe, Vol. II, 407.

[21] *Ibid.*, 328–406.

convenience.[22] Abul Fazl, who claims to have written a preface to the work, says, 'As His Majesty has become acquainted with the treasure of history, he ordered several well-informed writers to compose a work containing the events which have taken place in the seven zones for the last one thousand years. Naqib Khan, and several others, commenced this history. A very large portion was subsequently added by Mulla Ahmad of Thathah, and the whole concluded by Jafar Beg Asaf Khan. The introduction is composed by me. The work has the title of *Tarikh-i-Alfi,* the History of a thousand years.'[23] None of the known existing manuscripts contain the preface written by Abul Fazl. If it is found, it would, like his preface to the *Mahabharat,* throw considerable new light on the scheme of the work.

The portions of the *Tarikh-i-Alfi* comprising the history of Timur, Mirza Khalil, Mirza Shah Rukh, Ulugh Beg, Abul Qasim Babur, Sultan Husain Mirza, Babur, Humayun and Akbar (984/1577) seem to have been compiled into a separate continuous volume in the reign of Akbar shortly after the completion of the work by Mirza Jafar Beg Asaf Khan. 112 large miniatures, some of which cover two opposite pages, were added by the Emperor's order, Shahjahan in an autograph note on the fly leaf of the manuscript preserved in Khuda Baksh Oriental Public Library, Bankipore, Patna, wrote that the account of Timur and his descendants and that of Akbar down to the 22nd year of his reign, was composed in the time of Shah Baba (Akbar).[24] The work was subsequently entitled *Tarikh-i-Khandan-i-Timuriya.*

Tarikh-i-Alfi was based on the best available sources. Objectivity in approach and simplicity in expression were particularly emphasised. The work is arranged strictly in chronological order. The events have been recorded year by year beginning with the first years of Prophet Muhammad's death *i.e.*, 11th Hijri. Careless copyists

[22] C. A. Storey : *Persian Literature, A Bio-Bibliographical Survey* (London, 1935), 120–21 ; A Halim : 'Some Indian Collections of the Tarikh-i-Alfi,' *Indian Historical Records Commission Proceedings,* Vol. 18, (1942), 108–13. The paper does not include the manuscripts available in Sir Salar Jang Library, Hyderabad.

[23] H. Blochmann, English Translation of *Ain-i-Akbari* (Calcutta, 1927) Vol. I, 113.

[24] Maulavi Abd-ul-Maqtadir, *Catalogue of the Arabic and Persian Manuscripts in the Oriental Public Library at Bankipore,* (Patna, 1921), Vol. VII, 40–48.

have frequently confused the *rihlat* date with the *hijri* dates. Sir H. M. Elliot and Professor John Dowson have pointed out : 'But a much greater objection to be made to the *Tarikh-i-Alfi* is the plan of the work ; it is constructed in the form of Annals, like the tedious Historical Library of Diodorus ; and thus we are compelled to turn over page after page of this voluminous history, before we can trace the connection of events in any particular country which may happen to be the subject of our investigation. Nothing but an excellent Index could remedy such a defect.'[25] Elliot and Dowson have rightly pointed out that the compilers apparently availed themselves of all the best sources of information open to them ; often applying a very judicious criticism in selecting the most trustworthy records, and rejecting the fabulous legends with which so many of them were full.[26] Badauni, in his own peculiar style, has observed that Akbar did not approve of the legendary material being incorporated in the work. The earlier portion of the work is, on the whole, based mainly upon *Rauzat-ul Ahbab fi Siyar-un-Nabi wa'l Al wal Ashab*[27] of Amir Jamal ud-Din Ataullah b. Fazlullah al-Husaini al-Dashtaki-al-Shirazi (died 926/1520). He was an eminent theologian and flourished in the reign of Sultan Husain (873–911/1469–1506) at Herat. The third volume of the work was not, however, popular with the orthodox theologians in India. Badauni says that when he went to pay a visit to Makhdum-ul-Mulk along with Shaikh Abul Fazl and Haji Sultan of Thaneswar, he found that Makhdum-ul-Mulk had before him the third volume of the *Rauzat-ul-Ahbab*. He said to them : 'See, what mischief those who are followed in this land have wrought in the faith,' and he showed them the following couplet which occured in the encomium of Ali :

> This alone is sufficient to prove his resemblance to God.
> That it has been doubted that he himself was God.[28]

He said that the author had passed beyond *rifz*[29] and had

[25] Elliot and Dowson, *The History of India as told by its own Historians*, Vol. V, 156.

[26] *Ibid.*, 156–57.

[27] The work was completed in 900/1494–95 and is divided into three *maqsads* (Volumes). 1. Prophet Muhammad. 2. The First Three Caliphs. 3. Ali and the Twelve Imams.

[28] *Hami bus bud huq numai o,*
he kardand shak dar khudai o.

[29] Being a Shia.

placed the question of his misbelief to the stage of *huilul.*[30] He informed them that he had finally decided to burn the book in the presence of a Shia. Though Badauni had never previously met Makhdum-ul-Mulk, he boldly told him that the couplet was a translation of those verses which were attributed to Imam Shafi. Makhdum-ul-Mulk and Badauni tried to defend their points of view very enthusiastically. Mukhdum-ul-Mulk added that the second volume of the work also comprised passages which proved the heresy and misbelief of the author of the work.[31]

It was not possible to steer clear of the controversies and to face the intolerance of the orthodox. Mulla Ahmad,[32] the principal author of earlier portions, was a zealous *Shia*. It was probably to satisfy the orthodox susceptibilities that Mulla Abdul Qadir Badauni was asked to revise the portions written by Mulla Ahmad.

The accounts relating to the history of Sultan Muhammad bin Tughluq, of the Afghans, of the Provincial Dynasties of the fifteenth century and of the Sur dynasty have not been given chronologically under respective years, but the above have been dealt with continuously at different places. Adequate justice has not been done to the history of the Sultans of Delhi. The history of the Indian Timurids from Babur to Akbar has been dealt with at some length. The account of Babur is mainly based on the *Tuzuk-i-Baburi*, but the accounts of Humayun and Akbar, as also of Persia, Central Asia and Turkey, are based on informations available in the imperial archives and on those collected from oral evidence of eminent nobles and other people. The memoirs of Mihtar Jauhar Aftabchi, Bayizid Bayat and Gulbadan Begum, which provided valuable strands to the scholars who were interested in Humaun's reigns, were probably not available to the compilers of the *Tarikh-i-Alfi*. It seems that the compilers had an access to the works of Muhammad Arif Qandahari and Mir Ala-ud-Daula Kami Qazwini, but the concluding portions of the *Tarikh-i-Alfi* comprise the first official history of Akbar's reign, compiled under the Emperor's own supervision. Nizam-ud-Din

[30] Belief in the transmigration of soul.

[31] *Mantakhab-ut-Tawarikh*, Vol. III, 70–71, English trans. by Sir Wolseley Haig, 114–16.

[32] Mulla Ahmad bin Nasrullah Dai-buli Tattawi was converted to Shism in his early life and studied at Mashhad, Yazd and Shiraz. Before coming to Akbar's court (989/1581) he served at the court of Qutab Shah of Golkonda. He was murdered in 996/1588 at Lahore.

Ahmad has based his account of Humayun's reign mainly on the *Tarikh-i-Alfi,* and has extensively drawn upon it for an account of Akbar's reign. The work sprang from the tension that is fully reflected in the *Muntakhab-ut-Tawarikh* of Mulla Abdul Qadir Badauni, but it sought to ignore petty squabbles and prepared the people for adjusting themselves to the new values of life which were gaining increasing importance on account of Akbar's policy of 'peace with all.'

Portions relating to Babur, Humayun and Akbar comprise a detailed account of the principal incidents that took place in Iran, Central Asia and Turkey, and give a new dimension to the understanding of the policies and politics of the courts of Humayun and Akbar. The importance of India has not been unduly emphasised, but the leading role which the country had started playing in the policies of Iran and Central Asia is adequately reflected from the accounts of the *Tarikh-i-Alfi.*

12

Shaikh Abul Fazl

Historiography in Medieval India attracted the attention of scholars and learned men who cherished and cultivated it as an independent discipline in its own right. Some of them, such as Zia-ud-Din Barani, Nizam-ud-Din Ahmad, Abdul Qadir Badauni, Muhammad Qasim Ferishta and Khafi Khan were eminent historians and made contributions to Medieval historiography. They were influenced by earlier traditions of historical writings. But on account of their individual academic training and accomplishments, their position in society and their particular outlook on religion and politics, they chose to approach and treat historiography in their own way. Among them, however, Shaikh Abul Fazl occupies a place of distinction and has left his mark on the traditions of historical writings in Medieval India.

His chief claim to the title of a distinguished historian is due mainly to the predominent intellectual element in his writings, to his unfailing appeal to reason as against religious and cultural traditions, to his broader view of history, to his attempt to interpret the contemporary history in terms which took a note of the political and administrative realities of the period, to the new methodology which he sought to apply to his task and to the unique and masterly literary style of his prose. Finally, his most significant achievement as a historian is the fact that in the pages of the *Akbar-nama* and the *Ain-i-Akbari* he did succeed in giving Akbar's greatness a concrete and palpable form.

It may be contended that Barani and Badauni excelled him in capturing the spirit of their respective ages which they sought to depict. Similarly, Nizam-ud-Din and Ferishta can be regarded as more successful historians, because they approached their subject matter in a non-partisan way and recorded the facts more objectively and clearly. No one should hesitate to concede that Khafi Khan duly deserves the credit of perceiving and recording the important developments which brought about changes in society or in the administrative institutions and the relationship which subsisted between the two. Abul Fazl may be found failing in these qualities as a historian, but, except for him, no other medieval historian can lay a claim to a rational and secular approach to history and to the application of a new methodology to collect facts and marshal them on the basis of critical investigation. These are the hallmarks of Abul Fazl's historical writings.

Secondly, he widened the scope of history by recording a mass of facts pertaining to political, social, economic and cultural life, and by incorporating chapters on administrative regulations and procedures and topographical account of various provinces. He laboured hard for the collection of material, and selected important facts after careful enquiry and investigation, and then presented them in a clear and systematic manner. He questioned the validity of a source and accepted it only when it satisfied the principles of historical investigation formulated by him. In other words, he created a new idiom for understanding and interpreting history, widened its range and scope, and laid down the principles of historical investigation. It may, therefore, be suggested that in Abul Fazl's writings we can discover a philosophy of history, *i.e.*, a definite concept about the nature and purpose of history, principles for interpretation of history, and the critical apparatus for the collection and selection of facts of history.

Abul Fazl's achievements as a historian, summed up in the preceding lines, are by any standard quite impressive. However, in our evaluation and assessment of him as a historian some of his limitations need to be noted. His limitations owed their origin to his position as the favourite courtier and trusted secretary of Akbar to the official nature of his history, to his genuine of feigned veneration for Akbar as a perfect man and an ideal king. As a courtier and an official historian with the feelings of veneration for Akbar, Abul Fazl could not but defend and extol him and his activities, policies and measures. In his zeal for depicting his hero as a perfect man and ideal king he often fails to listen to the dictates of reason, moderation and restraint. This has made the account not only partisan but at times has degenerated into a panegyric.

Abul Fazl, the son of Shaikh Mubarak, was born at Agra on 14 January 1551. He was gifted with an extraordinary intelligence and showed signs of precocity in early age. He studied under the care of his father, one of the most accomplished scholars of the age. Shaikh Mubarak was widely respected for his learning, his broad and liberal views and his attachment to the mystic way of life. The impact of Shaikh Mubark's personality on Abul Fazl was profound and abiding. Abul Fazl mastered all branches of knowledge known as *manqul* at the early age of fifteen. He himself began to teach at the age of twenty.

The most important event which left a deep impression on the religious and political outlook of Abul Fazal was the protracted persecution which he and his family suffered at the hands of the powerful *ulama*. Shaikh Mubarak was suspected of being a Mahdavi and even a Shia. Abul Fazl, however, refutes these charges against his father.[1] The persecution continued for about two decades, and the family was compelled to lead the life of fugitives, whom nobody befriended or offered shelter and refuge. However, in the early 1570s, the days of suffering came to an end. Akbar received the family in 1574, and gave protection and patronage to them. Abul Fazl was himself presented to Akbar as Faizi's brother in 1574 and was received with special favour. After sometime Abul Fazl joined the service of the Emperor as a courtier.

It appears that Abul Fazl was torn by a deep and intensive inner conflict before he made up his mind to join the imperial service. He doubted the wisdom and propriety of becoming a courtier. The saintly and intellectual traditions of the age were very strong against seeking the royal service. Abul Fazl's intellectual predilections and the yearnings for the attainment of ultimate truth through meditation and contemplation further strengthened him in his resolve to lead the life of an ascetic and a philosopher. The life of a courtier was a complete negation of the tradition of Abul Fazl's own spiritual urges. However, the persistant persuation by Shaikh Mubarak and Faizi, combined with prospects and hopes of worldly advancement, set the conflict at rest. Abul Fazl was induced to accept the bondage of a courtier.[2] This proved to be a turning point

[1] Abul Fazl, *Ain-i-Akbari*, (Lucknow, 1893), Vol. III, 207–16.

[2] Abul Fazl, *Akbar-nama*, (Bib. Ind.), Vol. II, 387–89; *Ain-i-Akbari*, Vol. III, 217.

in his life and career. His rise in the imperial rank was slow and protracted. He began his career as a *mansabdar* of 20 and was in 1585 promoted to the rank of one thousand. Eventually he attained to the rank of five thousand, but the same year in August 1602 he was killed at the instigation of Prince Salim.

The chief interest of Abul Fazl's career does not lie in the rank which he attained or the offices he held, but in the great influence which he wielded over the Emperor in the initiation and execution of policies. The most significant role which Abul Fazl played was his skilful manipulation and exploitation of the religious discussions against the orthodox *ulama*. The persecution to which the family of Shaikh Mubarak had been put by the *ulama* had left a lasting impression on him and his sons. It had made them uncompromising opponents of the *ulama*. Abul Fazl and Faizi skilfully exploited the situation, discredited the *ulama* in the the eyes of Akbar by their superior reasoning and immense learning, and eventually brought about their fall from the position of power. Secondly, it was in this school of misfortune that Abul Fazl learnt the lesson of toleration, which brought about a profound change in his social and religious ideas. It also served as the basis of friendship with Akbar and provided Abul Fazl with a new concept of Indian history. The idea of religious toleration runs like a thread throughout his writings. Again, the same school of adversity stimulated him to unusual exertions in his studies, which subsequently proved of great value to him, and helped him to lead the opposition successfully and overthrow the orthodox *ulama*.

The decade between 1575 and 1585 constitutes the most tumultous and, at the same time, the most formative period of Akbar's reign. Political, administrative and religious issues of great magnitude and consequence came up before Akbar : most fierce controversies raged about religious questions and the position of the ruler in the Muslim community. The religious discussions held in the Ibadat Khana released the forces of critical enquiry. Abul Fazl undertook to champion the cause of reason and religious toleration. Eventually the opposition led by Abul Fazl and supported by Akbar completely disarmed the orthodox *ulama* ; they were compelled to acknowledge Akbar as the *Mujtahid* or the *Imam-i-Adil*—the infallible leader of the Muslim community and the final authority to interpret controversial issues of Muslim law and religion. The orthodox *ulama* were deprived of their offices and position of influence. They vacated the key positions in the administration of religious affairs ; and because of the drastic reforms introduced in it the power and prestige of the office of the *Sadr* decreased, and the political and economic stability of the *Madad-i-maash* holders, who were the staunch supporters of the orthodox *ulama,* broke down. Thus Abul Fazl had eventually won against his ideological and personal opponents.

His role in bringing about the fall of the orthodox was at once motivated by personal considerations as well as by his belief that the orthodox stood for fanaticism, blind acceptance of tradition and persecution of those who differed from them. The principles for which he stood and fought against the *ulama,* have been described in his writings on various occasions, sometimes casually, sometimes in detail and specifically. What is important for the present discussion is that his active participation in the religious debates clarified his views on religion and politics, and later were repeatedly reflected in his writings. The second important influence, which had a bearing on his historical writings, was his scholarly training and temperament and his preference for philosophical speculations. It induced him to choose what was sober and grave in life in preference to what appeared to be trivial and commonplace. Consequently, his writing abound in generalisations and philosophical reflections and form a part of his historiography. His intellectual bias also largely determined his style and literary value. He chose to write, as he declares in the *Akbar-nama,* for the elect few; it did not matter to him if the majority of the *llterati* of his age failed to understand his language and style.

Abul Fazl's political and religious views deserve attention for two reasons. In the first place, they determined his selection of important facts of history. In the second, they affected the treatment of subject matter. It is true that Abul Fazl ascertained the individual facts with great care, but both the selection of facts, which he recorded, and their evaluation and presentation were coloured by his outlook on the contemporary political and religious issues.

Abul Fazl postulates that the institution of monarchy is divine in its origin. It is a light which emanates from God. The monarch owes his position, without any intercession, to the grace of God. The institution is necessary, as well as desirable, in order to keep the antagonistic forces of society under control. In the absence of the institution the conflicting forces working within the society would destroy themselves in a self-consuming struggle. However, the monarchy should not be an instrument in the hands of the sovereign to seek his personal gratification, physical pleasure and lust for power and prestige. On the other hand, the sovereign should devote himself to the welfare of his people.[3] He should maintain law and order in a world which is full of conflicting forces. The monarch should be just, wise and brave, and he should possess great physical strength. Toleration, broad-mindedness and a strong sense of justice are the requisite attributes of an ideal monarch. Abul Fazl, to his great satisfaction, found such an ideal monarch in Akbar. What was more, Akbar possessed the requisite qualifications for looking after the religious as well as the temporal needs of the people.

His evaluation of the Mughal Empire under the leadership of Akbar, as a symbol of the forces of consolidation, stability and good government, ensuring economic prosperity, peace and safety, and religious freedom and toleration to all, was a natural corollary to his basic political views. From the above it naturally follows that the policy of territorial expansion was necessary as well as desirable in the religious, political and economic interests of the people. Thus Abul Fazl's political views, expounded again and again in his writings, serve to provide moral and intellectual justification for the imperialist policy of the Mughals.

Abul Fazl's religious views are an enigma to the student of Mughal history as they were to his contemporaries. The author of the *Maasir-ul-Umara* has summed up the views held by Abul Fazl's contemporaries about his beliefs.[4] Khan-i-Azam in a chronogram described him as a rebel against the Prophet. Jahangir held the same opinion about Abul Fazl. It was a commonly held belief that Abul Fazl was an infidel. He was also accused of being a Hindu, a fire-worshipper, secular and an atheist. However, according to the author of the *Maasir-ul-Umara,* it was more correct to say that he believed in 'peace with all' and was a free thinker, believing in the goodness of all religions. The author of the *Alamara-i-Abbasi* has described him as a *Nuqtavi.*[5] Urfi considered the two brothers

[3] *Ibid.*, Vol. I, 2–3; *Ibid.*, Vol. I, 201–02.

[4] *Maasir-ul-Umara*, Beveridge, Vol. I, 117–28.

[5] *Nuqtavis* : They considered the world to be eternal ; they denied Resurrection and the Last Day and retribution for the good and evil, and made paradise and hell to stand for prosperity and adversity in this world.

responsible for leading the people to apostacy. Abul Fazl himself confesses that he had attained the path of *sulh-i-kul.*[6] In a passage in the *Ain-i-Akbari* he has referred to the controversial views held about him by his contemporaries, both his opponents and supporters. It deserves to be quoted at some length.

'Although the son of Mubarak is at the present time the object of resentment and held up as a warning to mankind, and a strife of love and hate is kindled in his regard, the worshippers of God who seek truth give him the name of *Abul Wahdat* and account him a unique servant of the Supreme Giver. The valorous in the field of bravery style him *Abul Himmat* and deem him one of the wonders of carnal self-denial. Wisdom proclaims him *Abul Fitrat*, and considers him a choice specimen of that sublime house. In the writings of the vulgar herd which are noisy dens of ignorance, some attribute worldliness to him and hold him to be one of those plunged into this whirlpool, while others regard him as given up to scepticism and apostacy, and band together in reproof and condemnation.

Of me a hundred fictions rumoured fly,
And the world stares if I a word reply.

God be praised that I am not moved from these honourable dispositions by watching the strange vicissitudes of life, nor turn from well-wishing both to those who blame and those who commend, and defile not my tongue with reproof or praise.'[7]

A careful study of the *Akbar-nama* and the *Ain-i-Akbari*, however, will suggest that he was a rationalist and free-thinker. His final appeal was to reason. He ridicules those who appealed to traditions and conventions and to the opinions expressed in old religious books. He dubs these people as *taqlidi*, the followers of old traditions and precepts. He considers them as foolish and ignorant. In other words, the orthodox *ulama* were *taqlidi*, as they appealed to past traditions and to the holy law and practice of the Prophet. They failed to realize that with the passage of time truth expressed in books on religion and law had become obsolete and out of date. But at the same time Abul Fazi appears to have been a duly religious man. It is difficult to describe the exact views he held about God and other religious concepts. But his writings make it clear that

[6] *Ain-i-Akbari*, Vol. III, 218.
[7] *Ibid.*, 223–24.

he believed in the One Supreme God and respected the saints and their spiritual attainments. For formal religion and for its law and for the social practices inspired by religion, he showed scant respect, and in a way ridiculed them. Consequently, the Muslims in general and the orthodox in particular doubted his faith in Islam. However, the charge of atheism against him cannot be substantiated. While believing in One Supreme God he attached no importance to the formal religion, and emphasised the spiritual content in religion. His religious views naturally brought him in a headlong clash with the orthodox. In the contest Abul Fazl finally won. But in doing so he antagonised the majority of the *ulama* and the Muslims. He gained a reputation for being an enemy of Islam, the Prophet, Tradition and Muslim law. He realized the unenvious position which he held in the society, and was constrained to explain, elucidate and justify his ideological position in the *Ain-i-Akbari* and the *Akbar-nama*. Consequently, his work contains discourses on his liberal religious ideas, on the doctrine of 'peace with all', and on his faith in the supremacy of reason as against tradition.

His liberal views on religion have been set forth in a passage in the *Ain-i-Akbari*, entitled the conditions of the Peoples of Hindustan. The main points contained in the passage may be summed up as follows :

1. The main source of religious antagonism and bitterness between Hindus and Muslims was the belief that Hindus committed the *shirk*, *i.e.*, associated the attributes of God with human beings and their images. The charge against the Hindus, Abul Fazl asserts, was baseless. Careful investigation and enquiry has shown that the Hindus subscribed to the concept of one God.

2. Nevertheless, the misunderstanding was deep-rooted and led to bitter antagonism and even to bloodshed.

3. The sources of misunderstanding were many—

(*a*) Complete ignorance about the languages and modes of thought of each other.

(*b*) Reluctance on the part of the majority to know the inner truth through the path of research and investigation.

(*c*) General acceptance of established traditions, as against rational approach, because of the general belief that understanding acquired through careful enquiry amounted to *kufr*.

(*d*) Lack of a meeting ground for the learned and the wise of the different religions, where they could exchange their views in an atmosphere of sympathy and understanding and judge the controversial views on their merit.

(*e*) Failure of even the first king to take initiative and create the necessary conditions for a free exchange of views, enabling the learned to speak out the truth in clear terms.

(*f*) People lacked wisdom and good nature to abstain themselves from the level of vulgarity and barbarism. They interfered with the religion of others, killed them and dishonoured them. They failed to realise that religious persecution was irrational and futile. Even if the opponents were on the wrong path, it was because of ignorance for which they deserved consideration and sympathy rather than hatred and bloodshed.[8]

The views summarised in the above lines clearly bring out that Abul Fazl believed in complete religious toleration and regarded the Hindus as the worshippers of one God. In the second place, he refuses to accept the accepted views and traditional beliefs as valid truth unless and until they satisfied the demand of reason. The inner truth can be attained only through the path of enquiry based on reason. Persecution for religious differences was futile and irrational, because even those who were guilty of *shirk* committed the sin on account of ignorance and therefore deserved kindness. He advocated political action on the part of the monarch to create necessary conditions for free exchange of views among the wise and the learned of different religions, and thereby dispel misunderstandings which led to hatred and antagonism.

The intellectual and liberal outlook of Abul Fazl on religion considerably influenced his historical works.

VIEWS ON HISTORY

Abul Fazl has expressed his views on history and historiography at some length in the second volume of the *Akbar-nama*.[9] It appears from his account that for a long time his intellectual preoccupations were religion and philosophy. History offered him no

[8] *Ibid.*, 2–4, also see *Akbar-nama*, Vol. III, 659–60.

[9] *Ibid.*, Vol. II, 376–92.

attraction, and he looked upon it with scant respect. It was, for him, in no way better than any mythological account. To study history was futile and a waste of time. Its study did not lead to the realization of truth. Moreover, histories written in the past suffered from many defects. They were written by selfish and self-seeking persons who, in order to achieve their personal gains, had recorded incorrect statements and mixed up falsehood with truth. Those of the writers who were upright and honest, were well-meaning simpletons; they were also ill-informed. Consequently their accounts were foolish and ridiculous. Again, with the passage of time the original sources had disappeared. It was a great obstacle in the way of writing history, especially when historians lacked the spirit of critical enquiry. Moreover, some of the historians had added something of their own. Therefore, what was false and unauthentic passed as history. Histories containing false accounts had misled a large number of readers. Lacking a critical approach they had developed an attitude towards the past which was misleading and did much harm to the people.

This criticism of historical works in general terms obviously refers to the history of Islam and the Muslim rulers of India. The criticism would imply that Abul Fazl completely disagreed with his predecessors who wrote an account of the Muslim conquest of India and dealt with the activities of Muslim rulers. They saw Indian history as a conflict between Hindus and the followers of Islam. It was by this interpretation of Indian history that the preceding historians had misled the people and caused great harm to Indian society. Abul Fazl's criticism also seems to have been directed against those fact of Islamic history and institutions which appear to have been irrational in his eyes.

It appears that at a certain stage Abul Fazl began to question his own views about history. He pondered over the whole question thoroughly and accordingly revised his attitude towards it. Gradually the conviction came to him that past experiences and achievements of man, recorded in history books, were a positive source of enlightenment and wisdom. He points out that histories recorded the knowledge and wisdom of the sages and philosophers and thereby transmitted them to posterity. Therefore, in spite of the obvious limitations of history it was worth cultivating.

Moreover, according to Abul Fazl, the study of history is a

source of nourishment and strength to reason. He sees a definite relationship between *maqul* and *manqul*. He postulates that *Irfan*, *i.e.*, the realization of truth, was the ultimate end of man's life. It is possible only with the light of reason, but reason itself obtains light through senses, especially through eye and ear, *i.e.*, seeing and hearing. It is obvious that through seeing and hearing the accounts of those who lived in the past, reason is enriched.

Finally, the study of history helps the individual to overcome his feelings of grief and sorrow. Abul Fazl compares history with a dispensary where one can get medicine for sorrow and remedy for melancholy. It consoles the unfortunate and the grieved where in a world mutual relationships commonly lead to grief and pain.

An examination of the foregoing summary of Abul Fazl's views on history, written in the past, reveals that he attached great importance to a rational approach to history. He also had a clear idea that the facts and statements, incorporated in a historical work, should be based on original sources, and that facts should be recorded only after careful enquiry and investigation. In case a historian lacked, a rational approach and critical faculty to sift fact from fiction, his work would be worthless and in no way better than a collection of stories dealing with imaginary creations. Writings that mixed up facts with fiction can hardly be regarded as history.

In the second place, it is important to note that he does not regard history as an allied branch of the *Tafsir* or *Fiqh*. In fact, he is inclined to establish a close relationship between history and philosophy. For him they are not only allied subjects, they also complement and supplement each other. This idea about the nature of history constitutes a distinct departure from that which was cherished by Barani and Badauni. Moreover, Abul Fazl makes no reference to the generally accepted view of Muslim historians that history served to enlighten and warn the 'believers' only. Obviously, the note in his concept of history is secular rather than religious.

History, according to Abul Fazl, records the festivities and convivial parties as well as battles and campaigns. It embraces both what is serious and non-serious (but Abul Fazl did not deal with non-serious things); it deals with acts of kindness and cruelty, of generosity and meanness, of valour and cowardice ; it describes the condition of the people and the policies of governments, and it includes the wisdom of the sages and the learning of the scholar.

History also, according to Abul Fazl, embodies all the changes that take place in the world.

The *Akbar-nama* and the *Ain-i-Akbari* together constitute a single book. The first part of the *Akbar-nama* contains an account of Akbar's ancestors, including that of his father Humayun. The second part gives the most complete account of Akbar's reign upto the 46th year, in a chronological order. The work was undertaken in 1595, and after five revisions was completed in 1602. The *Ain-i-Akbari* is the third part of the book. 'It is a unique compilation of the system of administration and control throughout the various departments of government in a great empire faithfully and minutely recorded in their smallest detail, with such an array of facts illustrative of its extent, resources, condition, population, industry, and wealth as the abundant material supplied from official sources could furnish.'[10] It also contains an account of the religious and philosophical systems of the Hindus, as described in their ancient books, and of their social customs and practices. Thus, Abul Fazl widened the range and scope of history as no medieval historian before him had done.

Abul Fazl is the first medieval historian who realized and recognized the importance of original sources and gave his utmost attention and care to their study. He did not depend on a single source or account in order to ascertain a fact, but obtained as many versions as could be collected. They were put to a critical examination before they were accepted. He states that he has formulated a set of questions which were put to the reporter of an event or fact. This procedure, he points out, is of great help to the historian in ascertaining the truth.[11]

His source material consisted of accounts of events written by those who were eye-witness to them. Reports, memoranda, minutes prepared by the officers, imperial *farmans*, and other records were carefully consulted. He heavily drew upon the daily proceedings of the court recorded by the *Waqai Navis* since the nineteenth year of Akbar's reign.[12]

He obtained information, written accounts and reports about military campaigns, administrative measures and other events from

[10] *Ain-i-Akbari*, Jarrett, Introduction.
[11] *Akbar-nama*, Vol. II, 367–92.
[12] *Ibid.*, Vol. I, 9–10.

different sources.[13] He inquired from the principal officers, grandees, well-informed dignitaries and old members of the royal family. Not satisfied with the oral accounts, which were conflicting, he requested them to put their accounts in writing. He thus obtained written accounts from twenty persons who were well-known for their sobriety, moderation and integrity. He examined these accounts with care and put them to the test of reason. The conflicting accounts, furnished by distinguished persons, were reported to the Emperor, who verified a particular account or made suggestions for necessary corrections. Similary, the accounts which contradicted the personal knowledge and experience of the author were also referred to the Emperor. Through this process of historical investigation, the truth was ascertained and recorded.[14]

The measure of Abul Fazl's success and failure as a historian was largely determined by the conditions under which he worked. His limitations and achievements both may be traced to the position he held in society, to his acadamic training and accomplishments, to his experience as a youth and to his religious and political views. He took an active interest in the political and religious issues of the period, and his outlook on these issues gave a definite shape to the treatment of subject matter in his great work.

In the first place, as noted earlier, he was the most favourite courtier and a friend and supporter of Akbar against the forces which challenged the new concept of the Mughal Empire. He was Akbar's trusted secretary and confidant. At the same time, as his writings emphatically suggest, he genuinely entertained a feeling of adulation and reverence for the character and personality of Akbar. Such an attitude might have been partly inspired by considerations of personal advancement, but it is important to note that his own views on politics and religion were similar to those of Akbar. His firm belief in religious toleration owed its origin to his formative years, when he and his family experienced the worst type of persecution at the hands of the orthodox *ulama*. This belief proved to be the basis of a lasting friendship with Akbar. Moreover, few will question that Akbar possessed the highest and the noblest qualities of head and heart. No wonder that Abul Fazl found in Akbar simultaneously the qualities of a king, philosopher and hero. Whatever the reasons

[13] *Ain-i-Akbari*, Vol. III, 199–200; *Akbar-nama*, Vol. I, 9–10.

[14] *Ain-i-Akbari*, Vol. III, 199–200.

for Abul Fazl's adulation of Akbar, the fact remains that he completely identified himself with the policies and principles of government initiated by Akbar. He also subscribed to the religious views held by Akbar. A careful study of the contemporary sources suggests that Abul Fazl might not have been the real man behind the formulation of Akbar's religious and administrative policies; nevertheless, it was he who morally and intellectually sustained the emperor to remain firm and adhere to his policies which were quite unorthodox. His official position, as well as his personal views on religion and politics, required that he should defend, justify and extol Akbar and his activities. To record the activities and achievements of the ideal monarch was an act of worship for him.[15] Hence the account, although correct in matters of detail, was written in a partisan spirit, and aimed at extolling Akbar's achievements and glossing over his shortcomings and failures. To this task, he employed his extraordinary powers of intelligence, argument, learning and command over language. The vastness of the subject matter, the great issues which agitated the people of the age, and the extraordinary personality of Akbar, provided him with a theme and a subject well suited to write an epic. Abul Fazl, with his extraordinary command over language, attempted to combine history and epic into a single piece of literary creation. Few will doubt that he has not succeeded in his attempt. This is his measure of success as well as failure as a historian.

The result of this literary attempt is a most detailed and complete account of Akbar's reign available to us. The most remarkable achievement of Abul Fazl as a historian is to produce a book of history which reads like an epic. It possesses something of an architectonic greatness, and the personality of Akbar sits over this edifice like a coping-stone. In the pages of the *Akbar-nama* and the *Ain-i-Akbari*, the greatness of Akbar has been given a concrete form. It reflects the extraordinary moral courage, the spiritual yearnings, the great vision and profound sagacity of Akbar. The reader is overwhelmed with the physical strength and prowess of Akbar, as also with his kindness and stern sense of justice, and with the awe and majesty of his 'good fortune' (*iqbal*).

Akbar's new concept of the Empire, his unfailing interest in the improvement of the condition of the people through suitable and

[15] *Akbar-nama*, Introduction.

vigorous administrative measures, and his lofty concept and practice of complete religious toleration have been recorded in a language and a spirit which have immortalised Akbar. He has become a legend for the Indian people as one of the most benevolent and successful monarchs dedicated to the welfare of his subjects. This is no meagre achievement. Few historians can claim the same good fortune. Abul Fazl has evidently succeeded in the task he set before himself, as stated in the preface of his great book on Akbar.

This, to me, appears to be the most significant achievement of Abul Fazl as Akbar's historian. Equally important is Abul Fazl's treatment of contemporary history. He made a departure from the established and accepted historical traditions in many respects. He did not believe that Indian history should concern itself only with the achievements of the Muslim rulers in India; nor did he try to establish any relation with the past of Islam. He refused to agree with the view held by his predecessors that Indian history essentially constituted a record of the struggles between the forces of Islam and Hinduism. For Abul Fazl the conflict was between the Mughal Empire and the Indian Princes, Hindu and Muslim alike. In essence, it was a conflict between the forces of stability, consolidation and good government under an ideal monarch who was qualified to lead the people in temporal as well as spiritual affairs, and the forces of disintegration, and bad Governments led by the 'Zamindars'. For Akbar and Abul Fazl the Mughal Empire was an Indian Empire in the real sense, because it was no more an exclusive concern of a racial group or a combination of racial groups or only those of the Faithful. The religious, political and economic claims of the Hindu and Rajput landed aristocrats were fully recognized. These changed conditions left no justification for the Indian princes not to join the imperial confederation which would bring unity, stability and economic prosperity to the country. Abul Fazl's treatment and presentation of the important military expeditions against the Rajputs clearly brings out the point made in the above lines.

The new view of Indian history is best expressed by the change in the terminology for the imperial warriors. Abul Fazl describes them as *mujahidan-i-iqbal* and *ghaziyan-i-daulat*; they are no longer the *mujahidan-i-Islam*, and *ghaziyan-i-Islan* *i.e.*, victorious soldiers exerting in the way of Islam. The treatment of contemporary history in these terms struck a new note in medieval historiography;

it was a definite contribution to the idea of history. It is, no doubt, true that Abul Fazl's new concept of history failed to win many converts for some time. Nevertheless, his new outlook on Indian history proved to be of abiding value. It went a long way to popularise the secular nature of the Mughal government, and also considerably affected the outlook and attitude of the imperial officers and the Hindu landed aristocracy. In the long run Abul Fazl's secular interpretation of Indian history gained ground, and the historians of the later Mughals, whether Hindu or Muslim, looked on the political developments in the country in terms of the Mughal Empire and those who were opposed to it.

No less significant was Abul Fazl's deep interest in the ancient philosophical and religious systems of the Hindus and in their social customs and practices. He studied these aspects of the Hindu society with care and sympathy. These studies are the best examples of the historical objectivity and detachment in his writings. After al-Biruni, his was the first systematic attempt to understand the Hindu religion and society in a proper historical perspective. Moreover, his attempt to understand the contemporary Hindu society with reference to its past history of ideas was an approach which was original and resembles the modern sociological studies.

These achievements entitle Abul Fazl to an eminent position among the foremost historians of medieval India. However, in any realistic evaluation and assessment of Abul Fazl as a historian, it is but fair that some of his limitations may be noted. It is true that about details of individual events, which he seems to have investigated and ascertained with great care, he is reliable. But in his treatment of the subject matter he is subjective, rather than objective. His phrases and adjectives, and his construction of sentences, imply his own-assessment and evaluation of a particular event or situation. The narrative contains his judgment about an individual or an event or a situation. He invariably explains the motives which inspired Akbar in undertaking military action against a Rajput prince or a Muslim king, and these motives are described as just and laudable. Obviously such a treatment does not fulfil the conditions of historical objectivity.

Similarly, while Abul Fazl regards reason as his sole guide and precept, and ridicules those who follow the path of tradition as against reason, he does not apply the same standard to Akbar.

When dealing with the extraordinary spiritual qualities of Akbar, or referring to his qualities of prescience, which amount to prophecy and reach almost to supernatural powers, or recording the achievements of Akbar's 'good fortune,' Abul Fazl ceases to listen to the voice of reason. It is really painful to keep company with Abul Fazl in these weak moments. The apostle of reason appears to have fallen a victim to credulity and superstition.

Secondly, there is some evidence to show that at times he glosses over certain events and facts which might cast some discredit upon the wisdom or ability of Akbar. For example, the *Akbar-nama* does not say that the project of converting *jagir* lands into the *khalisa* and entrusting the administration of the *karoris* proved to be a fiasco; that it resulted in the ruin of large areas of cultivated land and of peasants, and eventually led to the harassment and punishment of the *karoris.* Abul Fazl's silence is ominous; he fails to write even a few sentences about the exertion of the *karoris.* Nor does he note that the grant of *jagir* lands was resumed by the 24th regnal year as the experiment had failed. These facts, however, have been recorded by Badauni and are corroborated in essentials by Nizam-ud-Din Ahmad. The internal evidence contained in the report of Todar Mal and Shah Fathullah Shirazi, incorporated in toto in the *Akbar-nama,* indirectly corroborates and confirms the accounts of Badauni and Nizam-ul-Din.

Similarly the reforms, spread over a long period, introduced in the department of the *Sadr,* do not find a place in the *Akbar-nama,* except a summary of the imperial order issued to separate the *madad-i-maash* lands from the *khalisa* and *jagir* lands. It is difficult to see why Abul Fazl chose to incorporate a brief account of the reforms in the *Ain-i-Akbari.* Even this account briefly refers to the corrupt practices that obtained in the department of the *Sadr* in general terms, and passes over the important issues which were responsible for the drastic reforms, aiming at the curtailment of the powers of the *Sadr.* Abul Fazl has also deliberately omitted the repercussions of the measures on the social and economic conditions of a section of the Muslim community and the deep resentment caused among its members. Badauni, as a spokesman of the class, gives comprehensive and convincing account of the adverse effects of the measure on the economic conditions of the *madad-i-maash* holders and their sharp reaction to these measures.

Again, the accounts of the religious discussions held in the Ibadat Khana, the origin of Akbar's disgust and breach with the *ulama* and the proclamation of Akbar as *mujtahid* or *Imam-i-Adil* can hardly be regarded as complete and truthful. Abul Fazl himself was a party to these religious debates and the main instrument to disarm and discredit the *ulama* in the battle of arguments, and thereby to bring about their fall from the position of power and influence. Naturally, his account of the fierce religious controversies cannot be accepted as impartial and objective. Moreover, the relevant passages are full of contempt and ridicule for the *ulama,* though they are couched in a sophisticated and dignified language. Nevertheless, the deep-rooted dislike of the *ulama* and of the values and principles for which they stood, has been underlined with vigour and eloquence. True that Abul Fazl scrupulously avoids attacking persons and individuals; but his old grievance against the class of *ulama* seeks full vengeance through his powerful pen. It may be conceded that the *ulama* stood for principles which had lost their vitality and validity in the new political contest; even some of their beliefs might have appeared to smack of a complete negation of reason and enlightenment. But even so they were, to argue in Abul Fazl's language, victims of ignorance and as such deserved consideration and kindness rather than persecution and eternal ridicule in the pages of history. In such passages Abul Fazl flagrantly violates those very principles of toleration and liberalism which elsewhere and in different context he so assidously postulates and propagates. The fact is that it was as much a struggle for power as an ideological conflict between the *ulama*, who occupied a position of power and influence, and the erstwhile mendicants who had been leading a retired life of asceticism and poverty. When the latter came to power they were as relentless with their sword and pen against the *ulama* as the latter had been to the former. They saw to it that the power of the *ulama* was completely broken and their names in history should go down as ignorant, selfish, mean and self-seeking individuals.

Many examples may be quoted where Abul Fazl has failed to do justice to his duty as a historian. The account of Sher Shah, for example, is a case in point. His achievements are belittled, and his success is attributed to treachery, fraud and deception. No modern historian will agree with such an assessment of Sher Shah. Some of his reforms are mentioned, but Abul Fazl hastens, in order to belittle them, that they were in imitation of those of Ala-ud-Din Khalji or of the rulers of Bengal.

Abul Fazl's preoccupation with Akbar and his activities has resulted in the omission of many facts which would have presented the other side of the medal and imparted a proper perspective to his account. We know almost nothing about the Afghan or Rajput side of the story, the position taken by these people and the nature of the triangular conflict in which Akbar did succeed but not without strenuous efforts of diplomacy, combined with necessary military actions. The result is that the political account, as presented in the *Akbar-nama,* fails to infuse life and colour to the grim struggle for the Empire of Hindustan. His narrative seems to be an attempt to convince us that Akbar's good fortune (*iqbal*) and superb military strength rode roughshod over the opposing forces, which were almost passive and served as a background to the triumphant military operations of the Mughal armies. Such an impression, which the account in the *Akbar-nama* invariably creates, fails to catch the realities of the political situation with which Akbar had to contend, for it was his foresight, diplomatic skill and the capacity to organise successful military operations that brought success to him and not only his good fortune, as Abul Fazl would like us to believe.

It is also important to note that Abul Fazl fails to give a faithful account of the political and social forces, which stood for regionalism, local patriotism and independence and racial conflicts which challenged the claims of Akbar as the rightful emperor of Hindustan. Consequently the depth, the magnitude and the intensity of the various types of conflicts of the period are not reflected in his writings.

Moreover, his preoccupation with the activities of the emperors, nobles, scholars and saints made his outlook on life rather narrow. He hardly took note of events and facts which appeared insignificant and trivial to the intellectual in Abul Fazl. These facts, if recorded, would have given a rare insight into the life of the common man and would have helped him in capturing the spirit of the age. His intellectual bias and his training as a scholar made him indifferent and contemptuous to what was non-serious, humble and ordinary in life. Consequently, he was generally interested only in those facts which were serious and consequential from the view point of a king, a noble, and an accomplished scholar given to philosophical speculation and reflection. And these facts when selected were presented in an equally sober, pompous and terse language, and in a medium well-suited for a philosopher who chooses to record the higher and deeper truths of life. The net result is that the life of the age in its broader sense, embracing the serious and the non-serious, the high and the low, the grim and the humorous, the simple and the colourful, does not pulsate in the pages of the *Akbar-nama* and the *Ain-i-Akbari*. It is true that the *Ain-i-Akbari* abounds in economic details, but these details read like a railway time-table or a departmental report, shorn of everything which can tell us something about the real conditions of the people and give an insight into the content, purpose and meaning of their life. Abul Fazl never speaks of the wages and prices, and the revenue demands in the human context of individuals and groups. The *Ain-i-Akbari* merely furnishes us with certain statistical details which can hardly be correlated with the living conditions of the people. Similarly, he deems it below the level of an intellectual to record the habits, customs, beliefs, social practices, and superstitions of common men and women. This limitation which arose from his personality, temperament and intellectual bias has left his story of the age one-sided and incomplete. The *Akbar-nama* is more a story of Akbar than a story of the society and the age in which Akbar and Abul Fazl lived. And it is in this sense that Abul Fazl has failed to capture the spirit of the age and to record in his book the story of a society as an integrated whole.

13

Persian Historiography in India during the 18th Century

Historical studies formed an essential part of the general academic discipline in India during the 18th century. Though not formally prescribed in the system of higher education, history held sway over humanistic studies as it provided great intellectual stimulus.[1] The output of historians in this period was consequently considerable. Besides formal political histories, many administrative manuals, and works on trade and commerce were compiled.[2] Interest in documents led to the compilation of many epistolary and other collections of historical significance.[3] Even the medium of poetry was not ignored by the historians and versified histories were produced in large number.[4] Apart from this literature, the biographical accounts of *amirs* and saints form a monumental and scholarly product of the period.[5] Above all, the 18th century is of particular interest on

[1] Nawab Shakir Khan, *Gulshan-i-Sadiq*, Patna, MS. f 44a; Nawab Sadr-ud-Din Muhammad Khan Faiz, *Kulliyat-i-Faiz*, Bodleian MS. Aligarh Rotograph, ff 122–25.

[2] Aitmad Ali, *Mirat-ul-Haqaiq*, Bodleian MS.; Mirza Muhammad Ali Khan, *Mirat-i-Ahmadi*, Gaekwad Oriental Series, 1927; Anand Ram, *Sivaq-nama*, Central Record Office, Hyderabad; Lachmi Narayan Shafiq, *Haqiqat-Hai-Hindustan*, Asufiyah MS. Hyderabad; Jawahar Mal Baikas, *Dastur-ul-amal-Baikas*, Aligarh MS.

[3] Musavi Khan Jurat, *Munshat-i-Musavi Khan*, Asafiyah Lib. MS. Hyderabad; Munshi Daya Ram, *Balmukand-nama*, Patna MS.; Saib Rai, *Khojistah Klam*; Bhagwan Das, *Aziz-ul-Qalub*, Aligarh MS.

[4] Nizam-ud-Din, *Nadir-nama*, Asafiya MS. ; Ahsan Ijad, *Shah-nama-i-Deccan*, Asafiyah MS. ; Mir Raza Zulfiqar, *Sharf-nama-i-Muhummad Shah*, B.M.MS.

[5] Keval Ram, *Tazkirat-ul-Umara*, Aligarh MS. Mirza Muhammed, *Tarikh-i-Muhhammadi*, Rampur MS. ; Shah Nawaz Khan, *Maasir-ul-Umara*; Rustam Ali Khan, *Tarikh-i-Hindi*, B. M. MS. ; Khwaja Gul Muhammad, *Takmilah-i-Siyar-ul-Auliyah*.

account of the enormous religious literature which include the celebrated works on the Quran, *Hadis*, Jurisprudence and mysticism.[6] For an understanding of the various aspects of social life and the different facets of culture, the *tazkiras* and the *diwans* of the poets yield valuable information. Thus the diversity and range of the writings of this period is very impressive. Perhaps in no other period of Indian history so much literature on the religious, political and social aspects was produced as in the 18th century.[7]

The main theme of historians during the period under review was politics, and subjects of secular character were given great importance. They devoted a fair amount of space in their works to military operations, achievements at the battle field and colourful activities of the Imperial court. Descriptions of administrative functions, acts of generosity and patronage of art and literature also absorbed their attention.

Khafi Khan wrote a political history, pure and simple, and he hovered around the Imperial court and camp to gather information. His work is a brilliant reconstruction of events, thorough, lucid and chronologically well-organised. His knowledge of facts is great, and the range of materials enormous. He has a conception of the continuity of Mughal history. Besides his erudition, the beauty of form and expression is remarkable. He has the skill to correlate events in a wider context, drawing parallels and illustrations from the past. Perhaps he is the only writer who gives a connected and precise account of the reforms attempted at different times to re-organise the *mansabdari* system which was cracking under the weight of its own vast structure.[8] His passages on central administration, Maratha affairs, and conditions of *jagirdars* are unique ; they not only contain new information, but show a deep insight of the author in these matters.

Analysing the process of decline that set in the Mughal

[6] For details of Shah Waliullah's works, vide, *Al-furqan*, Bareilly, *Islamic Culture*, 1951 ; K. A. Nizami, *Tarikh-i-Mashaikh-i-Chist*, Delhi, 1953.

[7] Writing in 1781, Muhammad Bakhsh Ashub says that during this period the art of history writing has fallen into disuse. But in view of the vast historical literature produced in the 18th century this statement seems to be incorrect. *Tarikh-i-Shahadat-i-Farrukh Siyar wa Julus-i-Muhammad Shah*, B.M. MS. f. 13.

[8] Khafi Khan, *Muntakhab-ul-Lubab*, Bib. Ind. Calcutta, 1874, Vol. II, 600, 769.

administration during the reign of Bahadur Shah, Khafi Khan states: 'Since the establishment of the Timurid rule in India, one title was not given to two persons, although a change of one or two letters was allowed. Safdar Khan Babi, posted at Aurangabad, possessed a hereditary title from the time of Aurangzeb. But Bahadur Shah gave this title to one of his old servants. Safdar Khan represented for the restoration of his title which he had lost without giving any cause of disobedience. The Emperor wrote on his application, granted, granted, granted, though the same title had already been conferred on another person. Since that day the evil practice of giving the same title to two or three persons developed. In like manner, the grants of *mansab*, elephant, *jaifah* and *serpanch* were no longer made in conformity with the rank and dignity of the recipient.[9]

The treasury officers observed with distress the rapid deterioration in revenue administration and felt the need of reforms aimed at making the *mansabdari* system standardized and efficient. The reformed system, they hoped, could cope with a situation in which expenditure outran revenue, and reckless grants of *jagirs* were made by the Emperor when lands available for the purpose were limited. Ikhlas Khan, the *Araz-mukarrar* reputed for his honesty and hard work drew the attention of Munim Khan, the *Wazir*, to the financial crisis caused by these problems.[10] He suggested that the *Wazir* should personally scrutinize every application before sanctioning an appointment or promotion.

A reform of this character was bound to meet resistance from the vested interests at the court. Munim Khan, through fear of his own popularity among the job-seekers, declined to discharge the unpleasant duty and asked Ikhlas Khan to undertake the work of reform himself. Without the assistance and co-operation of his superior, Ikhlas Khan found the task beyond his capacity. He refused to ride roughshod over the feelings of persons desirous to obtain ranks in the government.

In the end, the work of conducting an enquiry into the origin rank and dignity of *mansabdar*, was assigned to Mustaid Khan, the author of the *Maasiri-i-Alamgiri*. He was to check and certify all applications of *mansabdars* before the *Araz-mukarrar* and the

[9] *Ibid.*, Vol. II, 627–28.

[10] *Maasir-ul-Umara*, Vol. I, 350–52.

Wazir forwarded for final sanction of the Emperor. But his labours bore no fruits. The programme of reform was defeated not only by the resistance of fortune-seekers but also by the disinterestedness of Bahadur Shah. The Emperor would sign the applications of candidates presented by his two queens, Mihr Parwar and Ummat-ul-Habib, without first referring to Mustaid Khan. 'In consequence the signature of the Emperor lost its value. His Majesty would say to his officers that he had no alternative but to issue orders for the grant of jagirs to all applicants. His officers, however, were free to act as they thought best and as the occasion dictated.'[11]

Khafi Khan's knowledge of revenue administration at the local level seems to be authentic, as it stems from his practical experience in matters of revenue collection. He served the government for a considerable period as *Amil*, although he has nothing but outspoken contempt for the post. He calls the *Amil* wicked, corrupt and cruel. The revenue collector misappropriates the money of the government and plunders the helpless cultivators. The author himself confesses that he oppressed the peasantry and destroyed the property of Muslims. The work of leading pigs to pastures and herding dogs is, he thinks, better than that of revenue collection.[12]

Besides condemning the high-handedness of revenue collectors, Khafi Khan draws indictment on other officers who do not give serious thought to the worsening of the political situation, improving the lot of the peasants, planting new habitations and increasing the land revenue. He brings forth in plain words the abuses of *ijaradari* or revenue-farming by which the *raiyyat* is ground down to the dust of misery and the countryside desolated. He pungently criticises the wealthy who provide no help to the needy and live a self-centred and luxurious life.[13]

Another work on administrative details and description of commerce and trade is the *Mirat-ul-Haqaiq*.[14] Its author, Aitmad Ali Khan bin Aitmad Khan Alamgiri, was an inhabitant of Ahmadabad, where he passed the major part of his life. This voluminous work has been written on the pattern of the *Mirat-i-Ahmadi*. It is a diary of

[11] *Muntakhab-ul-Lubab*, Vol. II, 630.

[12] *Ibid.*, Vol. II, 677.

[13] *Ibid.*, Vol. I, 157–58 ; *Ibid.*, Vol. II, 600–769.

[14] Aitmad Ali Khan, *Mirat-ul-Haqaiq*, Bodleian MS. Sitamau Rotograph.

day-to-day events and news concerning Gujarat and Delhi, the capital of the Empire. It is a mine of information for details regarding prices that prevailed in different parts of the country, and the taxes imposed by the government in the reigns of the Later Mughals. Unlike the *Mirat-i-Ahmadi*, this work deals with the economic conditions not only in Gujarat, but also in Delhi, Agra and Allahabad. The author explains in various chapters the causes of the break-up of the *mansabdari* system. The conditions of the *mansabdars* who lost control over their lands or possessed no *jagirs* have been clearly analysed.

The historians of the period believed that the march of time could be explained by glorfying the accomplishments of the chosen few and by painting their portraits with a brush of hyperbole. For them the key to history lay in the rise and fall of individuals who played definite roles in determining the course of political affairs. The king or *amir* was the centre and main-spring of all events ; the different social strata were thrown into the shade. Although keenly aware of the material basis of Mughal civilization, these scholars failed to analyse the economic and social factors involved in the process of its decline.

While explaining the phenomenon of the decadence of Mughal power, these historians generally lay stress on the social and moral degeneration of the privileged few who grew indolent, self-satisfied and indifferent to their duties. For instance, Ahsan Ijad[15], the author of the *Shah nama-i-Deccan*, criticises the character of the nobility and attempts to interrelate its decline with the break-up of political power. His account of wars and administration given in the *Shah-nama-i-Deccan* is sketchy, but candid and accurate. He burns with indignation at the corrupt and luxurious life of Aurangzeb's successors, factional rivalries among the nobles, and their cowardly behaviour in dealing with the enemies of the Mughal government. He paints a lurid picture of the misery and poverty of soldiers, small *mansabdars*, low paid employees and other respectable and educated persons whose means of subsistence depended on government patronage.

With the capture of two strategic and fertile provinces, Gujarat

[15] Ahsan Ijad is also the author of *Farrukh Siyar-nama*, which deals exclusively with the political history of Farrukh Siyar, B.M. MS. Gr. 25 (Rieu 1273a).

and Malwa, by the Marathas, a large section of subordinate officers and servants, engaged in the work of revenue collection, were faced with unemployment. In discussing political issues Ahsan Ijad upholds a vigorous and forward policy towards the Marathas and other disruptive forces in the Empire. Like other writers, he censures the role of Raja Jai Singh who aligned himself with the Marathas, and who, in spite of the considerable resources placed at his disposal, was unable to protect the Imperial dominions from the Maratha inroads.

But his analysis of the complex causes—political, social and economic—that led to the disintegration of the Mughal Empire lacks depth and insight. He gives very simply the causes of what happened, but his investigation does not reveal the meaning or rationality behind the historical processes. He ignores the discussion of the conditions of the peasants and does not explain the evils which had crept into the Mughal military organization.

The age being one of political decline and economic destress, there runs a thread of gloom through the entire contemporary historical writings. The historians of this period rarely indulged in their rhetoric or florid style. Lucidity and simplicity alone could serve the objective they had in mind. Their concept of history was based on those moral precepts which had influenced the outlook and culture of the people. The historians liked to draw parallels from the past to compare similar situations facing the kings and nobles. Moral lessons derived from the past events were recommended to sovereigns and statesmen.[16] They sought to explain the course of history in terms of the struggle between the forces of good and evil. It was a philosophy teaching by examples, in the sense that those who followed cardinal principles of Justice and public welfare attained power and progress; and those who went astray from this straight path faced rack and ruin.

Most of the historians recorded mainly contemporary events and incidents. They either attended the Imperial court or served the ministers in the capital. Some of them were in the service of officials and governors in distant provinces. In this way they had excellent means to obtain adequate and authentic information about different events. The information about incidents in which they did

[16] Mir Muhammad Qasim Aurangabadi, *Ahwal-ul-Khawaqin*, B.M. MS. ff. 103–5.

not directly participate, they gathered from those who had first hand knowledge of the incidents. Iradat Khan, author of the *Tarikh-i-Iradat Khan*, served as *Faujdar*, first of Jagna and then of Aurangabad and Mandu in the time of Aurangzeb. Later he was appointed governor of Doab in the reign of Shah Alam Bahadur Shah. He says in his preface : 'As, on account of my office, and being engaged in these transactions, I have obtained a perfect knowledge of the sources of most events, and what to others even information must be difficult, it was planned and executed in my sight ; and as I was a sharer as well as spectator of all the dangers and troubles, I have, therefore, recorded them.'[17] In handling the historical material at their disposal, they were guided by their study of the earlier historians whose works abounded in their libraries. Animated by a passionate regard for truth, Khafi Khan emphasised the need of submitting the evidence to a thorough enquiry. He holds that a historian should be faithful and sincere in the presentation of facts. 'He (the historian) should show no partiality to one side or animosity to the other.'[18] Shafi Warid, author of the *Mirat-i-Waridat*, asserts that he has recorded events and occurrences which either he himself watched or heard from others. He took utmost pains in investigating the statements of others : those found incorrect after a close and thorough enquiry were rejected by him.[19]

These historians generally had independent and individual methods of collecting data; and though the facts were the same, their interpretations varied. This variation was determined by their particular situations, social background and political interests. In faction feuds among the courtiers and *amirs* they aligned themselves with one or the other of the contestants. This identification with the interests of their patrons affected their approach. Consequently, the

[17] Iradat Khan, *Tarikh-i-I-Iradat Khan*, Aligarh MS. f. 2 ; Elliot and Dowson, Vol. VII, 535. Khafi Khan was a government employee in the reign of Aurangzeb, when Farrukh Siyar came to the throne, he was appointed *Diwan* by Nizam-ul-Mulk. He gives his source of information in these words : "What he himself saw, what he heard from the tongues of men who from time to time were the associates of Farrukh Siyar, and from the Sayyids who were his companions at the banquet table and in battle, that he had honestly committed to writing, after endeavouring to arrive at the truth when statements varied." *Muntakhab-ul-Lubab*, Vol. II, 727.; Elliot and Dowson, Vol. VII, 44.

[18] *Muntakhab-ul-Lubab*, 726.

[19] *Mirat-i-Waridat*, Aligarh MS., 10.

element of subjectivity influenced their attempts to explain the interplay of political forces.

These historians shared the widespread belief that the Mughal crown was a divine institution, pre-ordained to rule the country permanently; and as such it was a symbol of solidarity and strength of the ruling class, and the ultimate shield to defend the people from the depredations of adventurers and power mongers. But during the period under review the king was reduced to an almost helpless pawn in the game of group politics. The deposition and death of Farrukh Siyar demonstrated the final triumph of ministers and nobles over the Emperor. The later Mughals had received no thorough education in the art of government. They proved unequal to the task of dealing with the crisis that continuously threatened the Mughal government.

The contemporary writers, who saw the Empire passing into the turmoil of civil strife, and its vast structure ultimately breaking down before waves of insurgency and foreign invasions, did not hesitate to condemn the unwise policies of the Emperors and their inefficient conduct of administration. They denounced the kings for their impolitic and inexpedient acts in regard to military operations and administration; even matters relating to their private life were subjected to severe criticism. Bahadur Shah was blamed for his extreme munificence in lavishing gifts and privileges of office and power on undeserving persons.[20] Jahandar Shah was depicted as a 'drunken profligate'[21] while Farrukh Siyar was called a prisoner of indecision.[22] Muhammad Shah was accused for his indolence and intemperance which made him incapable of holding the self-seeking nobles under control.[23]

Nevertheless, any act of insubordination on the part of the nobles was unbearable to the historians. They gave full vent to their indignation at the local leaders who made a bid to secure shares,

[20] *Muntakhab-ul-Lubab*, Vol. II, 601-2, 627-28 ; Kamraj bin Nain Singh, *Ibrat-Nama*, B.M. MS. Aligarh Rotograph, f. 36a.

[21] Nuruddin Farouqi, *Jahandar-nama*, B. M. MS. Aligarh Rotograph, ff. 36-38 ; Shaikh Muhammad Muin, *Farrukh-nama*, B.M. MS. Aligarh Rotograph, ff. 74-75, 89.

[22] Mirza Muhammad, *Ibrat-nama*, Patna MS. ff. 95-96.

[23] Yahya Khan, *Tazkirat-ul-Muluk*, B.M. MS. Aligarh Rotograph, f. 132b.

compatible with their might, in profits the Empire could offer.[24] In the struggle for supremacy between the centre and the provinces the historians are divided into two groups; some display enthusiastic partiality towards the Imperial centre, while others lend their support to the local chieftains and provincial governors. Historians like Qasim Aurangabadi, Mansa Ram, author of the *Maasir-i-Nizami*, Yusuf Muhammad Khan, author of the *Tarikh-i-Fathiyah*, and others who compiled their works in the Deccan, supported the Nizam-ul-Mulk in his conflict with the centre. But writers like Ashub, Rustam Ali, Shafi Warid, Mirza Muhammad held the Imperialist point of view. It appears, however, that their loyalty was to the Mughal crown and not to one who wore it.

The ruling class showed intellectual weariness and loss of creative vigour. The old spirit of service to the Mughal dynasty gave place to exploitation of the state for selfish ends. The big nobles monopolized all higher public employments, owned large lands as *jagirs* and undermined royal power.[25] The small *mansabdars* led a life of humiliation and poverty.[26] A class of newly-made nobles who could count on no claims of birth or merit rose to positions of power and prominence.[27] The corrupt and clique ridden nobility completely failed to respond to the challenges of the age. The political elite of the society sank into lethargy and remained throughout the period in a stagnant condition. Their intellect became morbid, their vision narrow, their morale undermined, and in its total individuality the entire class turned to be effete. The divisions among the nobility, its isolations from the rank and file of the people, and its indifference to the common good prepared the ground for the fall of the ruling class as a whole.

This degradation of the nobility has been presented by the contemporary writers with frankness and, sometimes, in strong language. Shafi Warid, discussing the Maratha affairs, records that in the province of Agra five to seven thousand *mansabdars* possessing big forces lived; a large number of *zamindars* inhabitating the area had ample resources in men and material. But this whole class of

[24] *Tarikh-i-Shahadat-i-Farruk Siyar wa Julus-i-Muhammad Shah*, B.M. MS., f. 43a, *Mirat-i-Waridat*, 644–45.

[25] For a detail discussion of this aspect vide, *Studies in Islam*, Delhi, January 1955, 33.

[26] *Ahwal-ul-Khawaqin*, f. 181b; *Mirat-ul-Haqaiq*, 92a.

[27] *Muntakhab-ul-Lubab*, 776 ; *Ibrat-nama*, Kamraj, ff. 46a, 54a.

mansabdars and *zamindars* could not prevent the Marathas from plundering the towns and villages of the Agra division.[28] The author of *Hadisa-i-Nadir Shah* writes : 'The affairs of the government had been upset. The ministers of the Emperor, intoxicated with the pride of the extreme wealth, and the increasing status of men like Qamr-ud-Din Khan and Khan-i-Dauran, had neglected the affairs of the government. They were indolent, commanded no respect, did not fear the Emperor, and except for indulging in corruption, they had no other work to do.'[29]

In an atmosphere filled with faction feuds, historians felt constrained to take sides and advocate the cause of their group leaders and patrons. This partisan politics marred their perspective and closed the horizon of their ideas. The canvas of history was narrowed down to a simple discussion of group alignments in the ruling party unrelated with the broader aspects of the community life as a whole. History was reduced to a mere collection of facts to be read like political pamphlets; it was used as an effective instrument to buttress the interests of one group of nobles at the expense of another section of the governing class. They lacked critical sense to investigate the truth and recognise the importance of objectivity in the collection and use of their historical material.

To illustrate this observation three typical examples of varied interpretations on controversial issues have been chosen. They are as follows :

(*i*) Conflict between Farrukh Siyar and the Sayyid brothers,
(*ii*) Contest for power between the Mughals and the Sadaat of Barha,
(*iii*) The role of different nobles when Nadir Shah invaded India.

A critical study of these particular issues may help us to ascertain the prejudices which influenced the minds of contemporary historians.

(*i*) The prolonged conflict between Farrukh Siyar and the Sayyid brothers kept the Imperial court in a state of almost continuous alarm and unrest. Engaged in a severe contest for survival, the Emperor and his ministers neglected the state administration,

[28] *Mirat-i-Waridat*, 644.
[29] *Ḥadiṣa-i-Nadir Shah*, (Anonymous), Asafiya, MS. f. 4a.

and set themselves to organise plots against one another.[30] With a combination of tact and firmness the Sayyid brothers were able to establish their domination and take the supreme control of affairs into their own hands. While recording these momentous events the historians of the 18th century seem to be sharply divided in their attitude to the selection of facts and their interpretation. A set of writers bitterly criticised the Sayyid brothers for their misdeeds; others, on the contrary, lay the entire responsibility for all the evils of the government on the shoulders of Farrukh Siyar. The Sayyid brothers are referred to in disparaging terms for their acts of insubordination, inordinate ambition for power, and their indifference to the actual discharge of administrative duties.[31] In like manner, Farrukh Siyar is accused of his feeble and fickle policies in dealing with the all-powerful ministers.[32]

Khafi Khan explicitly states that Farrukh Siyar committed a serious mistake in conferring the highest civil and military posts on Sayyid Abdullah and Husain Ali who were untrained and inexperienced in administrative matters.[33] On the other hand, Qasim Lahori, who calls himself a slave of the Sadaat, manifests enthusiastic partiality towards the Sayyids and holds the Emperor responsible for driving the Sayyids to desperation by his breach of faith and intrigues against them.[34] Mirza Muhammad[35] and Shafi Warid[36] allege that nobles like Mir Jumla, a Mughal, and Khan-i-Dauran, an Indian born Muslim, having become jealous of the rise of the Sayyids to power, resolved to preserve their privileges by means of backstage intrigues. These nobles instigated the Emperor against the *Wazir* and the *Mir Bakhshi,* and thus fomented strife at the court.

Yahya Khan, the *Mir Munshi* of Farrukh Siyar, adds other factors which contributed to the widening of the rift between the king and his ministers. He writes that, apart from the dispute over

[30] Kamraj. *Ibrat-nama*. f. 54b.

[31] *Ahwal-ul-Khawaqin*, f. 77a ; *Tarikh-i-Shahadat-i-Farrukh Siyar wa Julus-i-Muhammad Shah*, f. 42a.

[32] Mirza Muhammad, *Ibrat-nama*, ff. 102–3 ; Mir Qasim Lahori, *Tarikh-i-Saltanat-i-Farrukh Siyar*, B.M. MS. f. 62a.

[33] *Muntakhab-ul-Lubab*. 738.

[34] *Tarikh-i-Saltanat-i-Farrukh Siyar*, ff. 1b, 2a, 66b.

[35] Mirza Muhammad, *Ibrat-nama*, f. 30.

[36] *Mirat-i-Waridat*, 505.

appointments to the posts of *wizarat*, *sadarat*, and *diwan*. Farrukh Siyar expressly disapproved of the introduction of *Ijaradari*, and abolition of the *Jiziya*.[37] Muhammad Ashub surveys the whole situation from a sectarian point of view. He ascribes the cause of the conflict to an outstanding hostility between the Mughals and the Sadaat of Barha. According to him, the Sayyids monopolized all higher public employments, and the Mughals, the backbone of the Empire, faced unemployment and economic distress.[38]

Rustam Ali Khan, author of the *Tarikh-i-Hindi*, a highly summarised and condensed work, glorifies the spectacular feats of gallantry performed by Husain Ali Khan. His acts of generosity and liberal patronage to saints and men of letters are also praised.[39] But Ashub prefers to ignore these achievements and virtues of Husain Ali Khan. He takes pains to bring forth the vices of his character.[40] Worthy of note is the fact that nearly all historians fail to reveal the underlying pattern of Husain Ali's conciliatory policy towards the Marathas, Rajputs and Jats. They betray a spirit of prejudice against the Sayyids and misrepresent their methods of dealing with the *zamindars* and the regional leaders. True, their system of alliances with the local potentates was envisaged to isolate Farrukh Siyar, but this indirectly contributed to make the royal authority paramount in areas where disorders on a wide-scale prevailed.

The disgraceful deposition of Farrukh Siyar and his cruel treatment raised a storm of anger against the Sayyids. Not only the discontented nobles felt indignant at the wrongs done to the king, but the humble ranks of the society were also stirred to wrath.[41] The victorious ministers dishonoured the Mughal throne, filled public posts with their relations and adherents and inflicted severities on the person of the fallen monarch. Even those historians who had, hitherto, justified the stand of the Sayyids suddenly changed their attitude and used harsh language in condemning them for these wicked acts. This is particularly true of Mir Qasim Lahori[42] and Muhammad

[37] *Tazkirat-ul-Muluk*, ff. 122, 124.

[38] *Tarikh-i-Shahadat-i-Farrukh-Siyar wa Julus-i-Muhammad Shah*, ff. 70a, 43.

[39] *Tarikh-i-Hindi*, 772.

[40] *Tarikh-i-Saltanat-i Farrukh Siyur wa Julus-i-Muhammad Shah*, ff. 38, 42–43.

[41] *Shah-nama-i-Munawwar Klam*, f. 31b.

[42] *Tarikh-i-Saltanat-i-Farrukh Siyar*, ff. 76–77, 80.

Qasim Aurangabadi.[43] In contradiction to their earlier observations in regard to the irresolute and weak-kneed policy of Farrukh Siyar these writers now censure the methods followed by the Sayyids.

(*ii*) Another significant issue on which the narrators of these events differ from one another, is the bitter struggle for supremacy between the Sayyids and the Mughals. For an understanding of the origin, scope and nature of the clash of interests between the two groups of the ruling party, it is necessary to explain the historian's group alignments, his associations and source of inspiration which influenced his views. Most of the works were written either under the patronage of Muhammad Shah or the Nizam-ul-Mulk, the acknowledged leader of the Mughals. For instance Khafi Khan completed his work in the reign of Muhammad Shah and served for a long time under the Nizam-ul-Mulk. Muhammad Bakhsh Ashub was a Mughal, and he represents the Mughal view point in interpreting the scramble for power. Muhammad Qasim Aurangabadi, Ahsan Ijad, Yusuf Muhammad Khan, Munim Khan Aurangabadi,[44] Mansa Ram and others compiled their chronicles when the Nizam-ul-Mulk was at the zenith of his power.

These writers, as employees of the government in the Deccan, were bound by strong ties of personal loyalty to the Nizam-ul-Mulk who patronised and encouraged them. The Sayyids have few historians to advocate their case. Rustam Ali Khan and Ghulam Husain Tabatabai[45] might be included in this list of the Sayyids' supporters. Reflecting on these divergent opinions, Khafi Khan writes : 'In the times of Farrukh Siyar men have shown a partiality or animosity to one side or the other exceeding all bounds. They have looked to their own profit and loss, and turned the reins of their imagination accordingly. The virtues of one side they have turned into faults, while they have shut their eyes to the faults of the others.'[46]

Khafi Khan, in spite of his tall claims to honesty and frankness in recording events, could not conceal his sympathies for the Nizam-

[43] *Ahwal-ul-Khawaqin*, 88a, 145b, 152.

[44] Munim Khan Aurangabadi, *Sawana-i-Deccan*, Central Record Office Hyderabad MS.

[45] Ghulam Hussain Tabatabai, *Siyar-ul-Mutaakhkhirin*, (text), Calcu. II, 1836, 21-22, 30, 37-39.

[46] *Muntakhab-ul-Lubab*, 726.

ul-Mulk. He tries to gloss over the faults of his patron and finds faults with his enemies. He holds that the Nizam-ul-Mulk was averse to the idea of calling the Sayyid brothers as *namak-ba-haram* and *haram-namak*.[47] But the Nizam-ul-Mulk himself used these abusive terms for the two brothers in each and every *arzdasht* and letter he sent to the Emperor, and to his friends and subordinates.'[48]

(*iii*) The historians by no means agree whether Nadir Shah invaded India in 1738 on the invitations of Saadat Khan and the Nizam-ul-Mulk or it was Khan-i-Dauran who mishandled the situation and showed gross negligence in making preparations to stem the tide of Persian aggression. The anonymous writer of the *Risala-i-Muhammad Shah wa Khan-i-Dauran* and the author of the *Jauhar-i-Samsam* openly accuse the two leading Mughal nobles of treasonable attempts to invite the foreign invader and upset the established order of the country.[49] These allegations are contradicted by Ashub and Anand Ram Mukhlis who blame Khan-i-Dauran for his failure to support financially the governors of Kabul and Lahore in building up the defences of the North-West frontier. His policy of indifference towards Nasir Khan and Zakarya Khan produced an atmosphere of complacency and apathy, lulled the Emperor into a false sense of security, and aborted the efforts of government officials to meet the challenge of foreign invasion.[50]

[47] *Muntakhab-ul-Lubab*, 940. Khafi Khan was employed *faujdar* and *amin* in the *khalisa mahal* of Mustafabad in the Deccan. This *mahal* had been destroyed by the officers of the *Subedar* of Barhanpur ; the *raiyyiat* had fled away and cultivation stopped. Khafi Khan laboured zealously for the rehabilitation of the *mahal* and spend money in recruiting soldiers for the collection of revenue. In 1718 Husain Ali Khan, governor of the Deccan, decided to march to Delhi where his presence was urgently needed as new conflicts between Sayyed Abdullah Khan, the *Wazir*, and Farrukh Siyar, brought matters to a head. Hussain Ali Khan demanded twenty thousand rupees from Khafi Khan in order to meet the cost of his artillery. As the harvest time of *kharif* crop had not reached, Khafi Khan failed to deposit the required money. The governor collected money from other sources and dismissed the historian. Perhaps this loss of post he had obtained after surmounting serious difficulties rankled in the mind of Khafi Khan and made him biased against Husain Ali Khan, Vol II, 798.

[48] *Munshat-i-Musavi Khan*, ff. 48, 51.

[49] *Risala-i-Muhammad Shah wa Khan-i-Dauran*, Anonymous, B.M. MS. ff. 100, 103–105 ; Muhammad Muhsin, *Jauhar-i-Samsam*, B.M. MS. or 1898, Elliot and Dowson, Vol. VIII, 75.

[50] Anand Ram Mukhlis, *Tazkira*, Aligarh MS. ff. 119–20 ; *Tarikh-i-Shahadat-i-Farrukh Siyar wa Julus-i-Muhammad Shah*, ff. 162–64.

The *Risala-i-Muhammad Shah wa Khan-i-Dauran*, and the *Jauhar-i-Samsam* were written in a colourful and exaggerated style, and the avowed object of their authors seems to be exalt the status of Khan-i-Dauran, their patron. They bitterly criticise the role of his opponents, the Nizam-ul-Mulk and Saadat Khan, at the battlefield of Karnal. Anand Ram Mukhlis, *Diwan* of Qamr-ud-Din Khan, the *Wazir* and nephew of Nizam-ul-Mulk, and Ashub, a staunch champion of the Mughal cause, cast aspersions on the *Mir Bakhshi* and hold him responsible for the disastrous consequences of the foreign invasion. In view of mutual animosities among the nobles these statements of the historians should be submitted to a careful examination. There is no evidence, direct or circumstantial, to substantiate the charges of treason against Saadat Khan and the Nizam-ul-Mulk.

The historical literature of the eighteenth century is so extensive that it is not possible to analyse it fully in a single paper. However, this literature should not be evalued by the modern standards of historiography. The historians recorded what happened without going beneath the surface of things. What a historian could not explain or wanted to conceal on grounds of expediency, he attributed it to chance or the Divine will by saying that only God knew the reality of the case. Reflecting on rumours that Sayyid Abdullah Khan was poisoned to death at the instigation of the Nizam-ul-Mulk, Khafi Khan tried to defend the position of his patron. Without going deep into the matter and investigating the truth, he concluded that God alone knew the reality. These writers were the products of their age and mirrored in their writings the attitudes and traditions of the governing class which exercised a determining influence on the political developments of the period.

14

Muhammad Qasim and Khafi Khan

Muhammad Qasim and Khafi Khan are the two historians of the sixteenth century, a period characterised by feverished political activity, court intrigues and conspiracies, factional politics and changing loyalties of nobles and groups and, above all, the rapid political and economic decline of the Mughal empire.

Muhammad Qasim and Khafi Khan study this historical scene from two different angles, and a comparative study of their outlooks, attitudes, and prejudices, methods of collecting and representing the data can help us in forming an estimate of the historical writings of the eighteenth century.

Little is known about Muhammad Qasim in the contemporary literature. He was, perhaps, not well known as a scholar or a historian. He himself informs us that he was for sometime with the sons of Shah Alam (Bahadur Shah) in Bihar, where he was assigned the duties of attending on Ali Tabar and Bedar, the nephews of the Emperor. He served them well and won their favour. In consequence, they promised him high office in case any of them became Emperor of Hindustan.

Muhammad Qasim availed several opportunities to meet the Amir-ul-Umara, Husain Ali Khan, at Aurangabad, where he had gone to participate in the marriage ceremony of his own son. However, he was much disgusted owing to the former's arrogance.

Subsequently, he became *Bakhshi* in the army of the Nizam-ul-Mulk and served him while he was engaged against the Marathas. He enjoyed the favours and confidence of the Nizam-ul-Mulk and participated in his literary assemblies. The information supplied by him in the *Ahwal-ul-Khawaqin* is, thus, based on personal observation. He also cultivated *an intimate friendship* with Mulawassil Khan (d. 1158/1743–44), the Nizam-ul-Mulk's son-in-law, and the

Faujdar of Baglana.

The *Ahwal-ul-Khawaqin* is a history of Aurangzeb's successors upto 1151/1738–39 which is also the date of its completion. It is divided into two parts. The first part, which deals from the reign of Aurangzeb to Farrukh Siyar's deposition, was completed on 2nd Ramazan, 1147/1734–35. The second, which begins with the accession of Rafi-ud-Darjat, has been mainly devoted to the Nizam-ul-Mulk's conflicts with the Sayyid Brothers and his wars with the Marathas and ends in the year 1151/1738–39 before Nadir Shah's invasion.

Muhammad Hashim Khafi Khan, author of the *Muntakhab-ul-Lubab,* belonged to a respectable family of Delhi. His father, Khwaja Mir, also a historian, was an officer of high rank in the service of Prince Murad Bakhsh and later on under Aurangzeb. Khafi Khan grew up in Aurangzeb's service, and was employed by him for political and military affairs. In the reign of Farrukh Siyar, he was made *Diwan* by the Nizam-ul-Mulk.

The *Muntakhab-ul-Lubab* is a highly esteemed history, commencing with the invasion of Babur and ending with the fourteenth year of Muhammad Shah's reign. Since Aurangzeb had prohibited the recording of the events of his time, Khafi Khan completed a minute register of all the happenings of the period and published it after the Emperor's death. His work is very valuable as it contains an account of the entire reign of Aurangzeb.

Khafi Khan was Shia,[1] and therefore, showed partiality towards the Shia nobles in his work. He was prejudiced against the Turani nobles, excluding the Nizam-ul-Mulk, whom he was serving and for whom he is full of praise. Owing to this partiality he is sometimes nicknamed *Nizam-ul-Mulki.*

Khafi Khan informs us about the methods and principles which he has followed in compiling his work. He says that it is obligatory on a historian to be truthful. He should rise above all hope of reward and fear of harm. He traces the beginnings of partiality in historical writings to the reign of Farrukh Siyar, when interested people took advantage of the situation and got partial accounts prepared in which mutual jealousies determined the assessment of events. Such people considered only their interests and discarded the requirements of truth. The good qualities of the opposite groups

[1] C. A. Story, *Persian Literature,* Section 11, 464.

were represented as vices, and the vices of the party to which they themselves belonged were depicted as virtues. Khafi Khan then refers to his own approach and method of dealing with the subject.

'I have neither supported friends nor condemned the enemies for fear of harm. I have not followed anything particularly to please any *wazir* or *amir*. I have recorded whatever I myself have witnessed or heard from those persons who had access to the assemblies of Farrukh Siyar and the Sayyid Brothers and had full knowledge of their activities. After making a thorough investigation about the sifting of information received from different sources, I have recorded whatever seemed to me the truth.'[2]

It would appear from the above that both Muhammad Qasim and Khafi Khan were in the service of the Nizam-ul-Mulk and had, to that extent, identical backgrounds. In their works, they have dealt besides other things, with the contemporary political scene. Khafi Khan begins his narrative from the establishment of the Mughal Empire to the fourteenth regnal year of Muhammad Shah. Muhammad Qasim surveys the political developments from the death of Aurangzeb to his own day. In their historical approach, representation of data, analysis of situations, they differ on many vital points. To Khafi Khan history connoted a catalogue of events, neatly presented in chronological sequence. Muhammad Qasim believed in analysing situations, discovering casual connections and tracing the sources of all troubles to the political atmosphere of the court. Muhammad Qasim concentrates his attention on the court and considers it the basis of all troubles. He goes into details about the life of the emperors, the palace intrigues, the cliques of the court, and their repercussion on the life of the people and the administration in general. Khafi Khan nowhere puts his fingers specifically on the role of the Mughal Emperors in accelerating the pace of political disintegration and administrative chaos. To him history is merely a jumble of facts without any co-ordination and coherence.

Holding the emperors responsible for the chaos and confusion that prevailed in the country Muhammad Qasim says :

'The king is sitting like a woman within the four walls (of the palace). If the kings follow the manners of women and act on what

[2] Khafi Khan, *Muntakhab-ul-Luhab*, Vol II, 727-37, Bib. Ind., Calcutta, 1874.

the effiminate say, then it is the more necessary that the Muslims should take up the path leading to Mecca and Madina, and if they do not have travelling expenses, in that case, they should, it is better, commit suicide by taking poison.'[3]

Here he strikes a note of extreme anguish and despair and gives us an idea of the extreme helplessness of the people.

Muhammad Qasim analysed the character of the nobility more thoroughly than any other contemporary writer, including Khafi Khan. He finds the nobles of the period, in general, disloyal, treacherous and hypocritical. Their loyalty was skin deep and they could change sides without any qualms of conscience. He says that the nobles of the period not merely lacked in statesmenship but also in courage, which had been a distinguishing feature of the nobility during the earlier period. Muhammad Qasim thought that the source of all confusion, dissensions and instability in society lay in the court conflicts and intrigues which filtered down from the palace to the huts and surcharged the atmosphere with conflicts and tensions. He writes :

'A king whose nobles are at daggers drawn with one another and are thirsty for one another's blood cannot survive long. It is incumbent on the kings to abstain from the pursuit of luxuries. They should devote their time in attending to state affairs. Every matter of the state, whether significant or insignificant, should be personally looked into by them. They should not allow themselves to be governed by any noble. Merit and ability should be the criterion for their appointments and promotions, and not sycophancy. He should not take into account whether one is loyal or disloyal to the person of the king; belongs to this group or that group. Then only is it possible that the kings can escape the misfortunes and calamities which follow in the wake of court intrigues and conspiracies of the sycophants.'[4]

Muhammad Qasim also elucidates the functions of the kings which they had given up and had consequently brought untold miseries on themselves and their peoples on the one hand and disintegration of the state on the other. He observes :

'It is all the more necessary for the emperors to keep themselves

[3] Muhammad Qasim Aurangabadi, *Ahwal-ul-Khawaqin*, (British Museum Rotograph in the Aligarh Muslim University), f. 196 b.

[4] *Ahwal-ul-Khawaqin*, ff. 74a–75a.

busy (with administrative affairs), and should not waste it in trifling matters. Especially, he should devote more time to the pursuits of a soldier and reading of books on history, and should not deviate an inch from this dictum; for from such exercises the soldiers draw inspiration. It also increases the strength and stability of the army. The work of ten men cannot be expected to be done by one man. By reading history, a man gets access to past experiences and problems, and to the valuable measures of the (preceding emperors). For there exists animosity between loyalty on the one hand, and wealth, dignity, honour and high status on the other. These things are not bad so long as one does not assume the royal airs. In case he takes the path of arrogance and error, God Himself will punish him. He should not give up justice and equity as they are the sources of perpetual bliss, and should not allow wicked ideas to enter his heart.'[5]

Muhammad Qasim has also thrown valuable light on the causes of the conflicts and tussles between the old nobles and the new from the time of Jahandar Shah. Khafi Khan tells us only about the division of the nobles into two groups—the Turanis and Iranis. Muhammad Qasim, however, divides the nobility and their conflicts into the old respected Mughal aristocracy and the new classes of upstarts whom he calls *nau-daulatan* (upstarts). He says :

'Those whosoever they may be, acted on the advice of the black-faced, blockheaded sycophants, and tale bearers, they had to lose both *din* (religion) and *duniya* (country). Do we not see how many states and (administrative institutions) have been ruined due to these wicked scandal mongers ? They ruin the *fasal* (crops) of the Emperor for the prosperity of their *khirman* (the place where the crops are amassed after harvest).'[6]

According to Khafi Khan the conflicts of the period could be explained only in terms of the conflicts of the Iranis (Shias) and the Turanis (Sunnis). But in Muhammad Qasim's opinion it was a class of newly promoted people from obscurity and poor social backgrounds that had upset the political equilibrium. To support his thesis he gives the following example :

After being appointed *Wazir*, the Nizam-ul-Mulk, who was well acquainted with the administrative lacunae, pointed out to Muham-

[5] *Ibid.*, ff. 105 ab.

[6] *Ibid.*, f. 183a.

mad Shah certain measures to be taken to remove all those abuses which were sapping the very foundations of the state and bring about efficiency and order in administrative and financial departments. But the upstarts strongly and stubbornly opposed all attempts at reform. Muhammad Qasim critically examines the nature and the reasons for such opposition. He writes :

'How could they reconcile themselves to ride an ass instead of a horse ? The *nau-daulatan*, who suffered from over self complacency owing to their inferiority complex, though they had not even seen a donkey in a picture or on the screen, had all of a sudden become owners of horses, wealth and social status. How this group could tolerate any decrease in their *mansabs* and how could they reconcile themselves to ride an ass instead of a horse ?"[7]

Khafi Khan, however, gives a different picture of divided loyalties for he had connections with the Nizam-ul-Mulk and he had respect for the Sayyid Brothers. His attachment to the Sayyids was to some extent due to common religious affiliations. He, therefore, blames the Turani Party in order to justify the actions of the Sayyid Brothers. The circumstances under which the Nizam-ul-Mulk left for the Deccan have been discussed by both Muhammad Qasim and Khafi Khan. The reasons given by Khafi Khan give an entirely different background to the Nizam-ul-Mulk's decision to quit the north. The account leaves upon one's mind the impression that Khafi Khan was anxious to justify that the Nizam-ul-Mulk's continued presence in the north was not in the interest of the people. He says that there were several reasons which led to an estrangement between the *Wazir* and the Emperor Muhammad Shah. These reasons are :

(1) It was during this period that the Mughal Court received the news that there was political unrest in Persia, and Mahmud Khan, the Afghan, had overpowered Sultan Husain Shah and had imprisoned him. He had annexed a considerable part of Persia and brought untold miseries on the people. The Nizam-ul-Mulk recalled before Muhammad Shah all the past events, when the Sultans of Persia had rendered great service to Babur and Humayun. He advised the Emperor to send his forces to help the Shah of Persia. He offered his services for this purpose. But when the Emperor consulted his upstart advisers, they imputed motives to the Nizam-ul-Mulk, and thus the scheme of sending the forces to Persia was

[7] *Ibid.*

dropped.

(2) The Nizam-ul-Mulk advised the Emperor to abolish the *ijaradari* system and revoke the assignment of *jagirs* in the *Khalisa*. This proposal was also rejected.

(3) He advised the Emperor to stop the acceptance of presents in his name by his favourites, as it brought bad name to him. But the practice was not stopped.

(4) He desired the Emperor to agree to the re-imposition of the *Jiziya*, but the Emperor did not pay any heed to this proposal.[8]

On the other hand, Muhammad Qasim gives us an entirely different version. He says : 'It is said that once Muhammad Shah suggested to the Nizam-ul-Mulk to give up his claims over the Deccan. But how could the Nizam-ul-Mulk frankly say in the face of the Emperor that he had conquered that area by his sword, and therefore the emperor should leave it to his humble servant.' Instead he said : 'As Your Majesty desires.' But he was shocked and fell into a vortex of worries, and he argued with himself that the post of the *wizarat* was insignificant and meaningless if it could be retained at the cost of the Deccan, and besides, no one could say how long he would continue in that post. 'In case the Deccan slips away from my grip, I will be nowhere,' he said to himself and resorted to diplomatic tricks and stratagem and withdrew from the court and returned to the Deccan.[9]

Two or three incidents may be considered in order to bring the difference in the approach of Khafi Khan and Muhammad Qasim to the conflicting nature of data supplied by them regarding the death of Farrukh Siyar. The account of these two contemporary writers are basically different. They agree only in saying that Farrukh Siyar was seized in a most cruel and atrocious manner, but the two accounts vary in so far as the subsequent treatment of the Emperor by the Sayyid Brothers is concerned.

Muhammad Qasim says that immediately after his imprisonment, Farrukh Siyar was put to death by the Sayyids. Khafi Khan makes a subtle attempt to create an atmosphere in which the murder of Farrukh Siyar becomes inevitable and leads to a logical culmination of the tragedy. He says that during his imprisonment. Farrukh Siyar made an attempt to escape from the prison by offering bribes

[8] *Muntakhab-ul-Lubab*, 11, 947–49 ; 974–78.

[9] *Ahwal-ul-Khawaqin*, f. 186a.

to persons in whose custody he was placed. He offered a *mansab* of 7000 to Abdullah Khan, if he successfully manoeuvred his escape from the prison and took him to Raja Jai Singh Sawai, with whose help, he thought, he would be able to re-establish himself.

The circumstances leading to the death of Rafi-ud-Daula and Rafi-ud-Darjat are similarly a moot point. Khafi Khan says that they died a natural death. Muhammad Qasim, on the other hand, says that their death was the result of slow poisoning. He gives several reasons which motivated the Sayyid Brothers to perpetrate the crime.

1. As both of the Princes were devoid of wisdom, lacked valour and were illiterate, the Sayyid Brothers found that they could not carry on the administration, as they desired. In consequence they removed them by slow poisoning.

2. Till then they had achieved success in all matters, but now they feared lest any discomfiture should befall on them and disgrace them. So, the Princes were removed.

3. From Muhammad Qasim's account it appears that public opinion had played a very significant role in the politics of the period. The Sayyids feared that in case they murdered the Princes either openly or in secret, this would cause great resentment and commotion among the people, and in consequence they would fail to achieve their aims. They presumed that when no one in the line of Timur would be left alive, they would automatically occupy the throne. They made the following arrangement : Qutb-ul-Mulk was to govern northern India and the Amir-ul-Umara was to administer the Deccan and Malwa, with two different headquarters, as two independent Emperors. The authors make us believe that the Sayyid Brothers desired to destroy the race of Timur and occupy the Mughal throne.[10] Similar is the case with the accounts of the two historians regarding the assassination of Husain Ali Khan.[11]

CONCLUSION

Both Muhammad Qasim and Khafi Khan have critically examined the factors leading to the decay of the Mughal Empire. Both agree that court factionalism was the main cause of this decay. We find that Muhammad Qasim holds the Sayyid Brothers responsible

[10] *Ibid.*, f. 172a.

[11] *Ibid.*, ff. 176a–b ; *Muntakhab-ul-Lubab*, II, 904–09.

for the murder of the Emperor Farrukh Siyar and Khafi Khan agrees with the version. But while Muhammad Qasim explains in full the motives of the Sayyid Brothers in causing the death of Rafi-ud-Darjat and Rafi-ud-Daula through slow poisoning, Khafi Khan states that it was due to natural death.

Muhammad Qasim has, instead of giving details of wars etc., picked up only those problems which were adversely affecting the Mughal ruler and integrity of the state, and has suggested in detail, more than once, the measures and steps to be taken by the emperors to check the disintegrating forces. He is more critical, outspoken and has highlighted the intrigues, conspiracies and factional politics in the court and, above all, the rapid political and economic decline of the Mughal Empire. Khafi Khan, on the other hand, following the traditional style of writing history, has devoted himself more in describing the minutest details of wars and compaigns. He has avoided making suggestions to cure the malaise that was eating into the very vitals of the Mughal body politic.

A comparative study of these two contemporary authorities on the history of the Mughal Empire during its later years shows that the political conflicts and faction feuds had influenced the approach of the historians. Being a contemporary to a certain event or age is, therefore, not enough; the prejudices emanating from the social, political and religious sources have to be analysed in order to make a correct appraisal of the political developments during the eighteenth century. It is then that the authenticity or value of a historian's statement can be determined for reconstructing the history of the period.

15

Writings in Rajasthan and Gujarat

The early British and European scholars who directed their attention to the study of the medieval period of Indian history, (by which term they understood the period under Muslim rule only) based their studies almost wholly on Persian chronicles. The scope of these chronicles, which comprised the bulk of this body of source material, was extremely limited, in as much as their authors were mainly interested in recording primarily the lives and activities, the deeds and misdeeds, of rulers and conquerors alone. In their view it was not the business of history to take notice of the common masses, or of the various facets of the rise and progress of human society. These chronicles, however, admirably answered the purpose of the above mentioned western writers whose conception of history was not very different from that of the Persian chroniclers. Consequently history writing remained extremely limited in scope. No wonder that the picture of society which it presented remained extremely incomplete and lopsided.

But the view that India possessed no national history nor any historical compositions worth the name persisted despite the well-merited rebuke administered by Tod as early as the early thirties of the last century.[1] Apart from other reasons for the paucity of chronological works like those found mostly in Persian, Tod also had very aptly pointed out that to 'expect from a people like the Hindus a species of compositions of precisely the same character as the historical works of Greece and Rome' would be 'to commit the egregious error' of forgetting the peculiar tradition born of the outlook and attitude of the Hindus in respect of all their literary productions. Tod was not alone in giving this warning to students of Indian history and culture. Eminent scholars and savants like

[1] See Tod's Introduction to *Annals and Antiquities of Rajasthan*.

G. Buhler, Bhau Daji, Bhagwan Lal Indraji, Sir Aurel Stein, A. K. Forbes, L. P. Tessitory and others also from time to time drew attention to the fallacious notion that there was almost complete absence of historical literature in the pre-Muslim Indian literature of India.

Tod was followed by a band of scholars, like Kaviraj Shyamaldas, Bhau Daji, Bhagwan Lal Indraji, G.H. Ojha and others, whose writings should have served to dispel the popular idea of lack of historical literature in Samskrit, Hindi and other languages of the country. But during the last century an increasing amount of historical source-material has come to light which covers a far wider field than that to which the Persian historiographers generally confine their writings. This type of historical material which is literally bestrewn all over Rajasthan (and Gujarat and Malwa too), both in public and private collections, affords a wealth of information on the various aspects of the life of the people, their social traditions, their beliefs and institutions, their progress in the economic, industrial and commercial spheres, no less than on their unrivalled achievements in the fields of literature and sciences, both physical and super-physical, which is what mattered most in the context of the Indian historical process.

Simultaneously with the growing zeal for the discovery and preservation of these treasures, several institutions have been doing admirable service by bringing out learned and critically annotated editions of a large number of literary and historical works in Samskrit and other languages which have from time to time been the media of early writings. But with the brilliant and perhaps the single exception of the great Italian savant, Dr. L.P. Tessitory, no systematic attempt was made before, or since, to classify and catalogue the existing materials. But even Tessitory covered a limited field. A survey recently carried out in Rajasthan with this object in view, revealed the existence of hundreds of collections of manuscripts and other valuable materials. We may in passing also refer here to the very plentiful epigraphical material which continues to be enriched by the new discoveries made by the Department of Archaeology and other agencies engaged in this field. For the early medieval period, pertaining specially to Gujarat, the most outstanding name is that of G. Buhler, a polyhistor and scholar of stupendous learning who rendered invaluable service in the search and recovery of a large number of historical works and, indeed, laid the foundations of Indological Studies on a solid basis in Western India. He was followed by Bhau Daji of Sawantwadi and Bhagwan Lal Indraji, a Gujarati scholar.

During the last three quarters of a century the materials for the later period have been utitised by just a handful of scholars. After Tod, the pioneer work in this field was done by Kaviraj Shyamaldas, court poet of Maharana Sajjan Singh (1874–1884) of Mewar. Kaviraj Shyamaldas in his monumental history, entitled *Vir Vinod* which runs into nearly 2800 pages, has covered a very wide field of the history and geography of the whole of Rajasthan. The author has also brought together a large amount of statistical material on the political, economic and administrative aspects of Rajasthan. He has also given copies of many inscriptions as well as *farmans* etc., of the Mughal kings. Thus this great work will ever remain a standard work of reference on the political history of Rajasthan. Two other outstanding names among the modern historians of Rajasthan are G.H. Ojha and Harbilas Sarda. Ojha's work is literally of stupendous proportions. Besides his histories of Mewar, Marwar, Sirohi and other states of Rajasthan, Ojha's contribution to the cultural history of medieval India is extremely valuable. He wrote a large number of essays (*nibandhas*) which have been collected and published in several volumes. But his lectures on medieval Indian culture—*madhyakalin Bhartiya Sanskriti*—delivered under the auspices of the Hindustani Academy, Allahabad (1928), constitute perhaps the only comprehensive treatment of the subject. His most monumental contribution, however, to the study of ancient and medieval India is his *Bhartiya Prachin Lipimala* (The Paleography of India) (revised edn. 1918), the first book of its kind in Hindi or any other language. Harbilas Sarda, a versatile scholar and writer of note, made an exhaustive study of original Sanskrit and Hindi sources for his excellent history of Ajmer and his biographies of Ranas Kumbha, Sangram Singh and others. Following them an ever increasing number of scholars in the last couple of decades have turned their attention to these sources. Much creditable historical literature has been produced by Dr. Raghubir Singh, Prof. Dasrath Sarma, the Nahata brothers, and many others. The work done by these scholars has of late drawn the attention of younger researchers over a wider area to the urgency and importance of making use of this hitherto untapped source-material. It is gratifying to note, for instance, that a beginning in this direction has been made in the History Department of the Aligarh Muslim University, besides, of course, in the universities and other academic institutions in Rajasthan.

Nevertheless, what has so far been done is but a drop in the ocean, for a very large section of scholars, hidebound by outdated notions, both in respect of the time span of medieval India as well as the sources of its history, are still supremely ignorant of this body of source-material. This ignorance has also been responsible for the equally widely prevalent misconception that the age to which we give the name medieval was only the one covered by Muslim rule, that is to say, from about the 11th century to the middle of the 18th. The five or more centuries of our history preceding the 11th century, which constituted the seedbed of both the subsequent achievements as well as decline and decay of Indian society, are simply ignored as of no consequence and possessing no historical interest. This span of no less than half a millenium is dismissed as a historical vacuum. It is high time that those who have so far eschewed the study of the pre-Turkish period, and have confined themselves to Persian and foreign sources alone, denying themselves the profit to be derived from the vast wealth of indigenous material in the regional languages, acquainted themselves with Sanskrit, Hindi and its several sister languages to enable themselves to use the enormous amount of material extant in these languages. Our parochialism has naturally bred a cramped outlook and narrow vision in regard to the comprehension of our history and our heritage.

Besides a few monographs on the early ruling dynasties, such as the Gurjarapratiharas, Gahadwars, Chauhans, Chandels and Paramars, the most notable work on this period (early medieval India) was done by C. V. Vaidya and H. C. Ray[2]. But such is the dominance of deepseated traditional ideas and approach to the study of the so-called medieval age, that scarcely anything substantial has been done to carry further the new ground broken by Vaidya

[2] *History of Hindu Medieval India*, 3 Vols., and *Dynastic History of Northern India*, 2 Vols., both appeared in the 20s of the present century. In 1960 another scholarly work, *Socio-Economic History of Northern India* (1030–1194) by B. P. Mazumdar has come out. A few more monographs on the History Gahadvalas, Chandels, both in Hindi and English, have also appeared.

and Ray.

Comparative Values of Persian and non-Persian Sources. Among the many fashionable fictions relating to the medieval age and its sources which are widely current and accepted almost as axiomatic truths, and, which have greatly hindered historical enquiry and research, is the belief that Persian chronicles alone satisfy the standards of historical writing, while rarely does any such authentic or reliable historical work exist in the regional indigenous languages. Concerning the character and concept of historiography we have quoted Tod (*supra* para 2), to show that it would be a blunder to seek in Hindu literature the same pattern of historical writings as that of the Persian chroniclers, a large majority of whom never regarded any aspect of the life of the common people as worthy of being included in history. As a result, the bulk of the so-called Persian historical literature is loaded with jejune chronicles of the lives of the high and mighty. As regards their historical value, apart from many of them being sadly deficient in dates, what is far more important is the extreme unreliability of their narratives marred as they are, oftener than not, by their personal predilections, leading to *suggestio falsi* and *suppressio veri*, by their psychophancies and fanaticism and their likes and dislikes. These shortcomings of the chroniclers have provided to some scholars an easy excuse to reject what is unsuitable and to accept what is suitable to their preconceived purpose. On the other hand, the unquestioning and uncritical acceptance of the written word has resulted in the production of numerous works professing to be histories, but which on close scrutiny would appear to be more fiction than history. Thus the various shortcomings mentioned above are common to all classes of historical literature. The non-Persian historical literature, however, is in general marked by certain peculiarities which, of course, have their own merits as well as demerits. The first conspicuous characteristic of most of the Hindi (used in its wider sense) chronicles is that in their geneological lists they give not only the year and month of a significant event, such as birth, accession, death etc., of a person, but also the day, the hour and even the *pala*[3]. But this need not surprise any one who knows that a long standing custom with all those whose duty it was to keep such records, was to note all these minute details as a matter of sacred

[3] A *pala* is equal to 24 seconds.

obligation.

Another notable feature of a substantial body of this literature is that it throws light, directly or indirectly, on the various aspects of the life and achievements of the people. But many of the court histories and epigraphical records of the Rajput chiefs beat their Persian compeers hollow in the most ridiculous and impossible claims they make about the glorious achievements of their heroes. Nevertheless, there are many works more reliable and far richer in content, in Sanskrit, *Apabhramsha,* as well as in Hindi.

It has come to be well established by now that the dynastic lists contained in the Puranas such as Matsya, Vayu, Vishnu and Bhagwat, are quite authentic down to the Nanda, Maurya, Shunga, Kanva and Andhra dynasties. Thereafter although a small fraction of the enormous literary wealth of medieval India has survived, still a fairly large number of historical works come to light. We have said above that a large number of historical or semi-historical works were brought to light especially by the efforts of the celebrated German Scholar, G. Buhler and others—most of these are either *Charitas or Prabandhas, i.e.,* biographical sketches of Jain scholars or collections of historical legends. We give below the names of a few important historical works of the medieval period :

In his '*Life of Hemchandracharya*', Buhler (Eng. Tr. from original German by Mani Lal Patel), (Singhi Jain Series, No. 11, 1936) mentions the following *Prabandhas* :

Prabhavakacharitra, a collection of life-sketches of 22 Jain Acharyas, of Prabhachandra and Pradyumna Suri, (Circa 1250).

Prabandhachintamani of Merutunga, originally utilised by A. K. Forbes, in his Ras Mala (History of Gujarat) and translated into English by C. H. Tawney. Hindi translation by H. P. Dwivedi, (Singhi Jain Ser., 1929). This is a vast collection of historical legends which, according to Buhler, are of considerable historical value. The author Merutung of Vardhamanwa, Kathiawad completed it in 1305-06. The *Prabandhas* are stories of the lives of Jain saints and monks. Despite their legendry tone the *Prabandhas* do contain much that is corroborated by the inscriptions and other reliable sources (Buhler, *Life of Hemchandracharya,* p. 4).

Prabandh Kosh by Rajshekhar, a collection of the biographies of famous monks, poets and statesmen completed in Dhilli (Delhi) in

V. S. 1405 *i. e.*, 1348–49 A.D.

Kumarpalcharita, by Jinmandan Upadhyaya, completed in 1435–36 A.D.

There were three major biographies of king Kumarpal Chaulukya, all named Kumarpal Charit by three authors, viz., Jaisingh Suri, Charitra Sundar Gani and Jinmandanopadhyaya. But the renowned Jain Acharya Hemchandra made a compendium of more than a score biographies of King Kumarpal Chaulukya (b. 1092, accession 1142, d. 1173). This collection has been published under the title of *Kumarpal Charitra Sangraha* in the Singhi Jain Series (No. 41, 1956).

Hemchandracharya also wrote two more historical *kavyas* of the same name, *dvayashraya mahakavya*, one in Sanskrit and the other in Prakrit. The first gives a summary of the history of the Chaulukya dynasty, and the second contains an account of the life of Kumarpala.

Harsha Charit (S)[4] of Bana Bhatta, court poet of Emperor Harshavardhan.

Gaudvaho (Pr.) by Vakpatiraj (8th century) court poet of Yashovarman. Describes the conquest of Bengal by Yashovarman.

Navasahasankcharit (S), by Padma Gupta alias Parimal (Late 10th century). Life of Vakpati Munja, ruler of Malwa (975–995).

Bhoj Prabandh by Ballal—Early 11th century, contains an account of the administration of Raja Bhoja.

Vikramankdeva Charit (S)—Bilhana (Early twelfth century)—Life and times of king Vikramank, Chaulukya of Kalyani (1076–1126).

Rama Charit (S)—Sandhyakar Nandi (late 11th century). History of Rampal of Pal Dynasty of Bengal.

Rajatarangini (S) by Kalhana (1148–50)—History of Kashmir. The author says that in preparing his history he consulted as many as fourteen histories of Kashmir.

Rajatarangini (S) by Jonaraj, a contemporary of Sultan Zain-ul-Abidin of Kashmir (1411–1463), is continuation of Kalhana's work.

[4] 'S' stands for Sanskrit; and 'Pr.' for Prakrit.

Rajatarangini (S) by Jonaraja died in 1434, is Shrivara Pandit, pupil of Jonaraja, took up his teacher's unfinished work. Shrivara received patronage from Zain-ul-Abidin and his son and grandson, Haidar Shah and Husain Shah. Shrivara's history covers the period (1434–1479), up to the accession of Fath Shah.

4th Rajatarangini is the work of two authors, Prajyabhatta and Shuka. Shuka tells us that Prajyabhatta wrote a work called Rajavalipataka, which recorded the events up to the Kaliyuga 4589 *i.e.*, A. D. 1486. When Fath Shah was reigning. After this Shuka, who was a contemporary of Akbar, seems to have brought down the story of Kashmir to 1588, in which year, according to Abul Fazl, the *Rajatarangini* was presented to the Emperor when he first visited *Prithviraja Vijaya* (S)—Jayanak (Jairath), a Kashmiri, court poet of king Prithviraja Chauhan. Wrote his work sometime between 1178–1200. It is a reliable history of his patron.

Hammir madmardan (S)—Jaisingh Suri (12th century). Describes the war between Mohmmad Ghuri and Bhim II Chalukya.

Hammir mahakavya (S)—Nayachandra Suri. History of Hammirdeva of Ranthambhor who was defeated by Ala-ud-Din Khalji in 1298.

Vastupal Charit (S)—Jinaharsha Gani (13th century). Life of Mahamatya Vastupal, the wealthy merchant prince and minister of king Virdhawal of Dhavalakka (Dholka in Ahmedabad Dist.). Virdhaval was a feudatory of king Bhim II Chalukya of Anhilwada, Patan, in 13th century. (See Mahamatya Vastupal and his literary circle by B. J. Sandesan, (Bahadur Singh Memoirs, Ser. No. 3. 1953).

Mandalikmahakavya (S)—Gangadhar Pandit.

Most of these are in Sanskrit and some in Prakrit.

The above list comprises only a few of the historical and semi-historical works of the early medieval period. Almost all of them are concerned with north Indian history.

For the later period we have a large variety of historical literature which is divided under the following categories :

Abhilekh, Ilqabnama, Utpattigranth, Aitihasik, Tippan, Kursinama, Khyat, Gajjil, Charit, Jas, Janmpatri, Jivani, Tahqiqat, Daftar

Bahi, *Patta*, *Parwana*, *Ruqqa*, *Pattawali*, *Pidhiavali*, *Bat* or *Vart*, *Prashasti*, *Yad-dasht*, *Raso*, *Rasia* or *Rasa*, *Vigat*, *Vashavali* or *Bansavali*.

Besides these many terms signifying names of different classes of Government records were adopted from the Mughal administrative terminology, such as *awarija*, *parwana*, *rukka*, *sanad*, *siaha baqaya*, etc., all of which are preserved in Rajasthan archives at Bikaner.[5]

Finally, a few Sanskrit and Hindi works bearing on the history of the Mughal period may be mentioned with a view to drawing the attention of the students of history to the fact that these documents afford a wealth of data and information on those aspects which are generally ignored by Persian Chroniclers.

One of the most interesting and illuminating is a biography of a Jain saint, named Bhanuchandra Gani, who was a contemporary of the Emperor Akbar, by another Jain saint, Siddhichandra Upadhaya (published in the Singhi Jain Series). This is a most authentic and honest account as we know from the author's own confession.[6] Besides giving an account of the life of the saint, the author has given a most glowing account of the great Emperor and his numerous acts of social uplift and of the extraordinary qualities of the head and heart of the Emperor and of his great minister Abul Fazl. The author pays his homage to the versatile qualities of the Emperor in these words of profound appreciation : 'There is not a single art, not a single branch of knowledge, not a single act of boldness and strength which was not attempted by the young Emperor.'[7] The author is full of praise for the brilliance of intellect and wide range of knowledge of Abul Fazl, in whose company he had the opportunity to pass many years. He says : 'He (Abul Fazl) had gone through the ocean of the whole literature and he was the best among all men of learning. There is nothing in literature which was not seen or heard by him.'[8]

Another remarkable work which deserves notice is an autobiographical work by a rather extraordinary man named Banarsi

[5] For details see the author's *Descriptive Catalogue of Non-Persian Sources of Medieval Indian History*.

[6] 'Neither have I exaggerated out of arrogance nor have I underestimated out of meekness. Whatever actually happened has been described here.'

[7] p. VII.

[8] p. VII.

Das (1586–1643 A. D.) a contemporary of Akbar, Jahangir and Shahjahan. Born in a wealthy family of merchants of U. P., Banarsi Das went through many vicissitudes of fortune and was once reduced to utter penury. But he was also a poet of no mean parts. The most extraordinary trait however of this author's character is that in his autobiography (which is called Ardh-Kathanak, meaning half the story of his life because, when he wrote, in 1641, he was 55 years old, and expected to live the full span of five scores and ten although as ill-luck would have it, he died within two years, in 1643). Banarsi Das stands outside himself, as it were, and views the incidents of his life, no less his actions, with the perfect detachment of an observer and mirrors them with such conspicuous honesty and frankness that we are left simply amazed. He makes a clean confession of all the shady and puerile actions in which he had indulged, and of his living incognito as a penniless man at Agra. His memoir gives evidence on every page of that rarest of gifts, viz., to see ourselves as others see us and of having in ample measure that essential ingredient of humanity, the capacity to laugh at one's ownself. Incidentally he throws interesting light on conditions of trade and commerce, and on the security of roads and communications. He also furnishes first hand evidence of the extreme cheapness of necessaries of life, even in the capital of Agra.

Many more similar works can come to light if a proper and perseverant search is made. It may not be out of place here to stress the historical value of the writings, mostly poetical, of the large number of Hindu scholars and poets who were patronised by not only kings and emperors and provincial rulers, but also by nobles and other men of consequence.

It would suffice to mention only a couple of instances by way of illustration. Perhaps the most distinguished among the Hindu poets patronised by the great Akbar was Govind Bhatta, on whom the Emperor conferred the title *Akbaria-Kalidas.* From the writings of this poet, (which are generally prasastis or panegyrics) we learn of the generous and extensive encouragement given by the Mughals to the regeneration of Hindu culture through the medium of Sanskrit.[9] The name of Jagannath Panditraj is well known as the illustrious among the Hindu court poets of the 17th century. He was the recipient of great favours from Asaf Khan, as well as from the

[9] Cf. *Introducing India* (R.A. Soc. of Bengal; Monograph Part II), 84.

Emperor Shahjahan, and wrote *Asaf Vilas* in praise of his patron. The writings of these poets give us an insight into the trends of the so-called higher society, both Hindu and Muslim. They serve to reflect the confused and unsettled psychological state of the Muslim grandees on the one hand, and the sychophantic atmosphere of the later Mughal court on the other. But at the same time we may not fail to notice the closeness of different communities and the growth of a harmonious and healthy social fabric, oblivious of its sectional particularisms and differences, in contemporary Hindi literature, including the Hindi poetic efforts of some of the later Emperors. The *Nadirat-i-Shahi,* published by the Rampur State Library (1944), is a collection of Hindi (Hindustani) poems of Emperor Shah Alam II. The poems paint a lifelike picture of the social and religious life of the *darbar* and of the city people. We get here glimpes of how the emperor enjoyed the Hindu festivals like Holi and Diwali in the company of his Muslim and Hindu courtiers. We learn also about the many varieties of Musical instruments, fireworks, fruits and flowers, *nauroz,* wedding and birth day ceremonies and other festivities, in which both the communities joined with equal enthusiasm. The Emperor was so fond of Holi that he composed scores of beautiful couplets on Holi or Hori.

It is well-known that Shah Alam II was a most tragic figure among those who occupied the throne of the great Mughals. He gave most poignant expression to his pitiable and helpless state in a couplet which he addressed to Mahadji Sindhia when at the latter's call he discarded the British shelter at Allahabad and came over to Delhi.

A recent survey in some of the temples and other private collections of Rajasthan revealed the existence of manuscripts and other types of documents bearing upon economic, political, and social conditions, on art and architecture, weights and measures and a host of other interesting subjects. Above two hundred manuscripts and some printed rare works were selected and were utilised for preparing a model descriptive catalogue for the help and guidance of researchers. But the mass of such material in Rajasthan alone is so vast that it calls for immediate attention on the part of government and academic bodies so that it may be salvaged, preserved and suitably catalogued before it is destroyed by climate or neglect.

16

Sir Sayyid and Maulana Shibli

Sir Sayyid Ahmad Khan (1817–1898), the founder of the Aligarh movement, was remarkable in many respects; he was remarkable also in reviving the interest of his people in the Muslim past, both in India and abroad. This is clear from his preface to Shibli's *al-Mamun,* written in 1889. It is true that this did not represent something nostalgically romantic in his mode of thinking, but it is there and his academic pursuits, before he set out to launch his diversified reform activities, bear testimony to this. This trend assumed a concrete shape in Shibli (1857–1914), one of his close associates at Aligarh whose deep interest in literature, history and theology gave a definite direction and purpose to historiography in Urdu. This paper is an attempt to assess briefly their endeavours in the field.

Sir Sayyid Ahmad Khan was educated in the traditional manner. But he had imagination and initiative, and was a man of character and moral integrity. He decided against the wishes of his family and its spiritual guides (the people of the *Khanqah* of Shah Ghulam Ali) to enter British service. He was only twenty-one at the time. From then, till the great event of 1857, which proved a turning point in his life and career, his only activity of note was literary and academic. He had a keen interest in history and religion. He wrote treatises like the *Rah-i-Sunnat* and the *Kalmat-ul-Haqq* in the traditional style, which show that in the sphere of religious subjects he was still medieval and had not yet come under the influence of western liberalism. But in so far as history is concerned there are evidences to the effect that he was gradually being acquainted with western scholarship. There is no doubt that he was fully conscious of the happier days when Muslims had played an important role in the history and cultural development of India. His monumental work, the *Asar-us-Sanadid*, stands in support of this thesis. The preface of the book opens with the verse :

> *As naqsh o nigar-i dar o diwar-i shikastah*
> *Asar padid ast sanadid-i Ajam-ra.*

This indicates the depth of his feeling about the good old days when Muslim civilization in India was flourishing. It also shows a tendency in Sir Sayyid which impelled him to preserve what had been left behind, even in the form of relics, by the great caravan to which he himself belonged. This tendency in him, it seems, never died and we find the same note in his preface to Shibli's book *al-mamun*, in which he wrote :

> This is perfectly true that the nation which forgets or does not care to know the achievements of its great men, is the most unfortunate.[1]

But apart from this, the book also throws light upon Sir Sayyid's painstaking and planned scholarship. The first edition of the *Asar* appeared in 1847. This edition had certain defects. For example, the drawing of the monuments were complete, but the related inscriptions had remained incomplete, and were not correctly copied. The language of the book was ornamental and at places exaggerated. Sir Sayyid was aware of these shortcomings, and in the second edition publish in 1854 the final chapter consisting of an account of Delhi's poets, *ulama*, *sufis*, artists, etc., was omitted on the advice of Edward Thomas. In consequence of this, it became, a standard research work of history, both from the viewpoint of diction and pure academic pursuit. However, keeping the changed diction of the second edition apart, Dr. Habibullah's opinion about Sir Sayyid's writing of history seems, to a great extent, valid. He says : 'Traditions of the medieval Muslim historians impressed themselves even on original Urdu composition. This is evident in the earliest of such works—the *Asar-us-Sanadid* of Syed Ahmad Khan.... It is a descriptive account of the antiquities of Delhi—his native town—with drawings of the monuments, together with a chapter on the contemporary manners and society. Though not a narrative account of the past, yet its historical purpose is obvious, and it is clearly modelled on what Rosenthal classified as local history ...it is

[1] Shibli, *al-Mamun*, Qaumi Press, Lucknow, n.d., 1.

not impossible that Sayyid Ahmad Khan's urge to compile this account of Delhi was reinforced by two similar accounts of Agra (Akbarabad) written a few years earlier in Persian at the invitation of a British officer.... Such details usually formed part of almost all Persian histories and the *Tabaqat-i-Akbari* is a well-known example. An earlier writing of Ahmad Khan, *the Jam-i-Jam*, was in Persian (1839) and consists of a tabulated account of the period of reign, year of accession, birth and death, etc. of every Muslim king from Timur to Bahadur Shah, and is an obvious continuation of the *Taqwim* form of historiography.'[2] *Asar-us-Sanadid* also indicates its author's awareness about the importance of the use of source material in writing history. He has given a list of the original sources he used in preparing the *Asar*. From this it can be reasonably conjectured that, while making use of the relevant source books, he might have experienced difficulty in handling the neglected manuscripts and might have himself planned to edit and publish at least some of them. In 1855 he brought out the first lithographed edition of the *Ain-i-Akbari* of Abul Fazl, 'the text of which was based on a comparison of the texts available and to which valuable illustrations have been added. These two works (the *Asar* and the *Ain*) alone would entitle him to a high position among the scholars of the world.'[3] Later, in 1862, he edited Barani's *Tarik i-Firuz Shahi*, and in 1863–64 edited and published the *Tuzukh-i-Jahangiri*. All this was pioneer work which made the others realise the significance of western methodology in writing authentic histories. Particularly, Maulana Shibli seems to have been very much influenced by Sayyid's method and approach mainly based on 'the textual study of the original documents.'

Maulana Shibli was, however, a man of a different temperament. Like Sir Sayyid he had also been trained in the traditional learning of Islam and his knowledge of Islamic sciences and literature was deeper and wider than Sir Sayyid's. But Sir Sayyid was a realist and fully realized and understood the challenges of the modern age, while Shibli grew more and more idealistic and developed a sort of romanticism from which he never succeeded in weaning himself

[2] Habibullah, A. B. M., 'Historical writing in Urdu : A Survey of Tendencies' in *Historians of India, Pakistan and Ceylon* edited by C.H. Philips, London, 1961, 482–83.

[3] M. Mujeeb, *Indian Muslims*, London.

away. Unlike Sir Sayyid and Hali (1837—1914), he was not only interested in referring to the glorious past of Islam, but he worked out a programme of displaying it. 'He resuscitated and praised the great men of Muslim history and their times. A whole series of influential biographies of the Prophet, of great men of the early days of Islam and the flourishing 'Abbasi' Empire, of great theologians, and of the Iranian poets, reminded Muslims unforgettably of their great heritage.'[4] Besides, he also took upon himself the task of defending Islam and its great men, in which he succeeded considerably because of his vast knowledge, his painstaking researches and intelligent use of the relevant source material available to him. He was fully aware of what modern scholarship demanded of him, but his romanticism sometimes led him to resort to subjectivity and apologetics. However, he is perhaps the only Muslim historian of his time who has definite views about historiography. In the preface to his renowned work *al-Faruq*, he expresses a very high opinion of the early masters in the field of Muslim historiography, like Ibn Qutaiba (d. 276 A. H.), Waqidi (d. 230 A. H.), Al-Balazuri (d.279 A. H.), Tabari (d. 310 A. H.) and Masudi (d. 386 A. H.), but laments the degeneration of those who followed them since the beginning of the fifth century. He is very critical of all of them, with the exception of Ibn Khaldun (1332–1406) who, according to him, laid the foundation of the philosophy of history. He says that while writing history two things must be kept in view :

(1) All the events and conditions of a particular period, the history of which is being written, should be taken into account, *i.e.*, culture, social conditions, customs, morals and beliefs—everything should be given full weight.

(2) Attempt should be made to discover the chain of cause and effect in all the events.

He claims that in the early histories this methodology is missing. The reason is that early historians were generally unacquainted with philosophy and rational sciences ; they were also ignorant of the various sciences related to historical events. This, therefore, resulted in most cases in mere narration of political events battles, festivals and the rise and fall of dynasties. Moreover, there is another important point : To what extent the events generally described in history books are reliable ? There are two ways of

[4] W. C. Smith, *Modern Islam in India*, London, 1946, 43.

examining the events—*riwayat* and *dirayat*. The *riwayat* method, because of the full development of the sciences of *hadis* and *rijal* among the Muslims, has been critically and fully used by the early Muslim historiographers, but the *dirayat* method remained neglected. By *dirayat* he means, in brief, the application of common sense and reason in sifting the material and assessing the sources. He is also in favour of reasonable conjecture in interpreting the event in the light of the principle of causality but with moderation and caution, and here he finds fault with the European historians. As for language and diction, he is for simple narration of facts and advises to avoid all elegance of style.

These are the principles which should be, he says, followed while writing history. It was, however, unfortunate that he himself failed to adhere completely to these principles. Because of his traditional education, particularly his training in literature and scholastic theology, and the self-imposed task of defending and displaying the glories of Islamic civilization, 'history to him was mainly the history of intellectual and cultural development rather than of the political, social and material progress of human society.'[5] further, in *al-Mamun* he is apologetic and in *al-Faruq* subjective.

Shibli did not write much on Indian history, and here again there is a very salient point to note. He considered the world of Islam his *watan* and its history his national history. In his introduction to *al-Mamun* he says : 'A number of books on Indian history have been written, and the achievements of the Mughals and Timurids have been displayed in bright colours. But obviously the history of India is only a very small part of our national history.'[6] This is why he wrote abundantly about Islam and its heroes outside India. His monograph on Aurangzeb. *Aurangzeb Alamgir par ek Nazar*, is the only book that he wrote on Indian history. Besides this there are a few articles by him, for example, Gulbadan Begum's *Humayun-nama*, Jahangir's *Tuzuk*, Abdul Baqi's *Maasir-i Rahimi*, *Zebun-Nisa*, Musalmanon *ki Ilmi Betaassubi aur Hamare Hindu Bhayun ki Nasipasi* and *Hindustan men Islami Hukumat ke Tamaddun ka Asar*.

(1) *Aurangzeb Alamgir par ek Nazar*—This small book, one of the very few original works on Indian History in Urdu, is in defence

[5] Habibullah, *op. cit.*, 478.
[6] Shibli, *op. cit.*, Part I, 2.

of Aurangzeb, who has been, according to him, misrepresented and to whom great injustice has been done by the British historians and those who have blindly followed them. This is an original work and is based on authentic sources, of which he has made a reasonable use. His arguments are political in nature, but the religious bias is also obvious, and on the basis of the documents discovered later to which he did not have access one may refute him on a number of points. His criticism of the British authors like Elphinstone and Lane-poole is significant, as it represents his anti-British attitude which was due partly to his pan-Islamic ideas and partly to his difference with the Aligarh movement. In this book only certain controversial aspects and events have been examined and explained to show that the charges of intolerance and bad faith levelled against Aurangzeb are unjustified and Shiite historian and British writers have deliberately distorted the facts. The author, himself a Sunni Hanafi, in spite of his efforts to remain objective, has failed to remain impartial, because he seems to support Aurangzeb's religiosity his application of theological rules in matters of state and his dislike of Dara Shikoh's deviation from the Straight Path as understood by the Orthodox.

(2) *Humayun-nama*, *Maasir-Rahimi* and *Tuzuk-i-Jahangiri*—These three writings of Shibli are mainly in the form of literary appreciation and were published in *an-Nadwa* of Lucknow, respectively in 1907, 1908 and 1910. The main purpose seems to be to introduce these source books to the Urdu knowing readers, with the specific aim of presenting the glorious achievements of the Muslim rulers and *amirs* of India. Shibli's greatness lies in his historical sense and his anxiety to reconstruct the history of the Indian Muslims by an honest and reasoned appraisal of the original sources. He has examined these three source books mainly from the viewpoint of their importance as source material that gives reliable information about the cultural achievements of the Mughals. No doubt, there are shades of apologetics here and there, but on the whole these writings clearly indicate that Shibli 'was pre-eminently a historian by temperament and taught history to his people.'[7]

(3) *Zebun-Nisa*—This small article about the life of Aurangzeb's daughter, Zebun-Nisa, was published in *an-Nadwa* in 1909. Shibli was provoked to write on Zebun-Nisa by a cheap article based on

[7] Habibullah, *op. cit.*, 486.

hearsay and bazar gossip published in the *Indian Magazine and Review*. He complains that the errors committed by English authors generally become current and are received with popular enthusiasm. Then they spread from generation to generation, and ignorant people are led to form a bad opinion about the moral life of the Musalmans. After these introductory remarks he gives an authentic account of Zebun-Nisa's life, based on contemporary sources and reliable *taziras*. He quotes extensively from the *Maasir-ul-Umara*, *Maasir-i-Alamgiri*, *Sarw-i-Azad*, *Khazana-i-Amirah*, *Alamgir-nama*, *Yad-i-Baiza* and *Makhzan-ul-Gharaib*, and tries to give a true picture of the attainments, and character of the Mughal princess. The language is simple and the arguments convincing.

(4) *Hindustan men Islami Hukumat ke Tamaddun ka Asar*—The article starts with an introductory passage which, I think, mirrors Shibli's approach to history. He says :

> The conquest of a country by a foreign people is no crime; otherwise the great conquerors of the world would have to be termed as the greatest criminals. We should, therefore, study what impact the conquering people made on the culture and civilization of the conquered land. Chingez Khan, in so far as his conquests are concerned, is one of the greatest conquerors of the world, but every word of his life-story is stained with blood. There was a time when the Marathas dominated the Indian scene. But they came like a storm, plundered, exacted *chauth* and disappeared. Contrary, to this, when a civilized people conquer and occupy a country, there occurs a marked and sudden change in the civilization and culture of that country—the means of transport, way of living, diet, habits, clothes, houses and their upkeep, commercial goods, art and craft—everything undergoes a revolutionary change. May be the conquered people, due to their obstinacy and arrogance, do not express their gratitude and recognise the cultural benefits they have received, yet everything in that country becomes a living witness to the obligations they own to the conquerors.[8]

This attitude implies that the world was dark before the advent of Islam, and in India, in so far as the cultural goods and civiliza-

[8] *Maqalat-i-Shibli*, Darul Musannifin, Azamgarh, 1937, 194.

tional aspects of life are concerned, the Hindus had nothing worth mentioning. What a contrast to what al-Biruni has said in his *Kitab-ul-Hind.* But this is typical, and we find the same theme in Hali, Zakaullah and others. The article is, however, worth reading and Shibli has proved that the Muslims brought so many new things to India. Here again he supports his thesis with extensive extracts from original source books like the *Tuzuk-i-Babari, Khafi Khan, Tuzuk-i-Jahangiri, Ain-i-Akbari,* and the *Maasir-ul-Umara.*

(5) *Musalmanon ki Ilmi Betaassubi aur Hamare Hindu Bhayun ki Nasipasi*—This was to prove that Muslims were lovers of learning and were exhorted to discover knowledge wherever it was. They loved learning outside India, and when they came to India they brought the tradition with them. Shibli wrote this article also on provocation. The editor of the *Bharat Mitra* (Calcutta) wrote a review of Mulla Masih's *Ramayana* and made the following remarks :

> 'For centuries such a book was lying unknown. Perhaps, the reason is that the Muslims did not like it.'
>
> 'The Muslims ruled over this country for centuries and their rule ended, but they paid little attention to the literature and sciences of this country...Amir Khusrau took notice of the language of this land but just for a change. He never thought of studying the books of the Hindus; nor did he know about them.'
>
> 'But whatever was done in Akbar's time was on a very limited scale.'
>
> 'Dara Shikoh did pay attention to the books of high standard, belonging to the Hindus.... But because of his endeavours in this field, he was dubbed as *Kafir* and lost his life.'

Shibli gives extracts like these and is pained to see that even the fair-minded Hindus, like the editor of the *Bharat Mitra,* are sometimes led by their ignorance to make such baseless allegations against the Muslims. He has refuted the charge that no trace is available regarding Masih's life and achievements. He says that there is not a single *tadkirah* of the Persian poets where the name of Masih does not occur. The editor had said that Mulla Masih belonged to Panipat. Except this, nothing is known about him. Shibli says that among the nobles of Jahangir there was one Muqarrab Khan who originally belonged to Panipat but had settled in Kirana.

Masih was a resident of Kirana, but as he was attached to and patronised by Muqarrab Khan, he also came to be known as belonging to Panipat. Almost every *Tazkira* mention his *Ramayana* and the author of the *Maasir-ul-Umara* has given some selected verses from it. He has been forgotten by people because, as a poet, there was nothing meritorious in him. Firdausi wrote in his *Shahnama* about the valour and great deeds of the non-Muslim Iranians, and Saulat Turkistani wrote *Saulat-i-Faruqi* and praised the achievements of Abu Bakr and Umar. But what happened ? Firdausi is read by and known to every student of Persian poetry, while *Saulat-i-Faruqi* is known to none. Mullah Masih was just an ordinary poet, and had he written about the Prophet, even then he would not have been known by people.

Shibli, in this article, has refuted all the charges and has proved, again on the basis of sources, that neither the Turks nor the Mughals had any prejudice in this regard. But the question remains ; Whether both the Hindus and the Muslims alike have not generally, on purely intellectual basis, committed the folly of not studying and understanding, each other's religion. The historians of today are expected to answer the question. They are also expected to investigate the causes and consequences of this negligence.

17

Ananda Coomaraswamy

It is at once easy and difficult to write of Ananda Coomaraswamy as a historian of Rajput painting. It is easy because few obscurities attend either upon his person or his writings : he is so near to us in point of time that we know much about his life and nearly everything about his writings, and again, he has written of his themes on the evidence of materials to which he had no exclusive access. And yet it is difficult to write of his work not only because the last word has not yet been said on Rajput painting—every passing year brings to light new documents—but also because he is so brilliantly persuasive and writes with such unfailing tact that, even at his most emphatic, he somehow leaves room for our disagreements gently to coexist by the side of his theses. He wrote which such deep conviction and seemed to be able to move his readers so intensely that, while reading him even today, one falls unknowingly under a spell, and tends to suspend one's own judgement.

This ability to sway independent judgements, he displayed early in his writing career when he turned from the discipline of geology to interpreting the art and culture of India, and when he wrote his *Rajput Painting*[1], following a brief essay on the same theme in 1912,[2] he took the Western world by storm, as it were.

Fifty years have elapsed since his *Rajput Painting* first appeared. Much has been written on the subject since, and the studies of Indian

[1] Ananda K. Coomaraswamy, *Rajput Painting*, 2 vols., Oxford, 1916. The complete title of the work should be of interest to this study. It ran : *Rajput Painting. being on account of the Hindu Paintings of Rajasthan and the Punjab Himalayas, from the 16th to the 19th century described in their relation to contemporary thought, with texts and translations.* Referred to, hereinafter, as *R.P.*

[2] Coomaraswamy, 'Rajput Painting', *Burlington Magazine*, Vol. XX, No. 108, March 1912.

painting have registered a significant advance upon those pioneering days. It is time, therefore, to have a fresh look at Dr. Coomaraswamy's work, especially as it concerns Rajput painting, not only because our judgements have relatively matured as time has gone by, but also because even today almost all writers on the subject, however much it may be in fashion to affect disagreement with his conclusions, turn towards him for acquainting themselves with the soul of Rajput painting. The work that influenced a whole generation of writers still exercises powerful fascination.

To dwell on the merits of Ananda Coomaraswamy's work at length would be saying the well-known things over again : he was the true discoverer of Rajput art, and if several Rajput painting had been known and even published before,[3] they had never been collectively viewed or properly understood. They lay in a heap of material that went by the name of medieval Indian painting, and it belonged to Dr. Coomaraswamy to pick them up, dust and, then, insert them into the frame of his sensitive phrases. He proceeded, then, to distil for us the essence of Rajput painting, and in doing this brought to his task that brilliance of thought and that grace and facility of expression which he so powerfully commanded. He must, indeed, be regarded as one of the most eloquent writers on Indian art of all time. He created, again, by his consistent efforts, an atmosphere of new studies, clearing the air of the prejudice and nonsense of 'experts' like Baden Powell and James Fergusson,[4] and of the indul-

[3] Vincent Smith's *History of Fine Art in India and Ceylon* (Oxford, 1911). and E. B. Havell's *Indian Sculpture and Painting* (London, 1908), had already appeared before 1912 and included some Rajput paintings without, however, these being classified as such Dr. Coomaraswamy himself had noticed Rajput paintings in his own *Selected Examples of Indian Art*, (Broad Campden, 19 0), *Indian Drawings*, 2 Vols., (London, 1910–12), and *Arts and Crafts of India and Ceylon* (Edinburgh, 1913), but the *Burlington Magazine* essay and the two volume Oxford study gave a new meaning to Rajput painting.

[4] Dr. Coomaraswamy had a caustic note on these 'Anglo-Indian' writers, as he called them—

> 'That Rajput paintings have been entirely overlooked by Anglo-Indian writers may perhaps be explained by the remark of B H. Baden Powell: 'In a country like this we must not expect to find anything that appeals to mind or to deep feeling' (*Punjab Manufactures*. 1872, II, III). This is the normal standpoint of the Anglo-Indian writer. Fergusson for example, lays it down that, 'it cannot, of course, be for one moment contended that India ever reached the intellectual supremacy of Greece

gent or indiscriminate enthusiasm of several 'revivers' of Indian art.

We are principally concerned, however, with the work of Ananda Coomaraswamy as a *historian* of art, and here one runs into disagreements with him which it is partially the purpose of this brief paper to record. In doing this one may go wrong, but the following points are raised in the belief that it is important to offer points of view.

One feels forced to question, at the very beginning, the limits which Dr. Coomaraswamy thought belonged to the task of the art historian. 'The justification of the historian of art,' he wrote in his *Rajput Painting*,[5] 'is to be found in his ability to bring the reader into contact with his theme; and I,' he continued, 'have attempted no more than this.' This, it appears, was not simply a part of a general statement in which he sought the indulgence of 'later students' for the 'errors of commission and omission' in his pioneering work[6] : it was a considered definition of the task of the art historian to which he adhered more or less even in his later years. It becomes understandable in the context of those early times why in his *Rajput Painting* he chose to dwell more on the social and psychological explanation of that beautiful phenomenon ; but years later, he continued to regard this explanation as his central theme as an art historian. The differentiation between schools, the evolution of styles, their analysis and inter-relationships, remained in his studies on the fringe, as it were. This is not to say that he ignored these : in flashes of brilliance and insight he threw out suggestions and formulated theories that profoundly affected later studies, but they hardly ever became his principal concern. He was, for most part of the time, interpreting, one feels, rather than writing the history of Rajput painting.

To take an example. Rajput painting was divided broadly by Ananda Coomaraswamy into Rajasthani and Pahari. The former,

---

or the moral greatness of Rome.' Whether or not these are true judgements may be left to time to decide; here I only call attention to the, to say the least of it, unscientific attitude implied in the words, '*we must not expect*' and, it cannot, *of course*, for one moment be contended.' On this principle, the only object of research would be to confirm our *a priori* judgements !'

Rajput Painting, Vol. I, 6, n. 3.

[5] *Ibid.*, Vol. I, 6.

[6] *Ibid.*

in his *Rajput Painting*,[7] he split into local schools of production like Jaipur, Datia, Orchha, and 'presumably Udaipur and Ujjain,' etc., without entering into any long discussion about what separated them one from the other, apart from physical distance. In the Pahari group he drew the line between the two principal schools : Jammu and Kangra, fitting all paintings from this region into one or the other of these two centres although hinting, at the same time, at the possibilities of other centres like Chamba, Kulu, Mandi, Suket, Rampur, Guler and Garhwal being active.[8]

Nearly ten years after the publication of *Rajput Painting*, he sought to give more substance to the division of Rajput painting into local schools, and in the Rajasthani group included the Bundelkhand, Mewar, Western Malwa and Gujarat, and Central Rajputana (in which he put 'Jodhpur, Bikaner, and above all Jaipur') centres.[9] While this certainly looks very detailed and effective, it is of interest to dwell on the bases on which Dr. Coomaraswamy distinguished between them and identified the products of some of the schools. The early Ragamala sets are allotted to Bundelkhand, the suggestion being 'only based on the general character of the architecture represented in these paintings, and on the language of the inscribed poems.'[10] He expressed the honest fear while doing it that the suggestion 'may not be well founded.'

For Mewar painting[11] the main part of the evidence was taken by him to be the paintings of the theme of Shri Krishna as Shri Nathaji which could be traced to the Nathdwara shrine and which therefore it was 'natural to suppose' were produced in the state of Mewar. There also were the wall paintings in the island-palaces of Udaipur, and 'more recent portraits and other paintings' on the walls of the main Udaipur palace.

The Jodhpur work, again, Dr. Coomaraswamy said, was recognisable from 'the special form of the large turban,'[12] and, as for Jaipur, Amber, the old Kachhwaha capital, it was 'reasonable

[7] *Ibid*., Vol. I, 9.

[8] *Ibid*.

[9] Ananda K. Coomaraswamy. *Catalogue of the Indian Collections in the Museum of Fine Arts, Boston*, Pt. V, Rajput Painting (Cambridge, Mass., 1926) (referred to, hereinafter, as *Catalogue*), 3.

[10] *Ibid*., Pt. V, 3.

[11] *Ibid*., Pt. V, 4.

[12] *Ibid*.

to suppose......was already in the sixteenth and seventeenth centuries the main centre of Rajasthani painting,' partly because of the political contacts of Jaipur with the Mughal court accounting for the influence of its art on early Mughal painting, and partly because of the existence of a vigorous tradition of painting both on walls and on paper at Jaipur in the twentieth century.[13]

There may be much in what Dr. Coomaraswamy says in nearly all these cases, but one notices again and again that the considerations on which the differentiation is made between the various schools are not those of style but of matters which are other than internal, so to say, to the paintings. The evidence considered by Dr. Coomaraswamy, one should have thought, would form the beginning point of further analysis of each school, the basis on which unimpeachably to place a group of paintings in a particular school. It would have been natural then to proceed, after analysing *and describing* the elements of style in a school, to identifying more and more paintings of that centre of art production and trace the development of that school. But this, the more important part of the task, remains undone.

In Dr. Coomaraswamy's treatment of Pahari painting, one encounters the same reluctance to identify, on considerations of style, the paintings of the Punjab hills. The broad division of Pahari paintings into the Jammu and Kangra groups that he made in 1916 he retained in the *Catalogue* indicating at the same time that it 'may be possible with more exact knowledge to classify some at least of the Pahari paintings in accordance with another scheme.'[14] This 'scheme', however, consists of little else than the listing of political divisions of the hill states, following traditional accounts, into states of the Eastern or Jalandhar group and the Western or Dogra group, each consisting of eleven states, having their own ruling clans like the Katoch, Guleria, Jamwal, Jasrotia etc. There is little or no indication whether the existence of an independent political unit also necessarily meant the existence of an independent style of painting as practised there, and although Dr. Coomaraswamy thought that other states, apart from Nurpur, Guler, Kangra, Mandi, Suket, Jammu and Bandhralta, had their own local schools, he found it difficult in the state of knowledge at that time to identify their pro-

[13] *Ibid.*, Pt. V, 5–6.

[14] *Ibid.*, Pt. V, 6.

ductions.[15]

It becomes difficult to escape the conclusion that Dr. Coomaraswamy took both political boundaries and political importance as of central importance in the matter of the existence of local schools of painting; for it is hard, except in these terms, to explain the listing by him of all the states of the Punjab hills, and of the two main schools of the hills as belonging to Jammu and Kangra. In the case of the latter, he quite significantly notes down what may be his explanation of the phenomenon. 'It may be remarked,' he says, 'that Jammu and Kangra in the eighteenth century were by far the most powerful and wealthiest of all the Hill States.'[16]

The broad distinctions that Dr. Coomaraswamy made are no longer tenable, and we know fortunately much more about local schools now, but I am not suggesting that he is to blame if he did not at that time discover the importance of the developments in centres like Basohli, Mankot, Kulu and Bilaspur. What is suggested here is that the division made by Dr. Coomaraswamy was made in some haste, as it were, and on the basis of materials of evidence which even at that time could have been bettered.

This leads us to one of the sources on which Dr. Coomaraswamy relied for his information. For his analysis of the Pahari schools, it is not known with any certainty whether he made attempts to make enquiries in the hills themselves or saw royal collections, and there is mention by him of only one visit to the area and that to the old Kangra town. It becomes once again hard to resist the conclusion that even this broad division he made partly by attaching importance to the power and wealth of Jammu and Kangra, and partly by relying on the information supplied to him by the dealers in antiquities, more specifically by the 'Amritsar dealer,'[17] whom he prominently mentions in his writings. It was from the dealers that he acquired a large number of the paintings and drawings that went to form his magnificent collection; those were the days when the dealers carried about with them stacks of Pahari miniatures, quoting a flat, incredibly low, price for all paintings regardless of their quality.[18] The dealers also had 'authentic information' to pass on to

[15] *Ibid.*, Pt. V, 6–7.
[16] *Ibid.*, Pt. V, 8.
[17] *Ibid.*, Pt. V, 7.
[18] Rai Krishnadas ji is full of the most fascinating information and

the customer if he showed any interest, and it is enquiries from them, one is led to conclude, that formed a substantial part of the evidence of Dr. Coomaraswamy.

This does not on the face of it appear objectionable : the dealers, it is possible to argue, after all know most about their own collections. The strenuous search after paintings led them into the remotest corners of the hills, and they knew the collections, the source of each painting they acquired, the artists, and the traditions in their families. But it is at the same time important to bear in mind that it is precisely this information they do their utmost to keep back for a variety of reasons. The information which they supplied was either interested or calculatedly distorted, for the point with them was never to betray the true source of their supplies for fear alike of rival dealers and direct purchase by buyers. And, in some cases, the fear of the law, for we must be sure that a large number at least of sculpture was 'acquired' in violation of the laws which aim at the protection of monuments of importance. Stories current in the trade tell how the dealers often threw scholars off the scent about the objects supplied to them, the scholars nonetheless bravely pursuing the 'information' and building up a theory around it.

One knows only of one case where Dr. Coomaraswamy showed some suspicion of the Amritsar dealer's information, and that is where he doubts the description given by the dealer of what he believed to be the Jammu style pictures. These were referred to as 'Tibeti' by the Amritsar dealer, and Dr. Coomaraswamy only mildly suspects the accuracy of this description by referring to these paintings as 'the so-called Tibeti' pictures.[19] In other cases he took, I am afraid, the word of his informants too seriously, neglecting to examine the evidence with that sharpness which is characteristic of so much of his work.

In deciphering the inscriptions of the paintings to which one has, in the absence of other records, perforce to attach considerable

---

personal reminiscences of the days when Pahari paintings first came to the notice of scholars. He can recall with remarkable clarity the lack of deep interest in these paintings in the first two decades of this century, the manner in which the dealers went on their rounds, the most important of the dealers and their collections. I am deeply grateful to Rai Ji for much information and for many lively discussions.

[19] *Catalogue*, Pt. V, 7.

importance, he seems to have been in somewhat of a hurry again. One cannot find fault with his readings of the Takri inscriptions, for that is a script which is capable of defying the most patient of scholarships, but even in the Nagari inscriptions, most of which occur on Rajasthani paintings, Dr. Coomaraswamy seems to have failen into errors which could have been avoided with a little more patience reserved for the task. I have had occasion myself to re-read, elsewhere,[20] some of the inscriptions, and while all of us are liable to err in deciphering laconic titles like the ones we frequently find on Rajput paintings, it is still of the utmost importance that a reading should be beyond all doubt before a theory is raised on it.

In adopting a rather simplified scheme for the division of Rajput paintings into some principal schools, designated after easily recognisible state—or place names, it is possible that Dr. Coomaraswamy was attempting to save his readers from a certain degree of confusion, for it is almost sure that he had a definite audience in mind at the time of writing. He wrote clearly for the Western public—we must remind ourselves that his exposition of Rajput paintings as indeed so much of his other views occurred in books published for the most part in England or the United States—and it is probably for their benefit that he over-simplified and drew parallels to familiar names and phenomena. Again and again, in *Rajput Painting*, we run into evidence of the fact that he is trying to explain Rajput painting to the Western world with reference to themes and attitudes known to it. The classic period of the vernacular poetry of India is thus termed 'its age of Dante and Chaucer,'[21] to him where Radha hears, in a Rajput painting, the message of Krishna, the drawing recalls 'an Annunciation,'[22] the pastorals of the Kangra artists are different from the landscapes of Watteau or Millet.[23] While he achieved a laudable aim by addressing his writings to Western audiences—a considerable part of the West awoke now with a thrill to the beauties of Indian art—and there is no fault to be found with writing for a given audience, the unfortunate thing is that this attitude seems to have hardened itself as the years went by. The

[20] B. N. Goswamy, 'On Some Rajasthani Portraits in the Museum of Fine Arts, Boston', *Bulletin of the School of Oriental and African Studies*.

[21] *R.P.*, Vol. I, 2–3.

[22] *Ibid.*, Vol. I, 8.

[23] *Ibid.*, Vol. I, 24.

scheme with which Dr. Coomaraswamy began a rather simplified interpretation of the history of Rajput painting became, in later years, a pattern from which at least some part of the substance of art history remained excluded. The drawing of rigid lines is not always possible, nor are distinctions very sharp and emphatic when one is regarding a many faced phenomenon like Indian painting, and yet Dr. Coomaraswamy saw it as a matter of areas of pure and distinct colours.

In the insistent distinction between Mughal and Rajput painting, for instance. This he regarded as a distinction which it was 'no longer necessary to argue...for every addition to our knowledge makes it only more evident that there could scarcely exist two contemporary schools more diverse in temper.'[24] Mughal painting he regarded as the art of miniature painting, while Hindu painting was an art that stepped from the walls of shrines and palaces and public buildings; the one was of princely interest, the other universal; the one, 'aristocratic and professional' in form, while the other was at once 'hieratic and popular, and often essentially mystic in its suggestion of the infinite significance of the most homely events.' 'Mughal courtiers,' Dr. Coomaraswamy went on to say, 'would not have been interested in an art about herdsmen and milkmaids, nor Vaisnavas in pictures of elephant fights.'[25]

One discerns overtones in these statements, but also, to be sure, much truth. It is not thus possible seriously to argue even for a moment that there are no differences between the Mughal and Rajput schools; extreme examples of both schools can be recognised at a glance; one also recognises the diversity of temper and emphasis in much of the work of both these schools. But is it, one wonders, possible to argue that these are two different worlds the inhabitants of which would have to strain to recognise each other? If the extreme examples differ so sharply in the beginning, is it not also true that, as the styles progress, the lines of development, instead of remaining parallel, begin to converge towards each other a little? What conclusions does one draw from the fact that a large number of paint-

[24] *Ibid.*, Vol. I, 5. This appears to have been a favourite theme with Dr. Coomaraswamy, for there is much in this work and in his *History of Indian and Indonesian Art* (London, 1927) on this subject, showing the two schools juxtaposed to each other.

[25] *R.P.*, Vol. I, 6.

ings the scholars now find hard exactly to place and seek to solve their problems by designating them as 'Rajput-Mughal' ? What, again does one make of the facts, noticed among others but pushed into a foot-note by Dr. Coomaraswamy,'[26] that the majority of Mughal artists whose names are known to us was Hindus, that a very large number of Muslim artists worked at Rajput courts like Bikaner and Mewar,[27] and that it becomes impossible, *in terms of style alone*, to explain the turn that nearly all Pahari paintings book in the eighteenth century except with reference to Mughal painting ?

These are not rhetorical questions designed to emphasise a point by mere repetition. What is suggested is that the analysis of Dr. Coomaraswamy gains validity only if the points of difference between the two schools are thrown with a determined effort into sharp relief, and the points of contact and resemblance between them either ignored or played down. The two schools by no means stood at a distance and furtively glanced towards each other for a few centuries, and this is a fact that is now widely conceded.[28]

[26] The whole note is of interest and it runs :
'It is unnecessary here to discuss in detail the Rajput elements present in true Mughal painting. The Indian elements are apparent in several directions, (1) the illustration of Hindu themes in the first quarter of the seventeenth century, (2) the adoption of Hindu costumes at the courts of Akbar and Jahangir in the 'Rajput period', (3) the fusion of themes and styles in the eighteenth century, especially in Oudh, producing mixed types, and (4) the fact that more than half of the Mughal painters were native Hindus. All these conditions create resemblances between Mughal and Rajput painting quite superficial in the case of 1 and 2, more fundamental in the case of 3 and 4.' *History of Indian and Indonesian Art*, 127–28, n. 2.

[27] A whole family of Muslim artists worked at the Bikaner court and the name of the artist Sahibdin in Mewar is known. A series of sketches of the Bikaner artists is in the Motichand Khajanchi collection and was published not long ago in Karl Khandalavala. Moti Chandra and Pramod Chandra, *A Catalogue of the Exhibition of the Sri Motichand Khajanchi Collection & C.*, (New Delhi, 1960). For the Mewar artist, see Douglas Barrett and Basil Gray, *Painting of India* (Lausanne, 1963), 139–40.

[28] On the subject of the relations between the Mughal and the Rajput schools, Arnold and Wilkinson agreed with Ivan Stechoukine in arriving at 'the Hegelian conclusion' that a profound essential unity embraces the apparently wide differences between the two. See *The Library of A, Chester Beatty : A Catalogue & C.* (Oxford, 1936), Vol. I, p. XI, Basil Gray wrote on the 'Intermingling of Mogul and Rajput Art', (*Marg*, VI, i, 1953, 37).

'In the Mogul galleries it (the Indian genius) is turned outward, and

The point that there are differences of temper and feeling between the Mughal and Rajput schools loses validity rapidly when we move into the area of the subject matter of the two schools. There may be truth in the fact that while Mughal art excelled in portraiture, the Rajput painters 'also made' portraits, though it was an 'incidental aspect of their art', or that the Mughal artist evinced a lively interest in his environment as contrasted with the Rajput artist who had little or none of this interest. But it becomes impossible to argue on these lines beyond a point. Even quantitatively one may be able to prove that the paintings of secular, earthly themes from the Rajput states are by no means a negligible part of their art. Vaishnavas *were* clearly interested in elephant fights, and the Mughal artists did concern themselves, if not always, at least occasionally, with matters of the spirit. The vast number of portraits and darbar scenes, Music parties and equestrian groups, that one finds belonging both to the Rajasthani and Pahari centres, are things in which patrons and artists alike took obvious delight and are not merely incidental aspects of the art. There is no self-consciousness in these scenes, no hesitation, as there is none in that considerable body of Rajput painting which was frankly erotic, devoted to illustrating works like the *Rati Rahasya* with great relish and vividness.[29]

Dr. Coomaraswamy is so convinced of the philosophical bias of all Rajput painting and of the fact that it consistently leaned towards mystic suggestion that he strains the point, I think, beyond a limit, sometimes. All lovers in Rajput painting, one is able to see, are not Krishna and Radha; frequently they are only simple, mortal *nayaks* and *nayikas* whose faces were sometimes cast, in fact, in the image of the patrons of the artist. One comes up quite often

---

yet it does not forget the inner vision ; in the Rajput galleries it is turned inwards, but it remains intimately aware of the natural world.'

I find it unnecessary to refer here, in support of the statements made by me in the text in this context, to the whole body of work on the subject. The large collections that have of late years been examined and published, and the literature on the subject, is known to students of Indian painting only too well.

[29] One sees, practically in all collections, still intact in the hills, extensive sets of these paintings of erotic interest and living artists like Chandu Lal of Rajol and Puran Chand of Samloti in the Kangra district are clear about the tradition in their families that these were produced in response to specific demands of the patrons.

against a rather well-known royal face peeping from behind a bamboo-split curtain or proceeding from a loggia after a rendezvous, and in these cases even the pretence of making the lover look seemingly like Krishna is given up.

In his *Rajput Painting*, Dr. Coomaraswamy reproduced a nineteenth century lithographed book-title of a children's book called *Dil Bahlava*. This shows a scene at a well with women drawing or carrying water and engaging in ordinary conversation with nothing by way of a descriptive title given to the scene. This illustration Dr. Coomaraswamy calls 'The Well of Love' and then cites verses from Kabir and Vidyapati suggesting that the well is employed as a mystic symbol.[30] This, I submit, is a little unlikely : it is a plain *genre* scene without significance, and if one has to look back at all for its source to the Rajput tradition of painting, it must be linked with similar *genre* scenes that depict *piaos* or construction activity, or travellers gathered in a camp around a crackling fire.

What is of significance in this and other cases is that the meanings that Dr. Coomaraswamy reads in each individual scene or situation eventually piece together to form a complete picture of an unbroken continuity of tradition in Indian art of which he took Rajput painting to be an exalted expression. It is, in fact, towards establishing this that a great lot of his arguments tends all the time. One becomes gradually aware of the subtlety and the consistency with which he has been weaving a pattern. The reason why he so sharply distinguishes between Mughal and Rajput painting, and attaches so much of importance to the latter as a product of the soil, an art of the people, as contrasted with the superficial, court-inspired art of the Mughals, thus becomes obvious : in his scheme of things Mughal painting does not form a part of the pattern. It was 'but an episode in the long history of Indian painting' which remained unaffected by it. Mughal painting did not embrace life and religion together and remained therefore on the fringe. 'This Hindu or Rajput art' he wrote as early as 1910 to Sir William Rothenstein, 'is the descendant of Ajanta, its rise and zenith and decline seem to cover at least 1,500 years. The 200 years of secular Mughal art is but a breath beside it.'[31] Dr. Coomaraswamy

[30] *R.P.*, Vol. I, 76.

[31] See K. N. Towndrow, 'Sir William Rothenstein.' *Art and Letters*, XXV, *i*, 1951, 18.

was not deeply interested in the breath.

The emphasis on the folk affiliations of Rajput art[32] is of a piece with this reasoning; its links with the religion of the people or with the popular drama, the *yatra* or the *rasa*, of northern India are traced in some detail to indicate the depths of its roots in the land. Whether or not Rajput painting was an art of the people or an 'aristocratic folk art' is a matter which merits detailed study, but, to refer briefly to it here, it is arguable whether Rajput painting, at least as practised in the sixteenth to the nineteenth centuries and as known to us, belonged to the people in the sense in which Dr. Coomaraswamy understood it. While one could point to the general connection between the art and the courts of Rajasthan, from the Punjab hills there is incontrovertible evidence of the firmness of this link. I have had occasion to trace the movements of several families of artists of the hills in the course of the last few years, and it is fascinating to see how painting suddenly languished at a place where political power had declined, and how the artists attached to that court began to move away in search of other royal patrons elsewhere.[33] This is not to say that there was no connection between Rajput painting and the people, but one wonders whether the informality of these paintings, or their pastoral themes, are not sometimes mistaken for evidence of their existing independently of patronage.

To admit, however, that Rajput painting was also an art which, to a considerable extent, if not wholly, was a product of ateliers attached to the royal houses of Rajasthan and the hills, would have dimmed the distinction between it and Mughal painting, and introduced between the two a parallelism that would have affected the argument and, therefore, the purpose that Dr. Coomaraswamy had made his own : to prove that India had always had a national expression of her own, and that she countenanced for sometime, but eventually rejected all that did not agree with her spirit.

[32] 'Folk-art of the present day is a tradition handed down directly from the past : in Rajput painting, just as in the vernacular poetry of Hindustan, it is this folk art, fused with hieratic and classic literary tradition, that emerges as the culture of the whole race, equally shared by kings and peasants.' *R.P.*, Vol. I, 2.

[33] For a discussion see my 'Painting in Chamba : A Study of New Documents,' *Asian Review*, Vol. 2, No. 2, August 1965, and 'Sikh Painting : An Analysis of Some Aspects of Patronage,' in the *Oriental Art*.

This 'purpose' as we have called it, emerges clearly in the last chapter of his *Rajput Painting* which he significantly and somewhat unhistorically titles : 'Today and Tomorrow'. Here, frankly renouncing his role as a historian of art, he enters upon a marvellously eloquent plea for the revival in India of that unity of life and religion of which is born the flower of art, making at the same time an assertion of the faith that India may suffer but will find her voice again. To him Rajput art, a mystic, lyrical, continuing phenomenon that he had demonstrated as belonging to the people as a whole, symbolized at once all the values that stood threatened in his own days by forces powerful and destructive, and all that needed to be saved from the shadow of Industrialism and Bureaucracy and Western Ideals.

It needed a great deal of courage in those days to speak the way Ananda Coomaraswamy did, for he was being bitterly critical of the British Government's attitudes, but in doing this one wonders if he was not being a publicist at the expense of the historian in him. For when we construct an image in some haste and omit to take all the evidence available into account before pronouncing on the past as it was, we fail a little perhaps in our task as historians.

18

W. H. Moreland

W.H. Moreland was the first scholar to undertake an intensive study of the Mughal agrarian system, and his pioneer works have laid the students of the Indian economic history under lasting gratitude for having shown considerable enthusiasm for providing an over all picture of the Mughal age. However, his verdict is not final. Moreland was a keen student of economics and a trained English civil servant posted in the United Provinces in India. In his early work, The Revenue Administration of the United Provinces (published 1911), he made a genuine attempt to trace the legacy of the Indian land revenue system since the earliest times and its evolution under the British rule in the 19th and early 20th centuries. Moreland's approach was essentially dialectic. This general historical sketch served the purpose of showing some continuity of the agrarian problems inherited from the earlier times. Apart from it, the technique of comparing the land revenue system of the medieval age with the 19th-20th centuries revenue system in India, and the emphasis on the improvement brought by the British administration upon the former in various respects with historical illustrations was motivated by the keen desire to show the superiority of the British revenue administration over the previous Indian revenue administration. This book was also intended to serve as a handy guide for the English revenue officials in dealing with the 20th century agrarian problems relating to the landlords and the cultivators, especially when these problems were visualized in the historical perspective. However, it is doubtful if Moreland at this stage could clearly comprehend the clear-cut changes which had occurred during the course of the 18th century and had sufficiently blurred the main features of the Mughal land revenue administration. Despite all his shortcomings in the proper analysis of the 16th-17th centuries Mughal revenue administration, Moreland cut the gordian knot by undermining the mere narration of the political and the military history of India. He emphasised the primary role of the economic forces in Indian history. He stressed the fact that agriculture formed the main occupation of the people in the rural society, and was the chief source of revenue of an Indian state. This was a determinate economic factor in the past Indian society. An emphasis on this aspect permeates all his subsequent writings.

The evolution of Moreland from the role of an administrator to that of an economic historian is a gradual one. By the time Moreland and Yusuf Ali published their joint paper on Akbar's Land Revenue System on the basis of the *Ain-i-Akbari,* Moreland had developed a genuine interest in the Mughal land revenue administration. As a follow-up, India at the Death of Akbar, India from Akbar to Aurangzeb and the Agrarian System of Moslem India were essentially based on historical research and Moreland was par-excellence an economic historian. He gradually discarded the moral tone and comparisons of the condition of the peasantry during the British rule with the Mughal age. But although he developed the technique of historical research, he always remained eager to find such material as would suit his predilections and imperialist outlook. As an expert revenue officer, Moreland possessed considerable practical knowledge to steer through the difficult aspects of the problems in hand. Apart from this, he took to the comparative study of the different texts of the *Ain-i-Akbari* available to him, contemporary chronicles, accounts of the foreign travellers, a few Mughal farmans and dasturulamals. All the same, Moreland's technique of historical research was circumscribed by his narrow concept of interpretation. The reading of the technical passage of the *Ain-i-Akbari* is by no means an easy one. There is no denying the fact that when Moreland wrote, practically no archival revenue source material of the 17th century was available, and it is both very difficult and risky to formulate theories without understanding the correct meaning of the revenue terminology. In the absence of contemporary documents, a technical historian is obliged to be less rigid in his interpretation. The fact that Moreland had vast revenue experience of modern times in a way also proved a partial handicap, as in the interpretation of the ambiguous passages he was greatly tempted to rely on imagination. This can be well illustrated with a few examples. While interpreting *jama deh sala* (Ten Year Settlement) Moreland considers that the word jama in the passage does not stand for an assessed demand but refers only to the problem of the fixation of new valuation.[1] When the tables of the cash schedule rates (dasturs) immediately follow the description of the jama deh sala, Moreland gets involved in a difficulty. He finds that the passage starting with the problem of price-commutation further narrates the procedure of the fixation of valuation, and surprisingly ends with the tables of the cash schedule rates. Moreland does not consider the possibility of reading jama both as a valuation and an assessed demand (based on assessment schedule rates) to be interpreted in the context of the passage and still insists that the text of the passage stands for valuation. He gets disgusted with Abul Fazl and wriggles out with the solution that the Ain-i-Akbari is defective and the text must be corrupt. Here is an example of overconfidence on the part of a revenue expert who takes liberty with the technique of historical research. As regards the incidence of the state demand in Aurangzeb's reign, the royal farman to Rasik Das Karori (of Bihar) underlines the assessment to be enforced at the varying rates of 1/2, 1/3 and 2/5 (of the gross produce) according to the situation (dependent on the classification of land). Moreland contends that the aforesaid farman made only a theoretical enunciation of the variation in the assessment rates, whereas the actual demand was made nearer the maximum than the minimum. Even though Moreland had no contemporary documentary evidence to reject the statement made in the farman, he did so relying purely on his revenue experience for looking after the increase in the State revenues from the official viewpoint. The original pargana documents now available at the Rajasthan Archives, Bikaner, putting the above-mentioned variation in the state demand,[2] show Moreland was completely wrong in his presumption. Moreland did not understand as to how the revenue demand based on a detailed classification of the soil and the crops was levied under the Mughal regulations. His

[1] Moreland, *The Agrarian System of Moslem India*, (Allahabad ed.), 248–49, 251–54; Moreland and Ali, *Akbar's Land Revenue System*, as described in the Ain-i-Akbari, J. R. A. S., London, 1918, 1–42, for original text, see Ain-i-Akbari, Br. M. Add. 6552, fol. 145a, Ms. Hamilton, Berlin, fol. 136a; Akbar Nama, Br. M. Add. 26, 207, fol. 119a, Ms. Br. M.O.R. 27, 247, fol. 304a.

[2] Rajasthan Archives Jaipur (now at Bikaner). See Pargana documents of Aurangzeb's reign relating to Mal-o-Jihat wa Sair-Jihat and Yaddasht-i Haqiqat-i-Arazi wa Uftada.

reliance on the general statements embodied in the Ain-i-Akbari and Aurangzeb's farmans fixing the incidence of revenue demand at 1/3 and 1/2 of the gross produce under Akbar and Aurangzeb respectively as uniform rates, regardless of the nature of the land and the crops, is rather misplaced. In fact, these rates represent the highest pitch of the revenue demand for the grain crops, but the detailed sliding scale schedule rates were governed by the nature of the soil and the crops in a particular region and the variation in the demand could exist even within a single village. The schedule rates of the cash crops (jins-i-kamil) were comparatively much less, though based on the same principles of the classification of the land and the nature of the crops. This is ultimately bound to affect our estimate on the economic impact of the revenue demand on the condition of the peasantry during the Mughal age. Moreland's analysis of the methods of assessment of the Zabti and the Nasq, based on the reading of the Ain-i-Akbari, are far from accurate. Moreland has wrongly defined the Nasq as 'group assessment' or 'lump sum' assessment on the village or a pargana by agreement with the Headmen, while leaving to the latter the distribution of the assessed demand on the holdings of the peasants. He also takes a very rigid view about the scope and extent of the prevalence of the above mentioned methods of assessment during the Mughal age. He thinks that the most favoured method of assessment under Akbar was the Zabti and that the Nasq comprising 'village group-assessments', and 'annual summary assessments' had become the working rule during Aurangzeb's reign. The two fixed poles for his study are the Ain-i-Akbari and Aurangzeb's farman to Rasik Das Karori. He forgets that revenue practices do not disappear in such a sudden manner at the discretion of the monarchs. The Zabti method continued to operate throughout the Mughal rule and it co-existed with other methods of assessment.

Moreland was quite conscious of the generality of the terms like the zamindars and riaya, and preferred to put the term 'peasants' for the agricultural riaya. He correctly refused to be drawn in the theoretical and legal versions about the land ownership—a controversy which had engrossed most of the writers ever since the late 18th century.[3] But he was unable to run into the details of the various

[3] See details vide my Paper on Nature of Land-Rights in Mughal India, *The Indian Economic and Social History Review*, vol. I, No. 1, July-September, 1963, 1–23.

classes of the agriculturists connected with the land. He did not understand the varying nature of the land tenures in the zamindari and the riayati villages during the Mughal age.[4] He looked upon the question of ownership of land simply as vesting the peasantry with occupancy rights, and beyond this he had no contemporary data to throw any light on this issue. He left this important problem unsettled. Despite his reluctance to be drawn in an abstract discussion whether the Mughal system was based on the zamindari or ryotwari principles, his rough analogical association of a few features with either of the patterns is rather too vague. The obsession of finding intermittent periods during the Muslim era, when the state either directly dealt with the peasants or through the Headmen and the village 'group-assessment' method (especially after the mid-17th century), smacks of lack of clear understanding of the working of the Mughal revenue administration and the role of the landed intermediaries during the Mughal age. His worst error was the conformation to the traditional threefold division of the Mughal territories into khalisa, jagir and the semi-independent or autonomous chieftainships. Moreland could not properly comprehend the scope of Mughal land revenue operations in the territories of the Hindu chiefs (Zamindaran-i-Umda, etc.), the demarcation of the amli and ghairamli areas and the extent to which they were assignable to the Mughal state officials or to the chiefs (zamindars) themselves in lieu of their services to the Mughal state.[5] His belief that a Hindu Chieftainship (zamindari) like the Mewar continued to run revenue administration on purely traditional Hindu notions of governance uninfluenced by the Mughal system is not confirmed by the documentary evidence. Moreland failed to realise the changes in the position and the internal revenue organisation of the territories of the Hindu Chiefs which had occurred during the Mughal age. If the territories of the Hindu Rajput chiefs of varying degrees (Zamindaran -i-Umda, zamindars, etc.) are not considered a part of the Mughal revenues, it belies the entire understanding of the Mughal pattern of

[4] See details vide my Paper, 'Nature of Dehat-i-Taaluqa (Zamindari Villages) and the Evolution of the Taaluqdari System during the Mughal age', *The Indian Economic and Social History Review*, vol. II, No. 2, April, 1965. 166–77, *Ibid.*, vol. II, Nos. July, 1965, 269–88.

[5] See details vide my Paper, *Nature of Land Rights in Mughal India*, (vide f. n. 15), 10–14, f. nos. 60–70.

of the land revenue administration. Morever, Moreland's main thesis that the concept of the Mughal state like the earlier Muslim governments failed to provide political and social environment for the agricultural development and annual production of the country is completely fallacious. His assertion that the high pitch of the revenue demand, the constant conflict between the administration and the peasants, and the depopulation of the agricultural areas in one locality or another, strained the existing revenue system to the breaking point, and brought about general economic collapse after the middle of the 17th century, are all questionable surmises which are not essentially borne by the contemporary archival evidence. All these problems need a further probe, based on a scientific study, keeping in view the political as well as the sociological and ethnological background of the various regions of the Mughal Empire. Equal consideration has to be paid to the concepts of the agricultural production on the part of the state and the peasants, the ratio in the availability of the land for further tillage vis-a-vis population, the incidence of the revenue demand based on a detailed classification of the land and other socio-economic factors which played a dominant role during the Mughal period.

Moreland's reliance on the testimony of foreign travellers for an account of the life of the peasantry is partial.[6] The foreign travellers did not understand the concept of the land ownership in India and found institutional differences with their own countries. They asserted that, unless the land ownership be vested in the hands of the nobility, the agrarian evils were bound to occur.[7] They suffered from European complexes and made contradictory remarks about the people of India. Bernier's account of the hardship and the widespread flight of the peasantry is definitely exaggerated. Bernier had a motive in presenting an inaccurate picture of the patterns of the agrarian societies in the Asian countries in order to humour the French Government about the superiority of the European and especially the French landed structure and civilisation which was the apex

[6] For criticism of Moreland, see a review of the Agrarian System by Beni Parshad, *The Modern Review*, January, 1921; Brij Narain, *Indian Economic Life*, Lahore, 1929, 1–54.

[7] Eulogy of Father Jerome Xavier, S. J., a missionary in Mogor, tr. Rev. Hosten, S. J., J. A. S. B., New Series, vol. XXIII, Letter from Agra dated 14 September 1609, 121–22; Bernier Francois, *Travels in the Moghul Empire*, tr. Constable, London, 1891, 204–05, 211–12, 220–26, 233–34.

of the European culture during the 17th century. Unless the accounts of the travellers are subjected to scrutiny on the basis of their motivations and their limitations to understand the Indian way of rural life are borne in mind, a reliance upon them for the analysis of Mughal India is extremely risky. This was Moreland's greatest shortcoming. Moreland did not try to understand the ethnic and sociological background of medieval India. He has not dealt with the zamindari settlements based on tribal and clannish structure—a fact which gives a real clue to the understanding of the rural society and the agrarian history of Mughal India. Moreland did not try to go beneath the Pargana level. Even his account of the machinery of revenue collection is too sketchy. He made no attempt to analyse the socio-economic factors which affected the life of the people in the villages and qasbas, which in many a region came to be vitally connected with the cities. The spread of trade and commerce had tremendous impact upon the cultivation of cash crops and the role of cash nexus in the collection of the state revenues. Moreland's main merit was that he explained the land revenue system under the Mughals in the background of the ancient and the early medieval periods of Indian history so as to give a co-ordinated picture of the agrarian features through the ages. But he failed to realize the momentum of the socio-economic forces at work during the 17th century. Many a view and conclusion of Moreland on the agrarian droblems during the Mughal age need radical modification.

19

Early British Historians

For this paper, 'early British historical writing' covers the work of late eighteenth and early nineteenth century British historians.[1] The choice of this period of about ninety years for a study of the characteristics of British historiography on medieval India is not

[1] All the observations made in this paper are based on more or less a detailed study of the major relevant work of the following writers :

Dow, A., *The History of Hindostan*, 3 Vols., 1768-72.
Gladwin, F., *The History of Hindostan*, Vol. I, Calcutta, 1788.
Gladwin, F., *Ayeen Akbery*, 2 Vols., London, 1800.
Kirkpatrick, W., 'The Institutes of Ghazan Khan', *The New Asiatic Miscellany*, Calcutta, 1789, 149–226.
Hamilton, C., *The Hedaya or Guide*, 4 Vols., London, 1791.
Davy, Major, *Institutes : Political and Military*, Oxford, 1783.
Hamilton, C., *An Historical Relation of the Origin, Progress, and final Dissolution of the Government of the Rohilla Afghans in the Northern Provinces of Hindostan*, London, 1787.
Scott, J., *The Memoirs of Eradut Khan*, London, 1786.
Scott, J., *Ferishta's History of Dekkan*, 2 Vols., Shrewsbury, 1794.
Francklin, W., *The History of the Reign of Shaw Aulum*, London, 1798.
Gibbon, E., *The History of the Decline and Fall of the Roman Empire*, 7 Vols., 1776–88 ; edited, J. B. Bury, London, 1896–1900.
Jones, W., *The Works*, 13 Vols., 1807.
Price, D., *Chronological Retrospect, or Memoirs of the Principal Events of Mahommedan History*, 3 Vols., 1811–21.
Maurice, T., *The Modern History of Hindostan*, London, 1802–10.
Grant, C., *Observations of the State of Society among the Asiatic Subjects of Great Britain*, London, 1813.
Mill, J., *The History of British India*, 3 Vols., London, 1817.
Erskine, W., *Memoirs of Zehir-ed-Din Muhammed Baber*, London, 1826.
Wilks, M., *Historical Sketches of South of India*, 3 Vols., London, 1810–17.
Briggs, J., *History of the Rise of the Mahomedan Power in India*, 4 Vols., London, 1829.

arbitrary. The close connection of the historiography with the course of contemporary expansion of British rule in India and of the response to the problems created in British public life by that expansion, the intimate relation between the course and character of this historical writing and the major trends and methods of contemporary British historiography in general, the profound influence of the social and cultural environment of the historians on the character of their work, their general frame of reference, the logic in the development of this historical writing taken as a whole—all combine to impart to the work of the historians of this period a unity which is altogether its own.

The intimate connection between the work of these historians and the course of contemporary expansion of British rule in India is evident from their choice of subjects for historical treatment—the Rohillas, the later Mughals, Mysore, the Marathas, the Sikhs, for example. Furthermore, with the possibility first of and eventually with the establishment of British Empire in India, the Indo-Muslims came to be regarded as 'our predecessors'. Their empires became the most interesting subject for the new rulers of India.

The practical and public motives of the historians reveal their response to the problems created in British public life by the expansion of British rule in India. The servants of the East India Company in the late eighteenth century, for example, undertook constitutional and legal studies precisely because the Company was faced with the problems of ruling British India. The volume of British historical writing on medieval India began to increase considerably in the early nineteenth century largely because British India, the most important part now of 'the British Empire', was no longer a concern chiefly of the East India Company but of the whole British nation to whom, naturally, the writers had begun to address themselves. Nearly all the writers of this period were conscious of the use or practical implications of their work for British rule in India. Some

---

Grant Duff, *A History of the Mahrattas*, 3 Vols., London, 1826.
Tod, J., *Annals and Antiquities of Rajasthan*, 2 Vols., London, 1829-32.
Gleig, G. R., *The History of the British Empire in India*, Vol. I, London, 1830.
Elphinstone, M., *The History of India*, 2 Vols., 1841.
Cunningham, J. D., *A History of the Sikhs*, London, 1849.
Elliot, H. M., *Bibliographical Index to the Historians of Muhammedan India*, Calcutta, 1849.

of them overtly discussed the problems of government in the light of their knowledge of medieval India.

However, notwithstanding the dominance of its practical purpose, British historical writing on medieval India was closely related to British historiography in general. James Mill's study of Indian societies, for instance, was an extrapolation of the Scottish sociological studies, popularized chiefly by Adam Ferguson and John Miller. Similarly, Alexander Dow may be safely classed with the historians of the Enlightenment in so far as he tried to present easily available facts in a readable form and with a didactic purpose. A close examination of his work would show that his major assumptions were the same as those of David Hume and Edward Gibbon.

Though all the British historians of medieval India cannot be placed directly in one or another school of British historiography in general, its major trends were strongly reflected in British historical writing on medieval India. James Tod's work on the Rajputs was deeply influenced by the work of British 'medievalists'. Mountstuart Elphinstone too came to believe that the history of medieval Muslim India would throw 'a strong light on that of the Middle Ages in Europe.'[2] Joseph Davey Cunningham's conception of history came close to the 'science' and 'philosophy' of the Liberal Anglicans who had brought about 'a revolution' in English historical thinking in the early nineteenth century.[3] The collection and preservation of historical records—a reflection of the change in British historical outlook in the early nineteenth century, became as important in British India as in Great Britain. Historical scholarship as much changed the character of British historical writing on medieval India as of British historiography in general.

Indeed, the methods as well as the trends of British historiography influenced the character of British writing on medieval India. Unlike their predecessors, the early nineteenth century British historians of India, largely though they depended on literary sources, tended to treat them not as authorities but as sources. Their aim was, as one of them put it to another, 'to get at facts and to combine them with judgement so as to make a consistent and rational history

[2] Mountstuart Elphinstone to William Erskine, 18.7.1836, quoted, Colebrooke, T. E., *Life of Honourable Mountstuart Elphinstone*, 2 Vols., London, II, 345.

[3] Forbes, D., *The Liberal Anglican Idea of History*, Cambridge, 1952.

out of a mass of gossiping *Bukkurs* and gasconading *Tawarikhs*.'[4] The relevance of non-historical literature, archival records and archaeology for historical studies was recognized by many of the early nineteenth century British historians of medieval India. Thus, whereas Alexander Dow at the beginning of this period had been content to use Persian histories of European travels, Mountstuart Elphinstone near the close of this period used letters, *farmans*, memoirs, coins, the evidence of language and literature as well as histories and travels, both Asian and European. On the basis of a detailed analysis of the major works of these historians, it may be safely stated that they learnt their 'methodology' from the work of their contemporaries at home.

Without minimizing the importance of their purposes or of their schooling in methodology for the character of their work, it must be emphasized that the influence of the social and cultural environment of the British historians of medieval India was more subtle and, therefore, more decisive in determining the character of their work. Edward Gibbon's *History of the Decline and Fall of the Roman Empire* is in a sense 'a demonstration of the general ideas of the silver age of the modern European Renaissance'.[5] James Mill's *History of British India* has quite as much to tell us about the thought of the English Philosophical Radicals as Gibbon's *History* tells us about the ideas of the English Enlightenment. The work of the British historians of medieval India, reflecting the literary, aesthetic and religious as well as the intellectual currents of their time, mirrored the society in which they lived and worked. Conversely, in determining the character of British historical writing on medieval India, the rise of Romanticism and Evangelicalism in this period proved to be as deeply influential as the Enlightenment and Philosophical Radicalism. By far the bulk of this historical writing may be analysed in terms of these dominant movements.

What was commonly shared by all the British historians of medieval India was the assumption of an all round superiority of their own age in their own country over the age about which they were writing. Alexander Dow, for instance, contrasted the freedom and happiness of his fellow-citizens under a constitutional monarchy

[4] Mountstuart Elphinstone to James Grant Duff, 20.4.1822, quoted, Colebrooke, T. E., *Life of the Honourable Mountstuart Elphinstone*, II, 137.

[5] Whitehead, A. N., *Adventures of Ideas*, Cambridge, 1961, 13.

with the 'slavery' and misery of Indians subject to despotism. For Mountstuart Elphinstone, the general condition of medieval India in its most prosperous and best governed epochs compared ill with the general condition of even the indifferently governed states of contemporary Europe.

Indeed, the whole of contemporary Western Europe was generally believed to be morally and intellectually superior to all other ages in world history. In the last analysis, the rise of modern science with all its implications for thought and technology appeared to distinguish the modern European civilization from all other civilizations, whether Asian or European. Even Sir William Jones, for all his reputation as the greatest admirer of Asian peoples, thought of them as 'mere children' in sciences proper.[6] For him, Europe was the 'fair mistress' and Asia, at its best, the 'handmaid'.[7]

However, notwithstanding the general assumption of contemporary Britain's superiority over India, the attitudes of these British historians towards India and its past differed widely, and reflected largely their affiliation to one or another of the dominant schools. The historians of the Enlightenment, like Dow, could and did appreciate the vigour and political success of the Indo-Muslims ; they appreciated also the tolerant posture of some of the Mughals. They believed that in the interests of peace and political stability of the British Empire in India, as elsewhere, the ignorant multitudes were better left to their superstitions. The Utilitarians and the Evangelicals adopted from widely different standpoints nearly the same attitude towards India and its past : they hardly saw anything commendable in Indian societies ; India's past for them was a long tedious tale of unmitigated suffering ; and India's future in their view depended on the blessings Indians could receive or the British would bestow. The Romantics appreciated some of the aspects of Indian societies and cultures in isolation—religion, ethics, poetry, music, painting, sculpture or architecture, for example. Some of the Romantics came very near to saying that the Indian way of life was as valuable to the Indians as the British way of life was to the British. In their view, Indian institutions could be left intact until and unless the Indians themselves should wish to change them.

The British historians in this period, whatever their cosmologi-

[6] *The Works of Sir William Jones*, 13 Vols., London, 1807, III, 19.
[7] *Ibid.*, III, 1–9.

cal assumptions, accepted the concepts of State, Civilization and Nationality as their general frame of reference. However, the concept of State, remained uppermost with the historians of the Enlightenment; and with the Utilitarian and Evangelical writers the concepts of Nationality and State were subordinate to the concept of Civilization or Society. The Romantics, on the other hand, tended to subordinate the concepts of State and Civilization to the concept of Nationality.

It was their general frame of reference that endowed the work of Edward Gibbon and Sir William Jones (who did not write directly on medieval India) with a decisive influence on the character of British writing on medieval India. Gibbon found the method of 'grouping my picture by nations' the most meaningful for his treatment of Islamic history;[8] nonetheless, he underlined the unity of Islamic civilization which in his view transcended the regional peculiarities within the Muslim world. On this assumption the Indo-Muslims, for all the dividing lines of race and region, were in their way of life distinct from any other people in the world except the Muslims. Sir William Jones brought out the uniqueness of Hindu civilization as a peculiar product of the genius of the Hindu peoples, and made India for the West almost synonymous with Hindu India. Henceforth the formal division of Indian history into 'Hindu' and 'Muhammadan' was only a matter of time. James Mill, the first British historian to make this formal division, was proud of being a most serious student of Civilization. He was quick to acknowledge both Gibbon and Jones as his immediate predecessors.

Furthermore, since Gibbon and Jones had evaluated Muslim and Hindu civilizations, British historians of medieval India began to see those civilizations not only as distinct but also qualitatively different from each other. James Mill discussed the government, laws, religion, literature, historiography, philosophy, sciences, technology and morals and manners of the Hindus ; and, after a deliberate comparison, found the Muslims to be superior to the Hindus in all the spheres of civilization. Horace Hayman Wilson attempted to correct Mill's judgment by arguing that the Hindus were superior to the Muslims, except in historiography. Mountstuart Elphinstone, who is said simply to have described the Indian past

[8] Birkbeck Hill, G. (ed.), *The Memoirs of the Life of Edward Gibbon*, London, 1900.

and not judged it,[9] saw in fact a qualitative difference between the the Hindu and Islamic civilizations.

However, unlike Mill, Elphinstone did not subordinate nationality to civilization. Like the Romantics, he found the 'national' units within the frame of civilization more worthy of attention. Thinking of the inadvertance of inadequate judgments on Indians, he emphasized that there were ten nations in India, differing from one another in manners and language as much as those of Europe and possessing at the same time the 'general resemblance which is observable among the nations of Christendom.'[10] Already, James Grant Duff and James Tod had treated the Marathas and the Rajputs as 'nations' within the general frame of Hindu society. Joseph Davey Cunningham, who admired Elphinstone as a historian, treated the Sikhs as a distinct nation.

Late eighteenth and early nineteenth century British writing on medieval India, taken as a whole, appears to possess its own logic of development. The period started with the work of Alexander Dow, the first general historian of Indo-Muslim politics who has been regarded as merely a translator of Firishta's work, the *Gulshan-i-Ibrahimi*. Late eighteenth century servants of the East India Company, Dow's immediate successors, extended the field of inquiry by their studies of Indo-Muslim government and law as well as medieval Indian politics. While Gibbon created a new image of Islamic civilization with his asides and reflections on the economic, social and cultural aspects of Muslim history, Jones attempted a rediscovery of the whole of Hindu civilization.

With this background, and with very different assumptions and purposes, the Evangelicals and the Utilitarians, represented in the early nineteenth century by Charles Grant and James Mill approached medieval Indian history through the study of Indian societies and civilizations, past and present, to identify imperial responsibility with 'moral imperialism' in British India, thus marking a sharp break with the attitudes of their immediate predecessors on medieval India.

Reactions to their advocacy of radical social change appeared both in British India and Great Britain to influence the course and character of British historical writing on medieval India. Some

[9] Forbes, D., *The Liberal Anglican Idea of History*, 133; Philips, C. H., *Historians of India, Pakistan and Ceylon*, London, 1961, 7.

[10] Elphinstone, *The History of India*, I, 323.

Anglo-Indians, like John Briggs, underlined the insufficiency of evidence for moral judgments on Indian peoples ; others, like Vans Kennedy, questioned the validity of such judgments. The Romantics, like James Tod, repudiated moral imperialism in India by bringing out the best in the subjects of their studies. At the same time, they provided suitable material for the conservatives, like G. R. Gleig, whose opposition to radical social change in British India was little more than an extrapolation of their opposition to radicalism at home.

Mountstuart Elphinstone, the last general historian of medieval India during this period, represented several of its characteristic tendencies and summed up existing knowledge of medieval Indian history in Great Britain. His intellectual kinship with the Enlightenment enabled him to have a life-long appreciation for Hume and Gibbon and to accept their values of judgment. His emotional affinity with the Romantics is evident from the imaginative sympathy with which he studied the Indian past, whether Hindu or Muslim. Without subscribing to the moral imperialism preached by the Evangelical and Utilitarian apostles of radical social change in India, he wished and worked for a moral and an intellectual regeneration which should allow no sharp break with India's past. His view of Indian past buttressed his political liberalism which often prompted him to visualize a 'civilized' and an independent India in the future.

In summing up existing knowledge of medieval Indian history, Elphinstone had attempted to see 'Mohammedan' India in the round. The Rajputs, the Marathas and the Sikhs had formed as essential a part of his story as the Indo-Muslims 'nations'. The racial composition of the Indo-Muslims ; their national characteristics ; their attitudes towards the non-Muslims in India ; the influence of Indian environment on the government, administration, language, social customs, religious beliefs and practices, and manners of the Indo-Muslims ; the effect of Muslim conquest on the Hindus ; the influence of Islam on Hinduism—all these aspects of medieval Indian history had as much interested Elphinstone as the wars, government, literature, arts and prosperity of the Indo-Muslims. Although he had seen the Hindu and Muslim 'nations' as members of two markedly different civilizations, yet for him the significance of medieval Indian history lay in Hindu Muslim *rapprochement*. He had regarded Akbar as the creator of a 'national' state in India.

Elphinstone's interpretation of medieval Indian History was not acceptable to his immediate successor, H. M. Elliot, who appears to have planned a general history of medieval India with assumptions and purposes quite different from Elphinstone's. Elliot's *Bibliographical Index to the Historians of Muhammedan India* (1849) appears definitely to mark the beginning of a new phase in the history of British historical writing on medieval India. In his plan, we find the concept of 'Muhammedan' India crystallized and medieval India becomes a specialized study. But the scope of this study was narrowed down to the history of Indo-Muslims politics based on the testimony of 'native chroniclers'. Not his scholarship so much as his contemptuous approach and hostile attitude mark off Elliot from the bulk of his predecessors on medieval India.

Elliot found[11] the native chroniclers for the most part dull, prejudiced, ignorant and superficial ; they told him nothing of the social, political, and religious institutions of medieval India. Its history, he proclaimed, was yet to be written. He came to the significant conclusion that the medieval Muslim historians of India had glossed over the injurious influence of despotism on the lives of the people who, as Elliot indicates, were largely non-Muslims. These chroniclers, by confining their attention to the Indo-Muslim court and its splendour, had glossed over the evil effects of sanguinary laws too. Had they portrayed their Caesars with the fidelity of a Seutonius, almost always they would have portrayed Caligulas. Elliot would suffer no gorgeous illusions about Muslim rule in India. Five decades of British rule in India had done more for its people than what the Muslims had done for them in as many centuries. Unlike any of his predecessors, Elliot talked of 'our high destiny as Rulers of India'.[12] Thus, by the mid-nineteenth century the early period had come to its close. Its last major work, J. D. Cunningham's *History of the Sikhs*, had been published already in 1849, the year in which Elliot published his *Bibliographical Index.*

[11] Elliot, Preface, *Bibliographical Index*, VIII, XV.
[12] *Ibid.*, XXX.

20

Soviet Historians of Mughal India

The growing friendly relations between India and the Soviet Union have been accompanied by deep interest in Indian studies in the Soviet Union. Modern Indian history has been the object of their special study, but in order to understand and analyse the problems of British conquest and economic exploitation of India, the Soviet historians[1] have devoted attention to the economic life of Mughal India.

The Soviet historians, being the followers of Marx and Lenin, subscribe to the theory of Economic Determinism and mostly concentrate upon economic history. In regard to the feudal period they usually study the forms and techniques of production, the extent of the penetration of money-economy, the process of urbanisation and the nature of towns, the nature of land ownerships etc., and seek to answer the question whether the feudal economy contained elements of capitalism or not. In the present paper we will generally confine ourselves to a study of the views of Soviet scholars on the forms of handicraft production in Mughal India—a subject, which has been the centre of lively debate among them. On it largely depended the answer to the question whether the Indian economy during the Mughal period contained germs of capitalism or not.

The late Prof. Reisner, to whose credit goes the kindling of interest in the economic history of Mughal India among the present group of Soviet Indologists, took up the problem in his monograph, *Narodnie dvizheniya v Indii v XVII–XVIII vv.* (Popular Movements in India in the 17th–18th Centuries).[2] The movements of the Marathas, the Sikhs and the Jats form the central theme of the book, but

[1] *Contribution to Indian Economic History*, I, (Calcutta, 1960), 98.

[2] I. M. Reisner, *Narodnie dvizheniya v Indii v XVII–XVIII vv.*, Moskva, 1961.

Prof. Reisner has, in the first chapter, discussed certain features of the socio-economic history of the Mughal Empire in the second half of the seventeenth century. According to him the common features of the economic life were 'the community which combined agriculture with handicrafts, the diffusion of class and caste divisions everywhere, the conserving of the remains of slavery and communal-patrimonial structure. In India crafts had not been completely separated from agriculture and the development of commodity relationships had not yet led to the formation of markets embracing the territories of different peoples of India, not to speak of a common Indian market. The feudal division of the country into small parts had not been liquidated.' The author supports the view of Marx that this type of feudalism was characterised by the unity of small land-holdings and domestic handicrafts. The feudal property in India remained in the form of governmental holdings in land because of the need for common control over means of irrigation which were essential pre-requisites of agricultural production. The governmental property in land symbolised the monopoly in land and irrigational structures of the whole feudal class and the form which enabled the assertion of supremacy of the big feudal landholders.

The Great Mughal claimed about one-eighth of the arable land in his dominion as crown-lands. The system of *jagirs* served to concentrate the lands in the hands of a group of big feudal lords. The policy of the Mughal rulers of transferring the *jagirdars* after a short tenure encouraged them to extort money from the peasants by all possible oppressions. However, these *jagirdars* could not and did not have the time to expropriate lands of the earlier land-holders, who were mostly Hindus and who occupied them when they were the ruling groups in the country. These feudal lords often had an establishment in the cities. So the Indian cities were not the centres of commerce and handicrafts but were under the influence of feudal elements, who were serious obstacles to the growth of elements of capitalism in the cities.

In spite of the above facts Prof. Reisner agrees that progressive elements did appear in Indian society in the form of division of labour between the cities and the villages, acceleration of the process of exchange of goods between them, formation of regional markets which to some extent dealt with agricultural products. We have signs of regional specialisation in the produetion of agricultural products. The cities also increased in importance as centres of economic activities. All these factors could have undermined the isolationist character of the village communities in India. Although this progress did not as yet from the pre-condition for the change-over to capitalism, it did influence the class struggle going on in the society. The peasants and the craftsmen combined in their fight against the feudal lords, and out of this arose a number of popular movements.

Another important feature of the economic life was the role of the money-lender in villages. Prof. Reisner ascribes this to the introduction of the system of payment of land revenue in cash at the end of the sixteenth century. When Aurangzeb increased the land-revenue to more than fifty per cent of the gross harvest, the feudal exploitation of the peasants increased and the peasant became a constant prey of the money-lender. The productive forces were seriously impaired and the peasants were compelled to give up farming and leave their land. Prof. Reisner, following Marx, remarks that the growth of mercantile and usurious capital did not play any progressive role, since it simply worsened the condition of production and did not change the character of production.

As a result of exploitation, the peasant rose against feudal lords and the class war became acute. This was an important reason which caused the crisis of the Mughal Empire towards the end of the seventeenth century.

Another important fact which led to the crisis of the Mughal Empire was the sharpening of contradictions within the nobility itself. Used to luxurious living and lavish expenditure, they had to borrow frequently from the money-lenders and, like the peasants, they also fell into their clutches. This in turn adversely affected the peasants. The feudal lords, in order to supplement their incomes, began to engage in trading activities and money-lending. The feudal lords no longer wanted to share their income from the exploitation of the peasants with the central authority. The small and medium feudal lords, especially the Hindus, wanted to keep the 'right of exploitation of their own peasantry as their sole monopoly'. This development, along with the economic decline of the country, prepared the ground for the final disruption of the Mughal Empire in the middle of the eighteenth century.

Prof. Reisner also considers the role of European trading

companies in India in the seventeenth century, and concludes that the Europeans transformed India into an object of exploitation and accumulation of capital. They forced out the Indians from the maritime trade in the basin of the Indian Ocean. The opening of the trade route to Europe via the Cape of Good Hope caused the decline of Indian land trade to areas round the Mediterranean Sea and resulted in the ruin of many cities (specially of N. W. India). The European Companies combined economic penetration with piracy against the Indian ships.

Prof. Reisner holds that the economic policies of Aurangzeb not only deepened the crisis of the Mughal Empire but also led to its final collapse.

Prof. Reisner further took up popular movements against the Mughal Empire and discussed them in a series of articles. He specifically deals with the movements of the Marathas, the Sikhs and the Jats.

The disintegration of the village community, the penetration of money economy in the villages, the rise in the economic and military power of the feudal lords prepared the ground for further development of the institution of feudalism among the Marathas. The Maratha feudal lords were now prepared to extend their holdings not only at the expense of communal lands but also by fighting against the external grabbers. This became one of the causes of the Maratha uprisings. The peasants sided with the feudal lords because they were being exploited not only by their own feudal lords but also by the feudal lords of Ahmadnagar and Bijapur. The invasion of the Mughals in the second half of the seventeenth century threatened the peasants with complete annihilation.

Prof. Reisner calls the Sikh uprising a peasant movement, but holds that it began as a movement of protest by the well-to-do trading classes and craftsmen in the cities against the exploitation of feudal lords who even failed to guarantee the security of life and property. Being nearer to the capital they were always subject to a large number of extraordinary taxes. In the middle of the seventeenth century, when the crisis of the Mughal Empire deepened and the economy of the country worsened, the masses—thousands of peasants who had lost their lands and the craftsmen who had lost their livelihood—joined the movement.

The Jats, who led the second most powerful movement against

the Mughal Empire, also inhabited the areas adjoining the capital. Prof. Reisner points out that they were also subjected to intensive exploitation not only by the feudal lords but also by the traders, who flocked there from distant place to purchase indigo and cloth. Their miseries increased because, being near the capital, they were forced to work on Royal construction projects like palaces, forts, mosques and roads without wages. The Mughal armies, generally started their campaigns from Agra, and on such occasions they plundered the surrounding peasantry with impunity. This further impoverished the peasantry.

Thus Prof. Reisner has clearly brought out the rot that had set in the economy of the Mughal Empire in the second half of the seventeenth century and has shown that the three popular movements, of the Marathas, the Sikhs and the Jats, drew their sustenance from economic discontent.

Other Soviet scholars, on the whole, agree with Prof. Reisner's views on the economy of Mughal India. His statement that the Indian economy in the seventeenth century did not have those elements which would have enabled it to effect a change-over from the feudal economy to capitalist economy, while meeting with the approval of some Soviet scholars, has been challenged by others.

One of the most prominent supporters of Prof. Reisner's theory is Dr. (Mme) Antonova. Dr. Pavlov, Dr. Alaev, Dr. Chicherov, Dr. (Mme) Ashrafyan disagree with Prof. Reisner.

In her monograph on Akbar's India, Dr. (Mme) Antonova remarks that right up to the end of the eighteenth century Indian economy was based upon natural economy.[3] The feudal method of production and the feudal lords dominated the economy. The feudal lords actively participated in trade. The imported articles in the country were all luxury goods which were used by the *jagirdars*. The prosperity of merchants and money-lenders depended on the sweet will of the feudal lords. The merchants and the money-lenders had stakes in the collection of land revenue and, therefore, they were indirectly participants in the exploitation of the peasantry. Consequently, they did not oppose the feudal lords and thus failed to create in India the elements of a new social order. In the opinion of Dr. (Mme) Antonova, the highly developed trade and the system

[3] K. A. Antonova, *Ocherki obshchestvennikh otnosheni i politicheskogo story mogolskoi Indii vremen Akbara* (1556-1605), Moskva, 1952, III.

of money-lending hindered the growth of capitalism.

The author, however, agrees that internal trade in India was highly developed, and specially grains were moved from one part to another. Bengal had the lion's share in the export of grains to other parts of the country. The large number of markets and fairs, chiefly around places of pilgrimage, testify to the lively internal trade. The author ascribes the rise in internal trade to the great interest taken by the Emperor himself, who constructed a network of roads connecting the different parts of the empire. An important feature was the absence of participation by the *jagirdars* in the internal trade of the country as against the external trade, probably because it was less profitable. The author holds that these developments still did not pave the way for the change-over to a capitalist economy.

Money-lending expanded greatly, but the author quotes Marx in her support that it did not mean any change in the technique of production. Ultimately the system contributed to the decline of the Mughal Empire.

Speaking of cities, the author points out that they were of four types viz., (1) cities round the military camps ; (2) cities round the centres of pilgrimages ; (3) port cities and ; (4) cities round the centres of internal trade and crafts. Some of the cities, of course, combined all the four characteristics. All the cities had one element in common—they were dominated by feudal lords. The feudal supremacy precluded the possibility of the growth of a middle class in the towns. The merchants had no opportunity to participate independently in the political life of the country.

The craftsmen were also dependent upon feudal lords, who meddled in the production and sale of goods. The organisation of crafts was very primitive, and the instruments of production were very simple. There was no sign that the 'manufacture period,' that is, when a number of craftsmen come together and work under one roof for one common master, had dawned in India. Dr. (Mme) Antonova holds that in India this 'manufacture period' never came into existence. In the Royal Karkhanas, the workers were not hired in the true sense of the term. They were craftsmen, who had been forced to work on pain of punishment. There was no internal division of labour, and the Karkhanas did not belong to any private entrepreneur. Thus the elements of capitalism had been absent in the Indian economy.

Dr. (Mme) Antonova explains the lack of capitalist elements because of the insecurity of life and property, which deterred investment of capital in productive enterprises. On the basis of the above arguments Dr. (Mme) Antonova agrees with Prof. Reisner that Indian economy did not contain elements of capitalism.

Dr. (Mme) Antonova further developed this thesis in her article, *O genezise kapitalisma v Indii* (On the Genesis of Capitalism in India). According to her, in spite of the predominance of money economy, the feudal influence was so great that the rich traders tried to hide their wealth so as not to attract the greedy eyes of the feudal lords.[4] If one could find a rich merchant, it was extremely rare to come across a rich craftsman. Even this growth of money economy was unable to shatter the isolation of the self-contained villages. There was no uniformity in weights and measures, not to speak of a change in the technique of production. Division of labour in production, which is an essential element of the 'manufacture system', did not appear except in crafts, where it was absolutely necessary, like shipping and mining. The three basic elements for the rise of capitalism, (1) presence of a mobile labour force, free from personal dependence and lacking personal tools of production; (2) concentration of wealth into few hands; (3) the attainment of a definite standard of productive capacity, were absent in the Mughal economy. In India the first capitalist factory was set up only in the nineteenth century by English capital.

The position of Dr. (Mme) Antonova has been challenged by a host of Soviet scholars like Dr. Pavlov, Dr. Alaev, Dr. Chicherov and Dr. (Mme) Ashrafyan. Dr. Pavlov in his monograph, *Formirovanie indiickoi burshuazii* (Formation of the Indian Bourgeois), after discussing the economy of India in the seventeenth century came to the conclusion that there were elements of capitalism in Indian economy, but they were still not strong enough to start a consistent movement.[5] Dr. Pavlov pointed out that the shipping yards of Gujarat employed a number of workers, who worked for the master and thus 'the manufacture period' had already appeared. Detailed division of labour in production had come into being, and the isolationist character of the village community was fast disappearing.

[4] *O genezise kapitalisma v stranax vostoka*, Moskva, 1962, 181.

[5] Pavlov, *Formirovnie indiiskoi burzhuazii*, Moskva, 1958, 35–36.

Dr. Pavlov has been supported by Dr. Alaev. In his monograph *Uzhanay Indiya* (Southern India), and an article, *Razvitie indiskogo tkachestva do proniknoveniya v indiu evropeitsev* (Development of Indian Weaving till the Penetration of Europeans in India), Dr. Alaev refutes Dr. (Mme) Antonova. According to him the system of advancing money to the craftsmen on the part of the merchants or their representatives had resulted in the virtual enslavement of the workers, who had been in essence transformed into hired workers.[6] The hold of the merchants was so great that many craftsmen had lost their instruments of production.[7] The Indian merchants and the middlemen were so deeply entrenched that the Europeans, despite their best efforts, could not bypass them and establish direct contacts with the craftsmen.[8]

The main characteristic of the 'manufacture period', that is, a detailed division of labour in the production of a particular commodity, was present in India in the seventeenth century. In Gujarat and on the Coromandel coast specialists in dyeing and printing of cloth were flourishing. Shipping was an independent profession in Gujarat. Textiles manufactured in one city were bleached and dyed in other cities. According to Olaffsen, in the seventeenth century, near Tanjore, there were big factories for printing of cloth. The subjugation of craftsmen by merchant-capital created certain conditions for the development of capitalistic relations.[9]

Dr. Chicherov in his book *Ekonomicheskoy razvitie indii pered angliiskim zavovaniem* (Economic Development of India before the English Conquest) and articles *Nikotorie materiali o remeslenom proisbodstve v severo-vostochnikh raionov indii v XV–XVII vv.* (Some Materials about Handicrafts Production in the North-eastern Regions of India in the Sixteenth and Seventeenth centuries) and *Podchinenie remesla torgovim kapitalom severo-vostochnikh i ugo-vostochnikh raionakh Indii v XVII v.* (Subjugation Handicrafts by Merchant Capital in North-eastern and South-eastern Regions of India in the Eighteenth century), supports Dr. Pavlov and Dr. Alaev. He concludes, 'At the same time within the feudal economy of India in the 16th–18th centuries active processes were under way which led, in the

[6] Alaev, *Uzhanay Indiya*, Moskva, 1960, 59.
[7] *O genezise*, 176.
[8] *Uzhanay*, 61.
[9] *Genezise*, 177.

main, towards the end of this period to essential modification in the pattern of the relations of production without however changing them radically.

Qualitatively new forms of economic organisation of labour appeared in the crafts of feudal India in that period, alongside the old traditional forms. Deeper social division of labour, separation of the crafts from agriculture and the town from the village, and the development of commodity-money relations gave rise to the rudiments of capitalist relations both in the form of capitalist cottage industry and in the form of capitalist manufacture.[10]

On the whole, the Soviet historians have veered round the views of Dr. Pavlov, Dr. Alaev and Dr. Chicherov. The views expressed in *Novay istoriya Indii* (New History of India) confirm it. (The book covers the history of India from mid eighteenth century to the end of the first World War. It is a combined project of Soviet scholars and has been prepared by the Institute of the Asian People, Moscow, and therefore, may be said to represent the consensus of opinion among Soviet scholars.) The authors in the chapter on Social and Economic condition of India in the first half of the seventeenth and eighteenth centuries write : 'In different branches of crafts there appeared sporadically and in embryonic form elements of capitalism.[11]

The conclusion arrived at by the authors of *Novay istoriya Indii* seem to be correct and based on available historical evidence.

It would be wrong to accept the view that Indian economy had already effected the change-over to capitalism from feudalism in the seventeenth century, for there is evidence to suggest any change in the technique and organisation of production. Production was still carried on by the age-old methods and tools. The increased demand for goods was met not by any revolution in the technique and organisation of production but by more intensive specialisation, *i.e.*, many peasants, who had earlier devoted their time partly to farming and partly to crafts, gave up agriculture and concentrated on crafts as whole-timers. This is confirmed by contemporary evidence and accepted by Soviet scholars as well. However, it would be equally fallacious to hold that Indian economy was stagnant and incapable

[10] Chicherov, *Eknomicheskoy razvitie Indii pered angliiskim zavovaniem*, Moskva, 1965, 280.

[11] *Novay istoriya Indii*, Moskva, 1961, 55.

of responding to new challenges.

There is incontrovertible evidence that the Indian economy, based on self-sufficient villages', was being undermined. The practice of paying land revenue in cash, introduced in the sixteenth century, encouraged the growth of money economy and led to the production of goods for the market. In the seventeenth century money economy was widely prevalent in India.[12] The documents of East India Company and the accounts of European travellers in the country point to the growing importance of money-changers (*sarrafs*) and money-lenders—sure signs of the growth of money-economy. The Soviet scholars, especially Drs. Pavlov, Alaev and Chicherov, also accept this on the basis of evidence furnished by the documents of European Companies. Another pointer to the growth of money economy was the establishment of a number of mints for coining money.

The network of roads, contructed by Sher Shah and Akbar, besides consolidating the central authority, also helped to break the isolation of the villages and brought them into the vortex of city life.[13] The improved communications led to the exchange of commodities between far and away places. For example, Kashmir and Gujarat and Bengal exchanged through land routes not only manufactured goods but also raw materials.[14] Thus Drs. Pavlov, Alaev and Chicherov correctly mark the tendency towards the creation of an all India market—a development which was bound to affect the self-sufficient economy of the Indian villages and bring about a fundamental change.[15]

The fundamental change did not come about in the seventeenth century, but the symptoms for the change were pronounced. The

[12] Dr. Irfan Habib has dwelt at length on this aspect in his paper 'Banking in Mughal India', published in *Contributions to Indian Economic History*, Vol. I, 1–21.

[13] *The Cambridge History of India*, (Cambridge, 1937) Vol. IV, 57, K. A. Antonova, Ocherki........., 120

[14] Pant, D., *The Commercial Policy of the Moguls*, (Bombay, 1930), 95; Ed. Danvers, F. C., *Letters Received by the East India Company from its Servants in the East*, 1602–13, (London, 1896), Vol. I, 32; Pelsaert, *Jahangir's India*, (Cambridge, 1925), 19.

[15] We may also refer to the movement of food grains from one part of India to other parts—a normal feature in those days. Irfan Habib, *The Agrarian System of Mughal India*, London, 1963.

increased State demand and oppressions of nobility and merchants impoverished the peasants as well as the craftsmen. The peasants left their lands and an army of workers, who were ready to sell their labour in lieu of wages, had been formed.[16] A more important change took place in the status of the artisans.

Craftsmen were losing their independence. They had practically lost their freedom of marketing their goods, because they now worked against advances, paid by the merchants or the representatives of merchants. These advances were not only in the form of cash[17] and raw-materials,[18] but, in times of distress, in the shape of corn.[19] The subjugation of craftsmen by the representatives of merchant capital ushered in faint but significant changes in the organisation of the production system.

Independent craftsmen, now in great difficulties, became available for engagement as hired artisans. The Europeans took advantage of this situation. In their workshops and factories, Indian artisans began to exchange their skill for wages. There are a number of instances when Indian weavers were working in workshops set up by the Europeans.[20] The English established a Dyeing House at Ahmadabad, manned by Indian artisans.[21] Similarly, the English tried refining saltpetre in their own factories.[22] Hence, a new relationship, that of the owner and the employee—an essential ingredient of capitalism—was developing. Here was also the germ of the manufacture system (when a number of craftsmen work under one roof, with tools etc., provided by the master)—the forerunner of the capitalist system of production. Drs. Pavlov, Alaev and Chicherov have correctly emphasised this point while refuting Dr. (Mme) Antonova's contention that there was no element of capitalism in Indian economy in the seventeenth century and the manufacture

[16] The abundance of servants in cities and the flourishing slave-trade may be cited in support of this statement.

[17] *The English Factories in India*, 1622–23, (Oxford 1908), 116; *The English Factories in India*, 1661–64, (Oxford, 1923), 209; The *Diaries of Streynsham Master*, (London 1911), Vol. I, 113.

[18] Fryer, *A New Account af East India and Persia*, (London, 1909), Vol. I, Master, Vol. I, 135.

[19] *The English Factories in India*, 1630–33, (Oxford, 1910), 158.

[20] Master, Vol. I, 113, 139, 141.

[21] *The English Factories in India*, 1646–50, (Oxford, 1914), 27, 63.

[22] *The English Factories in India*, 1642–45, (Oxford, 1913), 164, 205.

system never developed in India.[23]

The important point remains that these buds of capitalist economy did not blossom in the seventeenth century. The reason was the stranglehold of feudal lords on the economy all over India. The lack of security of life and property discouraged the Indian merchants from investing their capital in setting up such enterprises. The European competition also acted as a deterrent. The Europeans had extracted various concessions from the feudal lords and were more favourably placed than the indigenous merchants in Indian economy. The Europeans used extra-commercial methods, like force etc., to ralegate the Indian enterpreneurs into the background. The result was that Indian capital was invested in money-lending, where risks were small and the returns not insignificant. The Europeans encouraged it because they were short of capital. This development, as Dr. Pavlov and Dr. Alaev have correctly pointed out, blocked the growth of capitalist elements in Indian economy in the seventeenth century.

Hence, the conclusion in the light of the above evidence is inescapable, and we must agree with the authors of *Novay istoria Indii* that, during the Mughal Period, the feudal economy was undergoing a change. Elements of capitalism had appeared, but they were sporadic and weak, incapable of achieving by themselves a complete transformation of feudal economy.

A NOTE ON SOURCES USED BY SOME SOVIET HISTORIANS OF MUGHAL INDIA

It may be interesting for the Indian readers to know the sources which have been relied upon by Soviet scholars to reach their conclusions.

The importance of a particular source has been determined by the nature of study made by the Soviet Scholar. Since Soviet scholars have been mostly concentrating on economic and social aspects, naturally they rate sources like the *Ain-i-Akbari*, accounts of European travellers like Pelsaert, Tavernier, Bernier and Thevenot as of

[23] We may also point out that the germs of manufacture system were already present in ship-building and mining. The accounts of European travellers testify this.

paramount importance.

The sources for the study of Mughal India are extremely extensive and it is humanly impossible for a single individual to use all of them. A choice has necessarily to be made and different Soviet scholars have laid emphasis on particular sources, as warranted by the type of their studies.

Prof. Reisner in his book *Narodine dvizheniyav Indii v XVII–XVIII vv.* set about to examine the popular movements and their economic roots in the second half of the seventeenth and eighteenth centuries and has depended mainly on the travel accounts of Europeans in the seventeenth century. His main reliance has been on Pelsaert and Manucci. The latter is indeed a store-house of information regarding the reign of Aurangzeb. While dealing with the movement of the Sikhs, Prof. Reisner also takes into account Persian chronicles like the *Muntakhab-ul-Lubab* which he has used it in Persian. Furthermore, Prof. Reisner has relied heavily upon the researches of British and Indian scholars in the nineteenth and twentieth centuries on Maratha and Sikh histories, for example, on works of Grant Duff, Kincaid nand Parasnis, Macauliffe, Elphinstone, Cunningham, William Irvine, Moreland, Jadunath Sarkar, S. N. Sen and Choksey etc. He has also consulted the French work, L. R. Krishan's *Les sikhs Origine et developement de la Communante.*

While reconstructing the agraian history of Indian communities—the Marathas, the Sikhs and the Jats—in the seventeenth and eighteenth centuries, Prof. Reisner has made extensive use of Indian gazetteers, published towards the end of the nineteenth century. This has to some extent led to the projection of later developments to the seventeenth and eighteenth centuries. Here it may be pointed out that Prof. Reisner was working under a severe handicap—he had no access to local materials. However, reliance on District Gazetteers for reconstructing the agrarian history of India in the seventeenth century is a marked feature of Soviet historiography.

Dr. (Mme) Antonova, whose monograph on social and economic conditions of India during Akbar's period was published in 1952, used primary and secondary sources in a number of languages, English, Persian, French, German and Russian. Among the primary sources used by her in Persian are Abul Fazl's *Ain-i-Akbari* and *Akbar-nama,* Badauni's *Muntekhab-ut-Tawerikh,* Nizam-ud-Din Ahmad's *Tabaqat-i-Akbari.* In order to treat the reign of Akbar in a correct perspective, she has consulted some earlier and later Persian chronicles as well. Some of them are—Barani's *Tarikh-i-Firuz Shahi*, Shahnawaz Khan's *Maasir-i-Rahimi*, Nihawandi's *Maasir-ul-Umra*, Amin Ahmad Razi's *Haft Iqlim* and Ali Muhammad Khan's *Mirat-i-Ahmadi*. (It may be pointed out that some of the above chronicles she consulted in manuscript form, preserved in the library of the Institute of Oriental Studies, Tashkent. The Library has a very fine collection of manuscripts relating to India. They are awaiting proper study by Indian scholars.)

Dr. (Mme) Antonova has also used reports of Parliamentary Committees on the affairs of the English East India Company, published in the nineteenth century to discuss the agrarian problem during Akbar's reign.

Other primary sources consulted by her are Tulsi Das's *Ramayana* (the Russian translation), *Adi Granth* (trans. by E. Trumpp), of Elliot and Dawson's, *One hundred songs of Kabir* (trans. by Rabindra Nath Tagore) and accounts of contemporary European travellers. Like Prof. Reisner, she also relies heavily on Pelsaert's *Jahangir's India* to emphasise her conclusions about the economic conditions of the Indian peasantry, artisans and masses.

Dr. (Mme) Antonova has used secondary sources in German, French and English. She has consulted works in German by Buhler. Glasenapp, Horn and von Noer etc. She has referred to works in French by Tassy and Menant. She has exhaustively used literature available on Akbar in English—works of Vincent Smith, Moreland, Ibn Hasan, J. J. Modi, Krishnamurthi and Varma etc. Thus the sources utilised by Dr. (Mme) Antonova are varied and extensive.

Dr. Pavlov in his book *Formirovanie indiiskoi burzhuazii* has exclusively depended on travel accounts of the European to describe the economic condition of India in the seventeenth century. He has completely ignored the documents of European trading companies, including the accounts of some important travellers like the Italian, Pietro della Valle, and the French, Carre and others. As a result, the author has been led to certain hasty conclusions about economic tendencies, which are not warranted by the evidence he adduces. Moreover, the author freely uses evidences of the late seveenteenth or even mid-nineteenth century to corroborate his statement relating to the seventeenth century.

In contrast to Dr. Pavlov, Dr. Alaev in his work *Uzhanay*

Indiya has been very meticulous about the sources. The period he has taken, fourteenth to eighteenth centuries, is a long one and the available sources are diverse and abundant. Dr. Alaev has tried to tap a wide range of primary sources—inscriptions, travel accounts, published documents of European companies (mainly of the English East India Company) and contemporary chronicles (trans. into English). He has also used district gazetteers, manuals and other informative materials, published by governmental departments from time to time in the present and the last centuries pertaining to his area of study.

Dr. Alaev has used practically all the research works published on South India, relating to his period, by Indian or European authors in English. He is careful about his conclusions, and has based them, as far as practicable, on contemporary evidence. Dr. Alaev's monograph is indeed a detailed piece of research.

Dr. Chicherov has extensively consulted primary and secondary sources in preparing his monograph *Ekonomicheskoy razvitie Indii pered angliiskim zavovaniem.* Besides studying all the primary sources available in English (published documents of European trading companies and published accounts of contemporary European travellers) he has also studied contemporary Persian chronicles, bearing on the topic (in Persian). He has also made use of some sources in the Bengali language to buttress his conclusions about the socio-economic condition. Relevant contemporary inscriptions have also been utilised. Like other Soviet historians, he has studied reports, published by the various departments of the Government of India in order to get a correct perspective of the agrarian system. Dr. Chicherov has critically used practically all the literature published on the subject by Indian and European scholars in English.

Thus this brief account shows that the Soviet scholars on Mughal India have based their studies on a wide range of primary sources. Credit should be given to them for tapping so many primary sources in so many languages. Unfortunately, due to physical limitations, they have not been able to tap local materials.

INDEX